alba house • DIVISION OF THE SOCIETY OF ST. PAUL
STATEN ISLAND, N.Y. 10314

Theology:
science of salvation

René Latourelle, S.J.

TRANSLATED BY SISTER MARY DOMINIC

NIHIL OBSTAT:
Joseph A. Komonchak, S.T.M.
Censor Deputatus

IMPRIMATUR:
Joseph P. O'Brien, S.T.D.,
Vicar General, Archdiocese of New York
July 31, 1969

Library of Congress Catalog Card Number: 79-94697

The nihil obstat, imprimi potest and imprimatur are official declarations that a book or pamphlet is free of doctrinal or moral error. No implication is contained therein that those who have granted the nihil obstat, imprimi potest or imprimatur agree with the contents, opinions or statements expressed.

Designed, printed and bound in the U.S.A. by the Pauline Fathers and Brothers of the Society of St. Paul at Staten Island, New York as a part of their communications apostolate.

TABLE OF CONTENTS

PART IV — THEOLOGY AND CHRISTIAN LIFE

PART V — THEOLOGY'S PRESENT ORIENTATIONS

Introduction

It has often been said, since the Council, that theology is in search of its *identity;* of its nature, its method and its function. It is trying to find out where it stands in relation to the world and to other sciences, and in relation to the other activities of the Church. People are asking whether theology is really *theology,* that is, talk about God, or whether it is not rather *anthropology,* or talk about man in the presence of God.[1]

In point of fact theology as it actually is today is rather like an enormous building yard. There are, in the renewal of biblical and patristic and liturgical studies, in the Council's declarations and orientations, in the appearance of new fields of research demanding theological reflection, in the widening and deepening of theological methods, in the opening out of Catholic theology to the world, to other Christian communities and to other religions, all the elements of a new construction planned on a magnificent scale.

It is not easy, moreover, for anyone who ventures into this

---

1. B. Lambert, "Les deux démarches de la théologie," *Nouvelle Revue théologique,* 89 (1967), pp. 257-280.

building yard to get his bearings, and still less easy is it for him to see what the new construction is going to be, what its lines of force will be or its style. All that is still in the realm of promises.

Now while theology itself is in search of its principle of operation, students continue to frequent the Universities and Seminaries, and to ask themselves what this new science which they meet is. Is theology capable of preparing them for their apostolic work, of forming them as servants of the word which will have an impact on the minds of the men of our times?

Without wishing to anticipate the future of theology, it is perhaps not impossible to give some idea of the building which is under construction. This is what we have tried to do, conscious of the risks we are taking and with no other end in view than that of *serving* the present generation of students in theology.

Such an approach could in practice be made in different ways. We could envisage theology under its genetic and evolutionary aspect, seize it at the moment of its birth and follow its development right up to our own day: in short we could give a history of theology. Again we could make in this history a certain number of, as it were, vertical cuts, in order to study contemporary theology in the light of what have been, in the course of the centuries, the great periods of theological thought. Lastly we could come to immediate grips with the questions which face present day students on the threshold of their theological studies. A certain number of these questions, notably those which concern the nature, the end and object, and the method of theology are in a sense classical questions and present themselves at all times and in all places, although with inevitable variations. Others, on the contrary, are peculiar to our own time and bound up with contemporary conditions. It is this final way of approach that we have chosen.

We discuss first (in Parts I and II) general questions, questions of nature and object and method. We have been at pains to approach them, not *in abstracto,* but by way of history, in the context of the contemporary mentality and with whatever light that it may be able to throw upon them.

Yet since the Council there is practically no one of the separate theological disciplines which has not been more or less touched in the very principle of its operations. Some disciplines, only yesterday non-existent, or at most in the process of being born, have obtained from the Church either a veritable charter or an official recognition — Pastoral theology, Missionary theology, Ecumenical theology for instance. A description of the new state of theological disciplines as it appears immediately after the Council is then of first importance in order that we may recognize the face which theology presents to us in our own day. This is discussed in part III.

Part IV studies a certain number of questions with which introductions to theology have not generally, up to now, attempted to deal. These questions, arising from a theology *en-situation -historique* whose method is being continuously renewed, are of capital importance for the student of theology today. If it is true that theological understanding must show how the Christian mysteries illuminate the spiritual life of everyman and the pastoral activity of the Church, how can one not speak of the relation in which theology stands to preaching, to the pastoral ministry and to the inner life? If it is true that the laity, no less than the clergy participate in the prophetic function of the Church, how is one not to study their role in theological teaching and research?

The last part, Part V, setting out from the main principles which have inspired the actual theological renewal of our time, studies what seem to be the chief axes of contemporary theological thought.

It is not without reason that we have chosen to call this book *Theology: science of salvation*. Indeed the God whom theology studies is the God who intervenes in history and who calls to salvation every man coming into the world. Theology deepens the personal relations which this living God wishes to establish with man in order that man may share in his life. For salvation is essentially the union of man with God in which man is divinized by God's communication with himself, a communication wholly free and wholly new.

If this is the object of revelation and the object of faith, theology, which is a reflection upon the living contents of the Christian faith, has as its task to make intelligible, in the context of the whole of revelation, the value for salvation, for *life,* of each of the Christian mysteries. Theology is a methodical reflection on the content of faith (the God who is savior manifested in Jesus Christ), and on the saving finality which is inseparable from this content. Insofar as theology does not manifest this value for salvation inherent in each Christian mystery, it does not fulfill its task. In the measure in which it loses sight of this salvific orientation which is inscribed upon the whole of revelation, it ceases to be theology.

The pages which follow try then to answer the principal questions asked by the student who comes to theology in a post-Conciliar context. It is a matter of *initiating* him into theology. Many other things, no doubt, could be said to him, but we have wished to draw attention to the essential things, considering that the experience of hard theological work will be able to teach them to him better and more quickly than a theoretical exposition.

As we come to the end of this introduction it is a pleasant duty to express our gratitude to our colleagues of the Gregorian University and of the Biblical Institute, who have helped us in so brotherly a spirit with their advice, particularly in the elaboration of Part III which is devoted to the different theological disciplines.

Part I.
THE NATURE OF THEOLOGY

CHAPTER I   FROM REVELATION TO THEOLOGY

1. *The double sense in which the word theology is used*

By "theology," in the wide sense, we understand the *knowledge of God*. This expression in its turn covers a double meaning, one objective, the other subjective. In the objective sense it means the knowledge which has God for its object; in the subjective sense the knowledge which God himself possesses, and which he communicates to men by grace. Let us be more precise about both senses.

1. In the *subjective* sense, theology is the knowledge which God has of himself and of the created universe. God, Subsistent Being, infinite and perfect, has as his proper and connatural object himself. He knows himself intuitively, and other objects in himself and through himself, as participations of himself. This consciousness which he has of himself, God, through grace, communicates to man perfectly insofar as this is possible to a creature, and according to different degrees, in the beatific vision; imperfectly, but, even so, wonderfully, through revelation and through faith.

Revelation is a complex reality, at the same time a manifestation and communication of God, a *dynamic reality* which accomplishes the designs of God in human history, and a *message* which is translated into human terms on the lips of the prophets and of Christ, in order to illuminate the hidden meaning of the saving events.[1] For the word of God does not merely speak or give information; it accomplishes what it signifies; it changes the situation of humanity; the life which it announces it also brings to pass. The revelation of God is an active word, efficacious and creative.

Faith brings about the meeting between God who is revealing himself and man. Through revelation God opens himself to man in a disclosure of love and invites him to an exchange of friendship. Through faith man responds to God's initiative, gives himself to God, allows God's word to penetrate and control him, enters into a living communion with him, a communion of life.

When God reveals himself to man he does so in a way proportionate to his condition as being in time and space, a being both individual and social, composed of both body and spirit. Consequently, revelation has certain markedly specific characteristics:

(a) Its destination is *universal*. It is addressed to the whole of humanity. It calls all the races of men to salvation and excludes none of them: "Teach all nations," said Christ (Mt 28, 19). "Go into all the world and preach the gospel to every creature" (Mk 16, 15).

(b) Revelation is *public* and *social*. It is not a secret confided to each individual in the depth of his heart to be hidden there, but good news, destined to be transmitted and proclaimed in the public square. Peter, on the day of Pentecost, cried out in a loud voice before a crowd of people the good news of salvation, in order to make it publicly and commonly known, to make it official (Acts 2, 14; Mt 10, 26-27; Rom 10, 14-17). Revelation impinges upon individual persons not as isolated units closed

---

1. Const. *Dei verbum* on revelation, n. 2; R. Latourelle, *Theology of Revelation* (Alba House, New York, 1966), pp. 457-463.

against one another but as members of the same body, in order that men may be aware of their communion with one another in revelation, as in faith and glory. It is made to men in order to make of them the people of God, the Bride, the Body of Christ, the Church.

(c) Revelation is *hierarchical*. It is not made immediately to each person, but through the mediation of privileged witnesses chosen by God, the prophets and the apostles (Acts 10, 41; Eph 2, 20-21). St. Thomas, in order to bring out the hierarchical character of revelation, compares it to a mountain torrent whose abundant waters, coming from God who is their source, descend to the plain only after forming successive river basins in the valleys. So revelation is made first to angels, following the order of the heavenly hierarchies, then to men, and among them to the greatest of them, the prophets and the apostles; it spreads analogously among the multitude of those who receive it through faith, those who have a deeper awareness of it being bound to transmit it to those who believe with less explicit faith.[2]

(d) Revelation is *progressive*. Man does not possess it all at once in a perfect form. Matter and spirit, he is subject to the conditions of corporality; his being unfolds progressively in space and time. Addressing himself to man, to this being of flesh and spirit, plunged in duration, God communicates with him through his senses and through history. From the very beginning of the world revelation has developed in quality and quantity through the centuries, maturing little by little as it makes man more mature, in order to prepare him for the fullness of time in Christ. "At various times in the past and in various different ways, God spoke to our ancestors, through the prophets; but in our own time, the last days, he has spoken to us through his Son, the Son that he has appointed to inherit everything" (Heb 1, 1).

(e) Finally, destined for man and destined to be received within a human intelligence, revelation has to accommodate itself to the *conditions of human understanding*. In God, revelation is a mystery

---

2. S. Th., 2:2: 2:6c.

of unity: unity of object, unity of operation, unity of structure. The design of God is unity, but our manner of conceiving and expressing this mystery is human and consequently imperfect. The human mind receives its object through the *senses;* that is why revelation is made to us by means of images, symbols, parables, allegories, and so forth. The human mind is *limited;* and so it is in the multiplicity of mysteries and enunciations that we become aware of the unique mystery, the mystery of the divine life. The process of man's mind is *discursive;* that is why we go from a general understanding to an understanding more precise and more profound without ever being able to exhaust the fullness of the mystery which is divine.

Such then is the *primary sense* of the word theology: it is the knowledge which God has of himself in his Word, in whom he knows all things, a knowledge which he communicates to men through revelation. While in creation the Wisdom of God is, as it were, imprisoned in things, in revelation this Wisdom is humanized in the word of the prophets; then it becomes incarnate in Jesus Christ.

2. In the *objective* sense theology is the knowledge which has God for its object. This knowledge can, in its turn, be conceived as the sum of human learning about God (*savoir humain, wissenschaft,* knowledge), or as man's assimilation and understanding of this *ensemble* of learning about God. Theology is, *knowledge about God* in both these senses.

But there is a triple knowledge of God: that which can be obtained by reflection upon the created universe; that which proceeds from God's word to men; and that, ultimately, which comes from the very vision of God. Consequently there is a triple theology: natural theology, or theodicy; the theology of *homo viator,* or theology proper; and the theology of homecoming or the awareness of those chosen by God. Each of these is knowledge of God but each differs from the other two in its way of attaining God.

Natural theology attains to God through the works of his creation and by the natural light of reason. Theology *proper* attains

to God through God's word and witness to himself and by the
light of reason illumined by faith. The theology of *homecoming*
knows God in his essence and by the light of glory. To each of
these forms of theology there corresponds a knowledge of God
increasingly profound. In natural theology God is known as
the source and end of the universe; in theology proper we know
the mysteries of his inmost life, but by report; in the theology of
homecoming we know the unveiled mystery, face to face.

In discussing the sources of our knowledge of divine things,
St. Thomas writes: "There exists a threefold human knowledge
of divine things. In the first, man, thanks to the natural light
of reason, *raises himself* to the knowledge of God by means of
creatures; in the second, divine truth, which lies beyond the limits
of our intelligence, *comes down* to us through revelation, not as
a proof to be followed but as a word to be believed; in the third,
the spirit will be *lifted* so that it may see perfectly what God has
revealed to it." [3] Thus in the first degree of knowledge, man *tends
towards* God as the source and end of the universe. In the second
degree, God himself takes the initiative, *stoops* and reveals to
man. God the transcendent and thrice holy, the hidden and the
invisible comes forth from his mystery and makes himself *Em-
manuel,* God close at hand: he speaks to man; he questions him;
he establishes with him a bond of friendship. At last, in vision,
man is *lifted,* by the light of glory, to the very sight of God.

2. *Theology in the strict sense*

Supernatural theology, or theology proper, is the science of
God, but a science which sets out from revelation. It speaks of
God, but of God as he is known to us through his revelation and
insofar as his revelation can introduce us to a deeper knowledge
of his inner mystery. Theology's point of departure then is the
living God, in the free witness which he gives of himself. To put
it in another way, since faith and revelation are correlative notions,

3. *S. C. Gent.,* L, IV, c.

it could be said that theology is the *science of the object of faith,* that is to say the science of what is revealed by God and believed by man. While the natural sciences are built upon the *données* (data) of experience, theology is built upon the *données* of revelation received by faith.

The theologian tries, by reflection, to arrive at a deeper understanding of the mysteries to which he already adheres by faith. What is, for the believer pure and simple, an object of assent, the theologian attempts to comprehend; what the believer pure and simple affirms as *true,* the theologian tries to see as *intelligible.*

There is, it is true, in every Christian an inherent reflection upon faith, a spontaneous reflection born of the shock of events and the pressure of environment; this is elementary theology, accessible to everybody, a theology in which faith tries to understand the why and how of what it believes. Scientific theology is the prolongation of this spontaneous reflection. It becomes a reflection *conscious of itself* (of its principles, its process, its status as a science, its conclusions), and it seeks to penetrate the object of faith in a methodical fashion. Theology, as a science, is the work of the believer who uses his reason in order to understand better what he already possesses by faith. Theology is faith lived by a thinking mind, and scientifically elaborated. It is faith "in a scientific state." It could be defined with St. Anselm, as *fides quaerens intellectum,* that is to say faith applying itself to understanding its object. Theology is the more faithful to its intention insofar as it not only receives the things which are given by faith but, over and above that, seeks always to penetrate and understand them more deeply.

St. Anselm said also: "I do not pretend to 'sound thy depth, O Lord, for how should I compare my understanding with thy mystery? But I desire to understand in some manner the truth which I believe and which my heart loves. I do not seek to understand in order to believe" (that is, I do not seek to understand first by means of my reason what I shall then, afterwards, believe), "but I believe first in order to try afterwards to understand. For I believe this — that if I do not begin by believing I shall never understand." [4] And St. Augustine writes: "I desired to see with the eyes of my understanding what I believed." [5]

Theology is faith assuming the language of reason in order the better to understand its object. For the very perfecting of Christianity it is important that there should exist in the Church this scientific reflection upon the object of faith. Christianity indeed permeates and orders the whole of human reality at so deep a level that it must be not only a making sacred of the secular world, not only a transformation of the inner life, but also a lighting up of the whole intelligible world itself. This influence on the intelligible world the Church at its outset, exercised with considerable discretion and even timidity, but in the course of time, under the guidance of the Holy Spirit, the understanding of faith has come to be pursued so resolutely and so continuously that no one now would question its legitimacy and necessity.

Before closing this chapter let us notice that the formula *fides quaerens intellectum* must not be applied too exclusively to the theologian in the technical sense. We have seen already that every believer is virtually a theologian. As a man he reflects in a spontaneous if not a scientific fashion on his situation as a believer. In our day especially, when the majority of Christians, thanks to the press, to radio and to television, are in possession of a relatively extensive human and religious culture, questions and reflections upon matters of faith arise of themselves from the concrete situations of life. It is of importance then that both clerical and lay theologians should translate without ceasing into contemporary language the inexhaustible riches of Christ, so

---

4. "Non tento, Domine, penetrare altitudinem tuam; quia nullatenus comparo illi intellectum meum, sed desidero aliquatenus intelligere veritatem tuam, quam credit et amat cor meum. Neque enim quaero intelligere ut credam; sed credo ut intelligam. Nam et hoc credo quia nisi credidero, non intelligam" (*Proslogion* I in PL 158: 227).

5. "Desideravi intellectu videre quod credidi, et multum disputavi et laboravi" (*De Trinitate* XV, 28, 51 in PL 42: 1098). See also *De libero arbitrio* II, 2, 5: "Id quod credimus, nosse et intelligere cupimus," in PL 32: 1243; *De Trinitate* IV, 1 in PL 42: 961; XV, 27, 40 in PL 42: 1096.

that they may set up more effective conditions for dialogue with the contemporary world.

Theology represents a constant effort on the part of the Church to live in contact with the world and its problems, its doubts and its desires. For theology constitutes a continual exchange between faith and reason, between the world and God, between the secular and the sacred. It confronts faith with the new problems which confront men. And it must live in ceaseless meditation upon the word of God so that it may see at what point that word may enter and penetrate into the world of our time.

To the question, what is the object of theology, or the subject of which it treats, Thomist theology answers: God *qua* God. Some other theologians, preoccupied with constructing a theology revolving, as it were, upon the very movement of revelation, reply to the same question by saying: Christ and the history of salvation. What then is the object of theology? Is it God or Christ? Is it God or the economy of salvation?

1. *The Thomist formulation*

The *material* object of theology is obviously God. The *formal* object of a science is the particular aspect under which it envisages its material object. Thus man can be the material object of several sciences: philosophy, sociology, psychology, anthropology, medicine for instance. Each of these sciences, however, envisages man under a different aspect. In philosophy, ontology considers everything from the point of view of *being,* whereas cosmology is concerned with the *becoming* of things. In order to indicate the formal object of theology, or its *subject* according to the terminology of his times, (*subjectum de quo aliquid scitur*), St. Thomas uses the expression, *Deus sub ratione Deitatis,* God under the very aspect of his Godhead, God as God. "In sacred science," he says, "everything is treated in relation to God, either because it is itself God" (the essence, the attributes, the persons of God), "or else because it is ordered to God as to its source and end" (creatures, human acts, laws, grace, virtues, sacraments).[1]

In theodicy, reflection arises from the world and reaches up from it to the ultimate principle, transcendent and personal, which explains the universe. Theology follows the opposite trajectory: its point of departure is the living God as he is in himself, as he knows himself and is known to us through revelation. The subject of theology is the living God whose word we believe and who, in the gift of himself, constitutes the joy of the blessed. It is the God who manifests himself to us visibly in the flesh of Christ, the sign, the utterance of his saving love. Theology studies God in the mystery of his inner life and in his design for our salvation. All theology, for St. Thomas, returns to the double mystery of the Trinity and the Incarnation, that is to the mystery of God in his inner life and to the mystery of the structure of means which lead us to him.[2] In terms still more personalist, we may say that theology treats of God himself and of Christ, as the efficacious sign of salvation.

This is why all theological treatises speak of God, of the God who is one and triune, of the God who creates and justifies, of the God who is made man and suffering servant, of the God who is the source of every grace and virtue, of the God who sanctifies through the Church and the sacraments, of the God who is the blessedness of those who love and serve him. Theology speaks always of the living and personal God, who has made the world, freed his people from the bonds of Egypt and made a covenant with them, who has so loved men that he has given his Son for them, and whom the Church in the Psalms invokes unceasingly as the God of salvation (Pss 23. 37. 87) or, in the prayers of the Mass, as the God who is and will be forever. The

---

1. S. Th., 1:1:7:c.
2. S. Th., 2-2:1:8; 2-2:1:5.

God of whom theology speaks is not an abstract concept, or a God who is dumb, but the living *God* whose words and actions fill the two Testaments.

Theology treats also of creatures, but it considers them in their relationship to God, as effects of God, or images of God, called to share his inmost life or to enter into the movement of cosmic renewal initiated by Christ's victory over sin and death. The attention which present day theology is paying to man and to the human condition as such is not a contradiction of this way of looking at things. If theology is bent over man it is to reveal to him that his secret is to be found in God. In the last resort the preoccupation and desire of theology is to *fulfill* man, by showing him his humanity renewed in Christ. It turns to man in order to turn man to God through the mediation of the new man. God remains theology's object.

The *objective* light or means by which the living God is thus accessible to theology (*objectum formale quo*), is revelation, or the disclosure which God makes of himself. From the subjective point of view, the light of theology as we shall explain in the next chapter, is reason illumined by faith, that is to say a light which emerges from the interplay of reason and the supernatural action of God, who connaturalizes man in the new world of the gospel.

2. *New formulations*

The expression *God under the aspect of his Godhead,* or *God as God,* used by St. Thomas to indicate the object of theology, can be interpreted in different ways. Here are the two interpretations most common today:

1. The formal object of theology, some say, is the *God of salvation*. Theology indeed is the science of the object of faith. Now the object of faith, and therefore of theology, is God, author of the supernatural order. If we ask what the truth is that God wished chiefly to reveal to us, what is central in the deposit of

revelation and what our faith aspires to know, we must answer that it consists in this: *God is our salvation; God saves us through Christ*. Even the mystery of the Trinity is revealed to us only in this perspective of salvation, in order to make us understand that the Father loves us and saves us through Christ in the Spirit of love. "Yes, God loved the world so much that he gave his only Son, so that everyone who believes in him may not be lost but may have eternal life. For God sent his Son into the world not to condemn the world, but so that through him the world might be saved" (Jn 3, 16-8). The essential content of "God's testimony" is that "God has given us eternal life and that his life is in his Son" (1 John 5, 11). In St. Paul the theme of salvation offered to men through faith in the gospel is the very subject of the Epistle to the Romans. Christianity is not an abstract metaphysic, but the history of salvation. In the Epistle to the Ephesians St. Paul tells us that God, in the design of his love wished to sum up all things in Christ, and that he has constituted Christ the only source of salvation for all men, Jew and Gentile alike.

Thus the dominating idea which directs the progress of revelation from the beginning of the Old Testament to the end of the New, and which gives the two Testaments their unity, is this: God saves us through Christ. We can have no conception of God other than that which he has revealed to us. But he manifests himself to us as the God who saves. The object of revelation, of faith, and consequently of theology, is, therefore, *God the Savior*. That is why the gospel is called "the word of salvation" (Eph 1, 13), "the message of salvation" (Acts 13, 26), "the gospel of grace" (Acts 20, 24), "the word of life" (Phil 2, 16).

2. Other theologians propose a formulation whose axis is the divine life. The formal object of theology, they say, is *the living God, source of life*. In practice this aspect of God is to be found athwart the whole of theology and in every theological treatise. The inner dynamic of the divine life is fulfilled in the generation of the Word and the spiration of the Spirit — hence the treatise *de Deo uno* and *de Deo trino*. But there is also in

God an external activity, in virtue of which the divine life is communicated to creatures: God creates man and raises him to a participation in his own life — hence the treatises *de Deo creante et elevante*. Through original sin this life has been destroyed in man but through the Incarnation of the Word and the sacrifice of Christ new life has come into the world — hence the treatises *de Christo legato, de Verbo Incarnato, de Deo Redemptore*. The divine life is diffused within the members of Christ's Body — hence the treatises *de Ecclesia, de Sacramentis, de Virtutibus*. There is a special treatise whose province is the study of the nature of this divine life communicated to men, the treatise *de Gratia*. Finally theology discusses man's last end, that is the everlasting possession or the everlasting loss of this life — the treatise *de Novissimis*. Each of these treatises studies an aspect of the divine life. Indeed it is always a matter of the mystery of the divine life, which takes its source in the Trinity, is communicated to men, destroyed by sin, restored by Christ and diffused within the Church.

3. *The position of theology and the theologian*

Theology then, is the science of God as God, taking revelation as its point of departure. That a science should thus have as the object of its inquiry the living and saving God cannot but affect profoundly its status or the status of the man who consecrates himself to it, the theologian.

1. If theology is able to speak of God in his inner life and in his plan of salvation, this is because God, first, in the superabundance of his love has come forth from his mystery to draw man into conversation, as friend with friend. At the source of every theological process lies this divine initiative, this manifestation by God of himself. Theology speaks of God, but what it says is founded upon what God has said of himself. It tries to understand God better, but it sets out from his own testimony. It follows that theology can never become an autonomous science.

Like the Church, of whom it is the function, it is "at the service of the word of God."[3] Theology is, and must remain, the humble servant of the word of God.

This can be said, no less, of the theologian. He, above all among the faithful, must listen to the word which he seeks to understand.[4] For the word of God is addressed to him in order to be received in a faith which engages the whole of his life. It demands of him docility of mind and docility of heart. The whole of his existence must be stretched to the dimensions of a truth which claims the final word upon man. From this point of view there is no difference between the teacher of theology and the student in theology. Both are under the word of God. Both are trying to penetrate to the depths and taste there the meaning of this word which is both the inspiration and the criterion of their life. Here, the object of the intellectual life and the object of the spiritual life coincide simply.

Among the sciences therefore, theology has a particular and privileged status. It carries on its work in a religious and sacred ambience, created by the deep affinity which unites teacher and student in communion with the same object. For the word of God which they are trying to understand better is the object of their faith and the foundation of their life. Both student and teacher are *given, surrendered* to this word. Theology can become then, for the student and for the teacher alike, a school of holiness. "Man does not live by bread alone but by every word which comes from the mouth of God" (Mt. 4, 4).

2. Since theology has as its object the living and saving God, it is characterized in certain ways which need now to be defined:

(a) It is *historical* in character. Since it has as its object God revealing himself in history and through history, theology is constantly related to the history of salvation. It reflects not upon a system of abstract propositions but upon the free intervention of

---

3. Const. *Dei verbum* on revelation, n. 10.
4. *Ibid.*, nn. 1 & 10.

God in history. Theology must, therefore, remain centered upon the history of salvation. There is no theology without reference to the economy of God's manifestation of himself.

(b) It is *christological* in character. Christ is the axis of the history of salvation. The Old Testament is an announcement and preparation for him, a prophecy and a pedagogy of him. In the New Testament Christ is the center and object of the Gospel, in his life and in his saving work. It follows that all theology is christological. We know God only through Christ: there is no theology, therefore, without Christology.

(c) It is *ecclesial* in character. It is within the Church that theology hears and receives the word of God: it is within the Church, and as an auxiliary of the Church and its magisterium, that theology seeks to understand and interpret the word of God; finally it is in communion with the theologians of the past and in dialogue with those of the present that carries on its work of reflection. There is no theology without reference to the Church.

(d) It is *anthropological* in character. The revelation of God is, at the same time, a revelation to man of his own mystery; for what is deepest in man is the mystery of God, who inclines towards him and overshadows him with his love. Whether he knows it or not, man is called by love Itself to share in the divine life. This is the secret of his being. Consequently theology cannot speak of God without speaking of man, just as it cannot speak of man without speaking of God. There is no theology without anthropology.[5] Moreover since God has chosen to manifest himself by means of the Incarnation, that is to say through the words, gestures and actions of the man Jesus, it follows that theology cannot understand the mysteries of the divine life without deepening its knowledge of man and of human experience. For it is man who has been assumed by the Son of God to express the Absolute. Finally, since the message of Christ is addressed not only to man, but to man *en situation-historique,* theological reflection cannot be constructed *in abstracto,* setting out from the notion of man *ut sic.*

---

5. E. Schillebeeckx, "Ecclesia in mundo hujus temporis," *Angelicum,* 43 (1966), pp. 346-347.

Just as Christ spoke the language of his time, theology must speak so that it can be heard by man today. The word of God asks to be made concrete for each generation through a theology which speaks *in each generation's terms*.

4. *Christ as the object of theology*

The formulations we have looked at up to now, that is: God as God, God the savior, God living and the source of life, all agree in recognizing that the formal object of theology is God. Other theologians, such as É. Mersch and the champions of kerygmatic theology, express themselves differently: the object of theology, they say, is Christ.

1. É. MERSCH'S OPINION

According to Mersch, the object of theology and its center *par excellence* is the mystical or total Christ.[6] The material object of theology, he points out, is two-fold: there is the principal object (God) and the secondary object (the works of God). The central object of theology, he goes on, must therefore embrace this two-fold object. This central object is none other than the total, or mystical, Christ. On the one hand, Christ is God; on the other, he is God-Man, with the whole of humanity which is united to him and incorporated in him. It is for this reason that it can and must be said that the total Christ is the central and integral object of theology. Moreover the mystical Christ is the *first intelligible;* for it is the mystery which opens the way for us to all the rest. This doctrine of the total Christ is eminently suited to give theology its own organic unity. It brings us to the center of intelligibility of the whole mystery of salvation. While the Thomist

---

6. É Mersch, "Le Christ mystique, centre de la théologie comme science," *Nouvelle Revue théologique,* 61 (1934), pp. 449-475; Idem, "L'objet de la théologie et le Christus totus," *Recherches de science religieuse,* 26 (1936), pp. 129-157.

systematization is theocentric, that proposed by Mersch will obviously be Christocentric.

Mersch's view, though it contains excellent elements, is ambiguous at certain points. It is true that Christ is central to the whole history of salvation. It is also true that the total Christ is the integral *material* object of theology. It is true again that the mystery of salvation becomes intelligible to us only through Christ. Finally it is true that, in respect of our actual union with God, the divine life is communicated to us only in Christ and through Christ. This granted, can one simply say without more ado that Christ is the formal object of theology? Our own answer to the question lies in the following remarks.

(a) Theology, as the science of the object of faith, must share the movement and orientation of faith. Now faith is, in the last analysis, wholly directed *towards God the savior*. "God's love for us was revealed when *God sent* into the world *his only Son* so that we could have life through him." That is why "we have known and put our faith in God's love towards ourselves" (1 Jn 4, 9-16). Our faith then is directed towards God who has sent his Son and thus witnessed to his love for us. It is in Christ that the loving design of God the savior manifests itself and draws us. In the *epiphany* of God's love Christ is *first*. But the ultimate object of our faith, and therefore of theology, is *God-who-saves-us-through-Christ* or God the savior.

(b) Theology seeks to construe the *datum* revealed according to the very *order* of the divine wisdom. Now the plan of the divine wisdom is precisely to sum up all in Christ in order *to draw men to God*. Christ himself and his mystical body are ordered to God: "All is yours; and you are Christ's; and Christ is God's" (1 Cor 3, 22-3); and, in the Epistle to the Ephesians, "Blessed be God the Father of our Lord Jesus Christ ... who has determined that we should become his adopted sons through Jesus Christ ... to the praise of the glory of his grace, which he gives freely to us in the Beloved" (Eph 1, 3-7). In Mersch's perspective, on the other hand, the mystery of the Trinity and the mission of the divine Persons is relegated to second place in order to concentrate attention on the primary object, the mystery of the mystical Christ.

(c) If we go back to what we said above about the object of theology, we can suggest now a definition formulated in more detail and with more precision: *God our savior, as manifested in Christ and through Christ*. Mersch's statement (that the mystical Christ is the first intelligible) can then be distinguished as follows. That the mystical Christ is the first intelligible for us in the order of our own discovery and mental acquisition, we concede. That it is the first intelligible in the order of the divine wisdom, we deny. For in this order the mystery of the mystical Christ derives its intelligibility only from its relation to the mystery of the living God one and triune, to whom it is its mission to introduce us. If it is true that we arrive at the mystery of the God who is revealing himself only by way of Christ, it is only through the mystery of God that we can understand and value the mystery of Christ.[7]

(d) This said, we can still ask ourselves whether a Christocentric systematization is preferable to a theocentric one. The Christocentric systematization proposed by Mersch is not only legitimate but perhaps even preferable from a pedagogical point of view since it corresponds more faithfully to the economy of salvation and its manifestation. Certainly it is a felicitous complement to the theocentric vision of the middle ages. But, we insist, the question of systematization cannot be confused with that of the object of theology. They are two quite distinct questions. Once it is admitted that the object of theology is God as God, there is nothing to stop one adopting a Christocentric systematization or a theocentric one, or an ecclesiocentric one or even an anthropocentric one. There are several possible systematizations, just as there are several types of theology. Each systematization has its own advantages and inconveniences. The principle inconveniences of the theocentric synthesis is that it can lead to an insufficient

---

7. F. Bourassa, "Sur le traité de la Trinité," *Gregorianum*, 47 (1966), pp. 260-264.

attention to the character of the structure and history or pedagogy of revelation.

2. THE POSITION OF KERYGMATIC THEOLOGY

The theologians who are called kerygmatic (from the Greek χηρύσσειν, to preach, to proclaim) have also proposed a Christocentric systematization; they have even proposed a double theology with a double object. One is aware of the historical context in which this kerygmatic theology appeared. Moved by the pastoral lamentations of those who deplored the ignorance and mediocrity of the life which they found among their flocks, a certain number of theologians (J . A. Jungmann, F. Lackner, H. Rahner, J. B. Lotz, F. Dander) thought that they had discovered the reason for this state of affairs in the defective way in which Christianity was being presented, or, at a deeper level, in the inadequate teaching of theology. They observed that preaching is often only diluted form of theological teaching, using the terminology, the arguments and the "objections" of theology. The catechism used in schools is too like an abridgment of the treatises of theology. Theology, itself, too devoted to demonstrations and refutations has come to forget that it is the science of salvation and that each of the dogmas of Christianity has its echo in personal religious life. There is a gulf between the theology of the academic and pastoral life. Faced with this problem Jungmann asked that one should distinguish clearly between the proclamation of the message of Christianity and scientific theology, and he hoped that preaching would draw its inspiration more from the sort of presentation found in Scripture and the Fathers, and that it would, consequently, have Christ and the history of salvation as its axis.

F. Lackner and J. B. Lotz claimed that the needs of the apostolate demanded more than this. They proposed to set up, side by side with traditional theology, what they called a kerygmatic theology, the first, the theology of the universities having as its object God *sub ratione Deitatis* and being a scientific, systematic theology preoccupied with research, and the second, the theology of the seminaries, having as its object Christ, and being a theology orientated to preaching and therefore historical, concerned with the progress and structure of revelation, and with the psychology and pedagogy of presenting the message of Christianity according to the example of Christ himself and of the Fathers of the Church in their homilies. While academic theology envisages the *datum* revealed under the aspect of the true, kerygmatic theology envisages it under the aspect of the good, of value. While the first expresses itself in technical language conformed to the exigencies of science, the second needs to express itself simply and evocatively through images; it aims at being the theology of the heart, a moving presentation of the fundamental themes of revelation because it has itself been moved by them. H. Rahner and F. Dander have themselves offered experimental types of this sort of theology.[8] What are we to think of the position which the kerygmatic theologians take up?

COMMENT

1. Immediately contested as it was (particuarly by M. Schmaus, A. Stoltz, C. Fabro and H. Weisweiler), the idea of a double theology (scientific and kerygmatic), with a double object (God on the one hand, Christ on the other) has been finally rejected and rightly so. Theology is the science of salvation. A theology which wants to be faithful to its object, to know the word of salvation spoken by the God who is savior, must, of necessity, bring out in each mystery this value for salvation and demonstrate its power to deepen Christian life. It is not simply by taking thought for edification or through pious corollaries that theology must be the science of salvation; it must be so in exerting itself according to the very requirements of the content of faith. Theology would not fulfill the demands of its object if it

---

8. H. Rahner, *Eine Theologie der Verkündigung* (Freiburg i Br., 1939); F. Dander, *Christus alles und in Allem* (Innsbruck - Leipzig, 1939).

neglected the aspect which manifests the word of God as the word of salvation. It would no longer be theology but rather a sterile metaphysic. That theology should certainly be more attentive to the structure of revelation, more Christocentric, more pastoral in its preoccupations, more conscious of its social function in the Church, all the theologians of the period, that is roughly 1936-1940, recognized gladly. The majority, nevertheless, were of the opinion that a special theology erecting itself in opposition to theology in the classical sense was superfluous; the task ought to be assured by scientific theology itself.

2. In reality, as often happens in the course of discussion, the debate had strayed from the subject. The crucial question, as Jungmann usefully reminded us is not one of theology, but of what is the proper relationship between theology and preaching.[9] F. X. Arnold observed for his part, "it is not to a kerygmatic theology but to the *kerygma* that a proper temper is coming back. So it is for the kerygma, for preaching, to take cognizance that it must, above all, conceive, order and concentrate the message of Christianity in a really kerygmatic way, but at the same time employ a particular method and language." [10]

In fact preaching, catechesis and theology all work on the *datum* of revelation but at different levels, towards different ends and consequently according to different laws. Theology is a science and a technical study. It is not a sermon; nor is it a school of preaching or of catechesis aiming at a popular exposition of Christian doctrine. Theology is the science of the object of faith, with all the exigencies of a science: rigorous analysis, technical terminology, exact method, coherent systematization. It would indeed be ungracious to refuse to theology what is willingly conceded to other sciences.

3. Although preaching, catechesis and theology constitute

---

9. J. A. Jungmann, "Le problème du message à transmettre ou le problème kérygmatique," *Lumen Vitae*, 5 (1950), p. 276.
10. F. X. Arnold, "Renouveau de la prédication dogmatique et de la catéchèse," *Lumen Vitae*, 3 (1948), p. 504.

three different levels at which the object of faith is presented and explained, preaching and catechesis pose problems which need to be solved in a scientific way. In relation to preaching for instance, all the problems concern its own nature, necessity and effectiveness, its own forms and laws.[11] These problems posed by preaching and catechesis and homiletics constitute the matter of these new sciences which we call *homiletics* and *catechetics*. And indeed the chief fruit of controversy about kerygmatic and scientific theology has been a more definite awareness of the necessary role of these sciences in the Church.

In conclusion, may we cite Fr. Yves Congar's judgment upon kerygmatic theology. "The kerygmatics," he says, "put their finger on a very real and very serious problem, but it is not quite certain that they saw it in its proper perspective. Preaching is nourished by theology but it is not theology." Each has its own law and its own end. "One doesn't engage a chemist as a cook," says Newman, "or a mineralogist as a mason." They are both necessary but each to his own end. "Certainly," Fr. Congar goes on, "there is nothing against composing treatises in which one uses theological material to answer to the characteristic end and exigencies of preaching — a legitimate and laudable undertaking, provided one does not wish to replace theology in the accepted sense by this utilitarian derivative, a thing moreover which the kerygmatics denied that they wished to do. We merely draw attention to two dangers: (1) the danger of a certain pastoral pragmatism, which would lead only too soon to the defects which an absence of real culture brings with it — a shrinking of perspectives, a loss of detachment, a risk of living vaguely and narrowly, a lack of humanism in the profound sense . . . . The ideal method, the method which would lead to the best results, would be to go by way of a disinterested theological culture and an analytic theology, seriously undertaken, and then to have the chance, the courage, the grace, the strength, to reassess everything in the light of a recourse to biblical studies and in the evangelical synthesis of the Christian mystery. (2) The danger of despairing too soon

---

11. D. Grasso, *Proclaiming God's Message* (Notre Dame, Indiana, 1965).

and superficially, of the living plenitude and possibilities of a true theology, an authentic science of faith. If one has really understood its supernatural, religious epistemological status, its unity, of whom it speaks, from what sources it draws its life, one will see that it has the means to answer, from its own point of view, the needs of a living *kerygma*. Such a theology, taking the word of God as its point of departure, is an unveiling of man and of things, a seeing of them, not from their own point of view but from the point of view of God, their source and end, from the point of view of his design for their salvation, which is, supremely, Jesus Christ .... Whether he sets out from a scientific theology or from a kerygmatic one, the apostle will still have to resolve the intrinsic problems of preaching, to accomplish the transition from knowledge to 'prophecy,' to delivering the prophetic message to man. For this he needs the mediation of contemplation and prayer, of spiritual perception and imaginative vision, of dialogue, of an inner understanding and lastly a means of outer expression, which is not for us to envisage here. It is a problem of the priest who is charged with the duty of preaching the word of God, not a problem of theology." [12]

5. *Theology or history of salvation?*

This dichotomy constitutes another way of attacking the question of the object of theology. Theology, says St. Thomas, has, as its formal object, or its subject, God as God, God as he knows himself to be and as he communicates himself to us through revelation.[13] Revelation on the other hand comes to us under the form of events which intervene in the course of human history and make up the history of salvation. The Old Testament recounts the *mirabilia Dei* on behalf of his people; and the New Testament is the good news of him who is present with us in Jesus Christ. Hence the question arises; is the object of theology

---

12. Y. Congar, *La foi et la théologie* (Tournai and Paris, 1962), pp. 186-188.
13. S. Th., 1:1:7.

the history of salvation or God as God? Should we talk of '*theology*' or of '*economy*' (God's plan of salvation)?

There is, to tell the truth, no break between theology and economy. Theology is Christological in its process and theological in its object. That is, the God who reveals is a God who involves himself in history and who reveals himself there in the very action in which he is involved. It is in the history of salvation and through the history of salvation that God, one and triune, makes himself known to us and makes known to us his plan of salvation. God manifests himself in the depths of a history, so that we can know him only by setting out from the economy of salvation. In order to know the goodness, the justice, the mercy of the God of the Old Testament we have to examine the history of Israel which recounts the experiences of God's people with their God, where the ways of God with regard to his people manifest something of his inner being.[14] In order to know the Father's love for his Son and for men we have to meditate upon the manifestations of his love in the life and actions and death of Christ. We can say nothing of God unless we take, as our point of departure, the history of salvation in which he has revealed himself. The way which leads to the inner mystery of God is the history of salvation, inaugurated in the Old Testament, and consummated in Christ and his Church.

Theology in its turn must meditate upon the history of salvation. It is talk about God, but about God known through economy. Two extremes threaten theology, that of reducing theology to the history of salvation and so refusing to penetrate to the inner mystery of God, and that of constructing a pure theology without reference to history, with the risk of forgetting that God reveals himself within an economy. If theology remains faithful to the movement of revelation and seeks to attain God where he makes himself known, that is, in the history of salvation which culminates in Jesus Christ, there can be no divorce in it between theology and economy. A theology attentive to the history of salvation is not opposed to a theology whose axis is God. And, inversely a theology of the living God could not be elaborated

---

14. Const. *Dei verbum* on revelation, n. 14.

independently of the history of salvation. Theology recognizes that God transcends the history of salvation and that the life of the Trinity is sufficient to itself. But it recognizes at the same time that we know nothing of this inner life of God except through the economy of salvation. There is no break between theology and the history of salvation, between theology and economy. Theology is reflection upon God, manifested in Jesus Christ. Its object is God known through the history of salvation.[15]

---

15. See on this subject: R. Latourelle, *Theology of Revelation* (Alba House, New York, 1966), pp. 343-358; E. Schillebeeckx, *Revelation and Theology* (Sheed & Ward, New York, 1967), pp. 325-39 and 109-13; F. Bourassa, "Sur le traité de la Trinité," *Gregorianum*, 47 (1966), pp. 254-85.

CHAPTER III   REASON AND FAITH IN THE THEOLOGICAL PROCESS

Up to now we have been considering theology mainly from the point of view of its object. Let us think now about the subject who applies himself to theology, the theologian. The question which arises immediately is: is the theological process a work of pure reason, a reflection of a philosophic kind upon something entitled to be described as "revealed," so that even an unbeliever, a heretic or an historian of religions can apply himself to it just as well as a believer? If, on the other hand, there is no theology without faith, by what right does faith intervene? To understand more clearly the respective roles of faith and reason, let us try to see the theological process at its different stages.

1. *Faith in search of understanding*

1. Theology is supernatural by reason of its source. At the origin of all theology there is a double gift of God, the gift of the word of God and the gift of faith to adhere to this word with absolute certainty. For faith is not the result of an apologetic proof or demonstration, but a gift of grace. "No one can come to me," said Christ, "unless the Father who sent me draws him" (Jn 6, 44-5; cf. Acts 16, 14; 2 Cor 4, 6; 1 Jn 5, 6). All theology rests on a double divine initiative, God's initiative in emerging from his mystery and entering into a dialogue of friendship with man, his

initiative in inviting us to believe, as if it were personally addressed to us, the word we hear. It is God who takes the initiative in speaking the word, and it is God who through the propensity and attraction he evokes within us, draws from us the movement of response, the response of faith. At the origin of theology, as at the origin of faith, all is the gift of God: all is grace.

2. Faith gives rise to theology, on the plane of the adherence of faith as on the plane of the object of faith.

Faith, whether as an act or a state of consciousness, is not yet the vision of God but knowledge *"ex auditu"* (Rom 10, 16). "We walk by faith, not by sight" (2 Cor 5, 7). We live in an economy of word and hearing, of witness and faith. We believe in the mystery on the word of witnesses, without seeing it. We have access to God only through the mediation of signs, signs of Christ's flesh, signs of his human speech. Faith is an initial possession, though an obscure and imperfect one, of the object we aspire to know. It reaches out towards a clear experience of the living God whose witness it has received. It wishes to contemplate unveiled him whom it knows to be the cause of its happiness. For this reason there is within faith itself an appetite for vision, a desire to know and to see. Adherence to what it has been told and a tending towards vision are the two essential aspects of the act of faith. Because it does not see, faith seeks to see, to understand. Theology is not better than faith, but it is an attempt to respond to this desire for vision which will be satisfied only in heaven. There is, then, in faith, both as an act and as a state of consciousness, in the measure in which it is the opposite of the act or state of vision, a dynamism which creates the mind's search to understand. The beginning of intellectual enquiry is always present in faith. In an inchoate way, belief already implies theology.

Faith gives rise to theology also in its object and content; for the unfathomable riches of Christ will never be exhausted (Eph 3, 8). In Christ are hid all the treasures of wisdom and knowledge (Col 2, 3). The human mind cannot remain indifferent to understanding what is virtually implied by revealed truth; for the truth in question has the answer to the most serious problems of our condition, both in time and eternity. "The mystery of man is revealed only in the mystery of the Incarnate Word." [1] The message of faith therefore creates in the mind a desire to understand, not through simple intellectual curiosity, but because the reality which it reveals appears as the supreme value in human life, as what gives it its ultimate meaning and makes it worth the trouble of living. The word of God is inexhaustible: it appeals for ever to both mind and heart. It is not a territory whose exploration will one day be over, but an abyss which deepens as the spirit deepens in response.

2. *Theological understanding in the light of faith*

Faith, even without charity, exercises a constant influence throughout the whole of the theological process, in the sense that the certitude of faith presides over it, and by its continued presence assures its validity. By faith the theologian holds as absolutely certain truths which he can not know either by experience or by reflection. It is because of that certainty that he applies himself to understanding the content of God's word. He seeks to understand, not only the formulas and propositions in which the mystery is stated, but the mystery itself; for his faith assures him that the propositions denote the divine reality itself. When the theologian affirms that there are, in Christ, two natures and one person, he holds as absolutely certain that the words are answerable to the reality, and that is why he seeks to understand the reality. The certainty of his faith is the motive and guarantee of his reflection. It is faith which gives theological reflection its *realism;* for faith apprehends the reality of the mystery. It is faith which keeps theology in contact with divine reality, and it is from faith that it derives its value as a science of the real. Without this permanent adherence which justifies it, theology would be without proper reference to the reality of the mystery at all; Christian statements would be only hypotheses, a human commentary relevant perhaps to the history of religion, but not to the knowledge of God. The

---

1. Const. *Gaudium et Spes,* n. 22.

theologian would be in the position of someone who pursues his research upon a religion different from his own (Buddhism or Hinduism for instance), without sharing its beliefs. Theology would no longer be the science of the knowledge of God or of divine realities revealed and believed. Without faith the statements of Christians would no longer be the certain principles upon which the theologian bases himself in order to construct the science of the living God. Theology would be a science without principles. That is why the formal heretic cannot be considered a theologian in the proper sense.[2]

Faith exercises its influence throughout the theological process not only because the certainty of faith presides over the theologian's enquiry and assures its validity, but also because of the

---

2. It is important to distinguish the formal heretic from the material heretic. The formal heretic is one who consciously and deliberately sins against faith because he denies one or more articles of faith. The material heretic is one who errs in matters of faith, but without wishing to do so: he has a good conscience.

The material heretic can have both faith and charity, and can really produce a work of theology. Grace by-passes the errors of the sincere Protestant just as it by-passes the errors of the parish priest who is materially deceived in matters of faith or does not know what the truth of faith is. The formal heretic, on the other hand, is not capable of being called a theologian in the proper sense. "The heretic," says St. Thomas, "who refuses to believe a single article of faith has not the habit of faith, neither of faith formed nor of faith unformed" (2-2:5:3:c). "The other articles of faith on which he is not in error, he does not hold in the same way as the believer holds them, that is to say by simple adherence to the first Truth, for which it is necessary to have the help of the habit of faith. The heretic retains certain points of faith by his own will and his own judgment" (2-2:5:3:1).

The position of the formal heretic is as follows: (a) He has not the absolute certainty of faith founded on the authority of God and the gift of grace, but a personal opinion, founded on his own will and judgment. He retains, however, his theological concepts and his theological manner of thought. (b) The articles of faith are not for the formal heretic, solid truths which serve as the basic principles of a true science of faith, but personal opinions. The work of the formal heretic will be a hypothetical construction.

In short the formal heretic, because he has rejected the authority of

continuous dynamic of the light of faith. The grace of faith connaturalizes man in the supernatural world of the Gospel. God imparts to the heightened human intelligence a propensity towards himself, the subsistent truth in person, and draws man into a conformity of consciousness with the very consciousness of God. From this infused impulse through which it is constantly bent upon God and drawn towards him, theological reflection receives its stimulus and its direction. The theologian seeks at the same time to understand and to conform his thought to the truth of

God and of the Church, because he has not the light of faith, and because he has no longer any principles on which to base his faith, cannot be described as a theologian in the proper sense. His work is no longer the work of a believer taking its point from the revealed *datum* accepted by faith, but a personal and hypothetical systematization. He can, however, be called a theologian in a derived and inaccurate sense, from the material similarity of his work to theological work in the strict sense.

If we now consider things as they look from outside, it can happen that there is no apparent difference between the work of the authentic theologian and the work of the formal heretic. But the position of the heretic cannot be judged on mere appearances, it must be judged from the point of view of his real and objective situation, just as the condition of the sinner has to be judged. Still it is difficult to imagine a work written by a formal heretic having in the concrete the same quality as the work of a believing theologian, just as the fruits of the sinner would not be the same as those of the just man. In actual fact, the formal heretic who rejects the authority of the Church no longer has a norm for judging matters of faith accurately; consequently he is easily mistaken, at least in small things and very probably in great things. His sin, moreover, deprives him of grace and of the gifts of the Holy Spirit. The believing theologian on the other hand works under the direction of the Church, and, in virtue of the light of faith, and of the gifts of the Holy Spirit, has a supernatural connaturality with the object of faith, which inspires and governs his work. That is why in the concrete, other things being equal in the sphere of intelligence and other natural gifts, it is to be presumed that the work of the believing theologian will excel that of the heretic. But, it must be repeated, the problem is not to be resolved from the point of view of appearances but according to the objective state in which the heretic and the believing theologian are.

God as obscurely foreseen and expressed in the grace of faith. Under the influence of this supernatural dynamic his faculties for discovery are stimulated: the revealed analogies take on warmth and life; new analogies suggest themselves to illustrate the richness of what is revealed. All theological work is accomplished in the light of God who bends and draws the theologian himself, and under the direction of the magisterium of the Church, the authorized interpreter of the word revealed.

Theology then is the joint work of the mind's activity and the light of faith, the work of reason, heightened and animated by faith: together they constitute a dynamic of knowledge human-divine and completely unique.

The intellect for its own part makes use of all the laws which govern human reasoning and human techniques and the exigencies of human science, particularly in matter of method, systematization and synthesis, exercising its activity in various ways: (a) it establishes the fact of revelation, or of the word of God in history, and the fact of the Church as the trustee and mediator of this word through the ages; (b) it defends revealed truth in showing that it is neither impossible nor senseless, but supremely intelligible; (c) it pursues that fruitful understanding of the mysteries of faith which the first Vatican Council described in the following terms:

> "When reason illumined by faith seeks within its limits with devotion and care, it arrives at a certain understanding of the mysteries which is very fruitful, and this may be either by means of analogy with natural knowledge, or by the relations which it establishes among the mysteries themselves or between the mysteries of the last end of man." [3]

3. *Theology and the gifts of the Spirit*

What we have said so far about the theological process would

---

3. Denzinger-Schömetzer, 3016. We shall examine the different forms which theological reflection can take in more detail in chapter 2 of part II, apropos of theological method.

be valid even for the theologian who had only faith, without charity. Let us think now about theological activity carried on not only in faith, but in a faith which expands and opens out in charity and in the gifts of the Holy Spirit. This is after all the normal state of healthy theology, and it is then that theology bears its best fruit.

With sanctifying grace, with living faith, we receive, in different degrees, the gifts of the Holy Spirit. While the theological virtues (faith, hope and charity) give us the power to act supernaturally, the gifts of the Spirit are to make us docile to his action. The gift of understanding particularly makes the mind more apt to penetrate the truths of faith. The gift of wisdom infuses into the theologian's soul, an affective connaturality with the object of faith which allows him to judge it accurately according to the divine thought. We are aware that connaturality with an object can be the fruit of the discursive activities of the mind, but it can also be the fruit of a communion of will which conforms it to the loved. The love of the object loved establishes then between the person who loves and the object loved an affinity which makes him espouse the state of the object loved in order to think of it accurately. The gift of wisdom infuses in us a connaturality of this sort with regard to divine realities. It establishes between us and the Gospel a communion of love. Its source is in the will, but its effect is in the understanding, which it makes capable of thinking and judging according to the thought and judgment of God.

This granted, we can say that theological enquiry, which brings into play all the resources of human reasoning, has at its disposition also, when it is carried on in normal conditions, a higher capacity for understanding, founded on the conformity of human will with the divine will which is the fruit of a living faith and of the gifts of the Spirit. "He who is united to the Lord is one spirit with him" (1 Cor 6, 17). "The man who is left to resources of his nature only does not receive the things of the Spirit of God" (1 Cor 2, 14). But he who is born of the Spirit and lives by the Spirit, judges according to the Spirit of the Lord. The grace of Christ, like an unerring instinct, draws the theologian toward

the object of faith making his thought coincide with the thought
of Christ and grasp its implications and resonances. As a friend
who, because he loves him, enters more deeply into the thought
of his friend than anyone else, so the theologian shares, in a
sense, the consciousness of Christ. He has within him Christ's
thoughts and feelings and judgments about God and man. Christ,
through his spirit informs and directs the processes of his mind
and gives him a living understanding of his mystery. The perfect
theologian therefore is both Doctor and Confessor. Such were
St. Augustine, St. Bonaventure, St. Thomas and St. Robert Bellarmine. In them faith opened out into charity and the gifts of the
Spirit.

In a lesser way, we must say the same of our own condition.
What is the object of theological enquiry if it is not the word of
God in Jesus Christ? And who can give us an understanding of
this word if not the Spirit of Christ? Theology will bear its best
fruit in us only if we live in love, under the guidance of the Spirit.
The only master who can open our eyes to the presence of Christ
in his word is his Spirit. He alone, if we allow ourselves to be
taught by him in prayer and to be led by him in our lives, will
give us that connaturality of love by which we can penetrate the
depth and taste the sweetness of the divine mystery. For theology
is the science of our life in Christ.[4]

---

4. Theology thus understood is one with the contemplation of the Greek
   Fathers, particularly Clement of Alexandria, who used the word *gnosis*
   for the deepening of faith which takes its initiative from the faith received in baptism. *Gnosis* is not just adherence to the truth but an
   understanding of faith acquired by study and by the exercise of
   charity. It is the desire to be united to God by an inner experience at
   once affective and contemplative. Through his faith, always seeking
   both understanding and the divine will, the perfect gnostic devoted
   himself to becoming the living image of Christ and, like him, the perfect
   teacher. According to Clement of Alexandria three things constitute the
   gnostic Christian: contemplation, the fulfillment of the Lord's precepts
   and the formation of perfect Christians.
   Cf. R. Latourelle, *Theology of Revelation* (Alba House, New York,
   1966), p. 112.

CHAPTER IV THEOLOGY AS SCIENCE AND WISDOM

I. THEOLOGY AS SCIENCE

1. *The context of the problem*

At the beginning of the *Summa Theologica* St. Thomas poses the question, "Is sacred doctrine a science?" If theology is a science is it so in the same sense as the human sciences we are familiar with or in a sense wholly or partly different?

Today, no one seriously doubts that theology is a true science, since it has its own special object, method, unity and systematization. But in the Middle Ages the answer did not seem so obvious. Some upheld the view that theology is not a science. Duns Scotus considered that if the concept of science were to be applied to theology, it would have to undergo such a modification that it would scarcely retain its original meaning. Others saw in theology a sort of middle term between faith and reason. This problem of the relationship between theology and the other sciences was no less important in the Middle Ages than is the modern problem of the relationship between faith and reason. But it has more than an historical interest, since it was the occasion for St. Thomas

to enlarge the concept of science and prepare the way for the idea
we have of it today.

In the Middle Ages the problem of theology as a science had
its origin in the Aristotelian definition of science. Science in the
mind of Aristotle, and according to the tradition transmitted by
St. Thomas and his contemporaries, is a knowledge which is certain and valid at all times, being the result of logical deduction.
It is *certain* because it proceeds from primary evidence which is
not itself demonstrable. It is *deductive* because it is capable of
drawing out its conclusions by means of necessary reasoning into
universally valid principles. Science is a perfect knowledge because it attains to things in their principles, in what is necessary
to them. It is a knowledge which is certain because grounded upon
the causes of being. To this type of Aristotelian science geometry
for instance belongs, with its theorems based on evident principles, on the axioms. Without this kind of initial evidence there
can be no science.

It is immediately obvious that it is difficult to apply such a
conception of science to theology, since revealed truth is not
seen but believed. Christian mysteries are not the object of
ordinary experience or observation, but are known by means of
witness and faith. Now it was considered in the Middle Ages that
a body of knowledge which depended on report (history for instance) does not correspond to the idea of science, for the report
of witnesses cannot lead to certainty but only to probability and
opinion. Hence the dilemma: either theology recognizes the
Aristotelian notion of science with the necessity for evident first
principles, and has then to eject faith from theology in order to
preserve its status as a science; or else theology denies the Aristotelian notion of science, and then theology can scarcely be
distinguished from faith. Either it sacrifices the scientific ideal
or else it sacrifices faith. The conclusion is that the man of science
and the believer should follow different paths. It was in this way
that the problem of theology as a science presented itself to the
Middle Ages.[1]

---

1. It is obvious that the answer to the question, "Is theology a science?"

2. *The answer of St. Thomas*

St. Thomas distinguishes, in the hierarchy of science, two types of science. Sciences of the first type are based on evidence inside the science itself, the first principles or axioms of geometry for instance. Sciences of the second type, on the other hand, depend on evidence which they borrow from neighboring sciences: thus physics depends on evidence drawn from mathematics, optics on principles which come from geometry. A science which obtains its primary facts for first principles from another science he calls a subordinate or inferior science. That on the other hand which lends its principles to another science he calls a subordinating or superior science. In this way every science rests on evident principles, either immediately or remotely.[2]

Let us now apply this dictinction to theology. It is true that theology has no immediate evidence of its first principles, that is of the truths of revelation; but these are evident in another "science," another body of knowledge, the very knowledge of God. That is why the status of theology as a science can be com-

depends to a large extent on what one's definition of science is. Science can be defined in at least three ways: (a) as certain and deductive knowledge as understood by Aristotle, in his three degrees (first degree, physics or philosophy of nature [what we call cosmology]; second degree, arithmetic and geometry; third degree, metaphysics); (b) as experimental science, physics and chemistry for example; (c) as a methodical and systematic body of knowledge unified by taking as its point of departure a given object. The method and the kind of unity will differ according to the object. They will obviously not be the same in history, sociology, anthropology and theology.

2. "Sciendum est quod duplex est scientiarum genus. Quaedam enim sunt quae procedunt ex principiis notis lumine naturali intellectus, sicut arithmetica, geometria et huiusmodi. Quaedam vero sunt quae procedunt ex principiis notis lumine superioris scientiae, sicut perspectiva (optica) procedit ex principiis notificatis per geometriam, et musica (harmonia) ex principiis per arithmeticam notis. Et hoc modo sacra scientia est scientia, quia procedit ex principiis notis lumine superioris scientiae, quae scilicet est scientia, Dei et beatorum. Unde sicut musica credit principia tradita sibi ab arithmetica, ita doctrina sacra credit principia revelata sibi a Deo." *S. Th.*, 1:1:2c.

pared to the status of the sciences called subordinate; it is subordinate to the "science" or knowledge of God, for it receives its principles from God by revelation. These principles, the object of vision in the infinite knowledge of God, are assumed by theology in faith.[3] The position of theology as a science remains legitimate, since by faith it is in continuity with the knowledge of God and shares in his certainty, which is vision.[4]

In short St. Thomas's answer to the question, "Is theology a science?" can be put in this way. Theology is a true science, but it belongs to the type of science called a subordinate science, for it receives its principles from the knowledge of God. Its status is legitimate because the principles of theology, that is the revealed truths, are evident in the knowledge of God, and because theology, being in continuity with divine knowledge through revelation and faith, participates in the evidence of divine knowledge. Theology is then, in its own way, a certain and deductive knowledge.[5]

3. *Comment on the answer of St. Thomas*

St. Thomas's explanation, if it clears the air, does not dispose of all the difficulties. For the resemblance which exists between

---

3. "Theologia est inferior (subalternata) scientiae quae est in Deo. Nos enim imperfecte cognoscimus id quod ipse perfectissime cognoscit; et sicut scientia subalternata a superiori supponit aliqua, et per illa tanquam per principia procedit, sic theologia articulos fidei, qui infallibiliter probati sunt in scientia Dei supponit et eis credit et per istud procedit ad probandum ulterius illa quae ex articulis sequuntur. Est ergo theologia quasi subalternata divinae sapientiae, a qua accipit principia sua (*Sent.* Prol. a. 3. sol.).

4. "Ille qui habet scientiam subalternatam non perfecte attingit ad rationem sciendi, nisi in quantum eius cognitio continuatur quodammodo cum cognitione eius qui habet scientiam subalternantem" (*De Veritate*, 14: 19: 3).

5. On the problem of theology as a science, see M.-D. Chenu, *La théologie comme science au XIIIe siècle* (Paris, 1945). C. Dumont, La réflexion sur la méthode théologique," *Nouvelle Revue Théologique*, 83 (1961), pp. 1034-1050; 84 (1962), pp. 17-35; P. Tihon, *Foi et théologie selon Godefroid de Fontaines* (Bruges & Paris, 1966).

secular sciences and sacred science is in the order of analogy. Christian theology will always overflow the Aristotelian categories. The resemblance consists in the fact that the theologian receives from God the mysteries which he applies himself to understanding just as the subordinate science receives its principles from the superior one. The difference lies in this: the man who learns an inferior science (optics for instance) can just as well learn the superior science (geometry for instance); the theologian on the contrary cannot enjoy the beatific vision but only hope for it in the life to come. St. Thomas in having recourse to explanation by subordination in order to establish the status of theological science, does not then speak in an univocal, but in an analogical sense.

His explanation, however, covers a deeper intuition. St. Thomas, it seems, wanted to suggest a new type of scientific subordination, which was not known, and could not be known, to Aristotle. According to this new conception of things the proto-type of science is not human knowledge but divine knowledge. And all the human sciences act as imperfect approaches to this infinite knowledge, theology occupying a privileged position. In virtue of the supernatural dynamic with which it heightens and gives life to the theological process, faith establishes between the knowledge of God and the reflection of the believer a profound organic continuity. The divine knowledge is prolonged and lives in the human reason. Theology is thus bound to the divine knowledge by an inner relationship which it would be impossible to find to the same degree between inferior and superior human sciences.

St. Thomas did not break entirely with the Aristotelian conception of science, but he drew attention to a new type of subordination. He enlarged the notion of science, and by that very fact, became the forerunner of the modern concept.

4. *Theology and the modern notion of science*

Modern thought has accustomed us to an idea of science

much more receptive and comprehensive than the Aristotelian one. Today the term science is used for any discipline which has the advantages of its own object and method and leads to a communicable synthesis. The object studied may be of the experimental, historical or speculative order. From this point of view theology obviously qualifies as a science, since it has its own object, method, unity and systematization.

In modern scientific demonstration experience and reason are inseparable. But a science can be described as experimental or rational according to whether it is the recourse to experience or the part played by reason which dominates in it. Hence there are the positive sciences where fact and experience predominate, and the rational sciences where reason predominates. To which of these types, according to modern thought does theology belong? Theologians here are divided. Some, faithful to the Aristotelian-scholastic idea of science, makes theology a clearly speculative science. Others, remarking that theology is characterized above all by being a science of something given, the revealed *datum,* and that it demands the setting up of a positive type of research, consider it as a science "fundamentally positive" but "positive integral," that is as a science which recognizes that theological deduction has a place, but within a process of which the design remains in itself inductive, and which aims at an understanding by other procedures than those only of Aristotelian demonstration.[6] From the point of view of modern science it seems to us legitimate to classify theology among sciences of the positive rather than the speculative type, since theology is the science of what is given in revelation (on which it is based and to which it makes constant reference), but on condition that the characteristically reflective function of theology should not be considered a function of secondary importance, for which in practice one need show little esteem. For that would be to destroy the very nature of theology as an understanding of faith.

---

6. T. Tshibangu, *Théologie positive et théologie spéculative* (Louvain and Paris, 1965), pp. 391-392.

II. THEOLOGY AS WISDOM

1. Generally speaking the wise man is he who, in a given order of things, fastens upon its essential principles, and gives to each of the elements of the order its just significance and value in relation to the whole. But theology is knowledge of every reality, divine and human, through the first of all causes, the Cause of causes, God himself, the source of the universal order. Theology proceeds from the fact of God and of his manifestation of himself to man. It tries to penetrate and reconstitute the divine design setting out from the elements which have been communicated to us by revelation. Like the prophet, it tries to see and judge all things according to the divine vision, in the light in which God himself sees them. It tries to find the intelligibility of each creature, as it exists in God and his creating and saving design, that is to say not only in its ontological structure but also in its concrete existential reality, and in its destination from the point of view of salvation. It wants to be God's interpreter in the midst of the world, setting out from his revelation. In the history of men it makes it its study to discern the action of God; in the signs of the times it tries to see the calling of God.[7] Because theology seeks in this way to understand the sense of beings and events according to the very vision of God it deserves the name of wisdom, and can fill, even with regard to human science, a role of unification and synthesis. It recapitulates in Christ all the realities of the universe, eternal and temporal, spiritual and material. For Christ is the Alpha and Omega, "the apex of human history, the point towards which the desires of history and civilization converge, the center of the human race, the joy of every heart and the fullness of every aspiration." [8] In medieval society, a society not yet secularized but still impregnated with religious wisdom, theology was the supreme science and illuminated the

---

7. Const. *Gaudium et Spes,* n. 4; M.-D. Chenu, "Les signes des temps," *Nouvelle Revue théologique,* 87 (1965), pp. 24-39.

8. Const. *Gaudium et Spes,* n. 45.

whole conspectus of culture.[9]

Yet theology must remember that the plane of wisdom which has been revealed to us is that of salvation. It is this plane which God's saving design communicates and not the secret of matter. That is left to man's own creative effort. Theology must respect the autonomy of human research in the sphere which is proper to it. Its own competence is in what concerns the ultimate meaning of things, including that of the universe, that is to say, their relationship to God and to his supernatural purpose of grace.[10]

2. Theology is wisdom also in the sense that it reflects upon its own principles just as philosophy, the supreme science of wisdom in the natural order does. In philosophy, criticism or epistemology has as its function the study of the objective value of our knowledge and of our natural certainties. In theology, the supreme science and wisdom in the order of revelation, there exists in the same way a reflective function whose task is to study the basis of our knowledge and certainty in matters of faith. This task is fulfilled by apologetics, which establishes the fact of revelation or of the Word of God in Jesus Christ, and consequently the rationality of the choice of faith. If God has indeed spoken and if the fact of this Word is firmly established, then what is spoken by the Word is rightly believed.

---

9. *S. Th.*, 1:1:5. The scholastics are in the habit of saying that philosophy is the servant of theology, meaning that philosophy is an aid to theology in trying to understand the divine mystery. It obviously does not follow that this auxiliary role is the only one exercised by philosophy. For philosophy is queen in her own province, not a simple servant. The expression means that theology, in order to fulfill its task as the science of the living, self-revealed God, makes use of philosophic reasoning and of the data of philosophy, and in this context philosophy is auxiliary to theology. Besides all the sciences are in turn principal sciences and auxiliary sciences. In their own sphere they are principal; outside it they are at the service of other sciences and become auxiliary.

10. Y. Congar, *La foi et la théologie,* p. 189.

CHAPTER V THEOLOGY, FAITH AND THE MAGISTERIUM

Without being itself either faith or the magisterium, theology has vital and many sided relationships with both.

1. *Theology and Faith*

What we have said so far is enough to indicate that faith and theology, although they are intimately united, are two distinct realities.[1]

1. Theology, as the understanding of faith, presupposes faith, by which man abandons himself wholly and freely to God, in complete homage of intellect and will to God who reveals and in a free assent to what is revealed.[2] Faith is the total adherence of a man to Christ, and his communion of life with him.

2. The motive of our assent in faith is the authority of God who reveals; in theology the motive is the quality of the demonstration. Certainty therefore varies in theology according to the value

---

1. K. Rahner, *Science évolution et pensée chrétienne* (Bruges & Paris, 1967), pp. 55-56.
2. Const. *Dei verbum*, n. 5.

of the arguments. It is even subject to error. In faith, on the other hand, certainty is absolute and irrevocable, based upon the rock of the Word of God.

3. Faith has as its object what is formally revealed by God. The object of theology includes not only revealed truths but also the conclusions and deductions which it draws from them, as well as all the truths connected with what is revealed.

4. Faith and theology constitute two distinct attitudes. While faith is the result of an existential engagement of the whole man, body and soul, mind and heart, in a choice which issues from the very center of his being, theology, as a science, is first and foremost the understanding of faith. Believing and reflecting upon belief are distinguished in the same way as living and reflecting upon life. They are two necessary attitudes within the same life but they are distinct. Just as human life is life which thinks about itself in order to discover its own meaning and orientation, so faith is a life which admits of reflection upon itself for its own good. Theology does not then seek to empty faith of everything but what is intelligible, but to serve faith by deepening our initial knowledge of it.

5. Faith attains God by union and communion with him. Theology is knowledge of God, but by way of the intelligence and the discursive reason. This discursive understanding certainly benefits from the greater clarity given to it by the light of faith, but it remains a scientific and rational process. Theological understanding though it is imperfect, obscure and slow in acquiring, is nonetheless, in the Church's witness, productive.[3]

2. *Theology and the Magisterium*

1. Theology and the magisterium have resemblances. Both indeed have a common origin, the revelation entrusted to the Church; and both pursue one and the same end, that of con-

---

3. Denzinger - Schönmetzer, 3016.

serving, penetrating always more deeply, defending and offering to men the deposit of faith, and so of helping men forward on the way of salvation.

2. On the other hand theology and the magisterium have different functions and different gifts. The relation between them should not be conceived as a relation between a charismatic understanding of revelation, proper to the magisterium, and a purely rational reflection proper to theology, but rather as a relation between two activities each animated by a different charism. It is the task of the magisterium in virtue of the mandate received from Christ, and by a gift of the Spirit proper to it (the charism of assistance), to preserve the deposit of faith (Tradition and Scripture) in its integrity, to protect it against all error or contamination, to judge authoritatively theology's interpretations of revelation, and itself to offer new and deeper understanding of the faith. Theology also receives a charism of the Spirit adapted to its function in the Church. This function is to investigate revelation under the guidance of the Holy Spirit and to bring to the knowledge of the Christian community, and in particular of the magisterium, the results of its research, so that through the doctrine taught by the ecclesiastical hierarchy these results may give light to the whole people of God.[4]

It is also the task of theology to collaborate with the magisterium in the teaching and the defense of the faith. In determining the relationship between the charism of the magisterium and the charism of theology, two points should be stressed: on the one hand, the gift of the Spirit given to the theologian and to all Christians does not dispense them from submission to the magisterium; on the other hand, fidelity to the magisterium does not mean passiveness and absence of initiative as if all impulse to research should come from the magisterium.[5]

---

4. Paul VI to those taking part in the international theological congress held in Rome in September 1966 (Latin text in the *Osservatore Romano* of October 2nd 1966).

5. Z. Alszeghy and M. Flick, "Il movimento teologico italiano," *Gregorianum*, 48 (1967), p. 18.

3. Theology exercises a function of mediation between the magisterium and the Christian community, first of all in the sense that it seeks to discern the signs of the times. It listens constantly to the voice of faith as lived by the community, so that it may know its rhythm, its accent, its problems, and so too that it may grasp "the orientations which the Holy Spirit creates within the people of God." [6] Sensitive in this way to the problems of the community, theology applies itself to solving them by investigating the word of God afresh. It offers its solutions to the magisterium to aid it in its task of guiding the Church. Without theology the magisterium could doubtless teach and preserve the Christian faith, but it would with difficulty arrive at the understanding of the faith necessary in order to respond to the ever changing needs of the people of God. For the charism of the magisterium is not an infusion of new knowledge, a revelation, but an assistance in using the means, natural and supernatural, which are placed at its disposal.

Another function which theology has in relation to the magisterium is that of striving to form the faith and the moral life of Christians as a whole. The magisterium could maintain the Christian community in a state of orthodoxy and prevent it from allowing itself to be blown apart by every wind of doctrine, but without theology the Christian community could allow the faith which it had received to be etiolated or to fall into a certain slumbrous immobility of thought. It is the mission of theology constantly to give new life to the Christian faith, to clarify it, to deepen it, to show its concrete implications and to discern also where it is in danger of going astray. In this way theology becomes service of the Church: service of the community, of the magisterium and of faith.

3. *Fidelity and Liberty in the Theologian*

Theology being a service, it follows that it must be given in a communion of thought with the magisterium, with the

---

6. Paul VI to the theological congress in Rome, in September 1966.

Christian community and with all the other theologians engaged in the same tasks of teaching and research. A theologian therefore is something other than a franc-tireur,[7] or a man trying to build up his own personal reputation with no regard for the scandal or anxiety which his words may cause in the conscience of other Christians.

He is, before everything else, a responsible servant of the Word of God, bound by a two-fold fidelity to Christ and to his Bride the Church. To seek the truth far from the magisterium, by arbitrary and unauthorized ways would be to expose himself to the danger of working in vain, without producing any fruit for the life of the community, or to run the risk of taking for truth the mirage of his questing imagination.

On the other hand, granted this loyalty to the *magisterium* there still remains an intense field of knowledge where it is recognized that "the clergy no less than the laity, have a proper freedom of inquiry and a proper freedom of thought, and also a proper freedom to make known, with courage and humility, how within the sphere of their competence, things appear to them."[8] If the theologian is the prophet of the future, preparing the way for the magisterium to the solutions of tomorrow, a proper liberty is indispensable to him. In the new and difficult matters in which he is habitually involved, a certain diversity of opinion is quite compatible with unity of faith and loyalty to the magisterium. For the rest, history is a witness to the fact that there has always been room in the Church for very different theologies and theologians. The faith is one, but what a difference there is among the theo-

---

7. Hans Küng justly points out that the *franc-tireur* theologian must be carefully distinguished from the avant-garde theologian. The *franc-tireur* cares nothing for the community. He works for himself. He does not represent the Church. The *avant-garde* theologian works first and foremost for the Church. He prepares the way as a precursor or pioneer. If he moves in advance of the rest it is in the manner of a commando, exposed to receive the shocks, in order the better to serve the community.
See Hans Küng, *Liberté du Chrétien* (Bruges & Paris. 1967), pp. 135-138.

8. Const. *Gaudium et Spes,* n. 62.

logies of Justin, of Cyprian, of Origen, of Augustine and of St. Thomas Aquinas. This diversity is good for the Church and a source of progress.

It must be added that in this process of inquiry, in which he serves the magisterium and the Christian community, in this continual facing of contemporary problems, the theologian is obviously exposed to the possibility of making mistakes. How indeed could one conceive that in his work of interpreting and applying the data of faith, he should never do so? It may be that faced with new facts he will be led to change his opinion, to alter his position. It can also happen that some of his opinions, long resisted within the Church, are recognized as the truth, as has happened in the conciliar debates. These fluctuations of thought and risks of error are the necessary result of a theology which wishes to engage in a dialogue with the world. They are part of a theology subject to historical conditions.[9]

The Biblical Commission has already, in its decree of April 21, 1964, asked understanding and indulgence for the exegete; for, it says, he has to face difficult questions which even exegetes of great reputation have been unable to solve. Has not the theologian good reason to claim like treatment, since the risks which face him are no less considerable? It is true that the theologian, as a son of the Church, consents to be judged by the supreme jurisdiction, that is by the magisterium instituted by Christ as the infallible interpreter of his word. But between this supreme jurisdiction and the theologian there exists an intermediary jurisdiction composed of all the theologians engaged on the same lines of research. Normally it is at this level, in a brotherly exchange of ideas and opinions, that the sifting has to be done, the separation of the chaff from the good grain, of the valid solutions from those which have no future. If the theologian is always conscious of being under the threat of summary judgment, how can he work with all his heart and soul and strength in the service of the Church which is his whole life? In theology, as elsewhere, joy and love

---

9. K. Rahner, "Historicidad de la Teología," *Selecciones de Teología,* 6 (1967), pp. 147-156.

are the normal climate for really fruitful work. If they are absent
it may happen, as history is our witness it has happened in a not
so distant past, that Catholic theology, in order to avoid the risk
of condemnation, takes refuge in the study of futile subjects, allowing itself on the points of real importance to be outstripped by
Protestant research.[10]

---

10. The Commission set up by the recent synod of bishops (Rome, October,
1967) has happily stressed the importance of holding a balance between
the proper liberty of theological research on the one hand, and, on the
other, faithfulness to the magisterium and to the word of God. The
Commission's report puts it like this: "Though theologians have no
mandate to teach with authority (this magisterium belongs to the
successors of the apostles), they have a distinguished role to play in
the Church and do her an indispensable service. It is for them to seek
by unremitting effort a more perfect understanding and expression of the
revealed mystery, and so to provide, as far as they are able, an answer
to new questions as they present themselves, as they do continually —
questions which are often of crucial importance for Christian life itself.
So that they may accomplish their task in a normal way, they must
surely be allowed a proper freedom, both to follow new paths and to
see the acquisitions of their predecessors in a new perspective. They,
for their own part, must put themselves at the service of the word of
God, faithfully and in humility, and not use it as a means of advancing
their own opinions. Their proper freedom must always remain within
the limits of the word of God as it has been preserved in unbroken
tradition and as it is taught and interpreted by the living magisterium
of the Church, in the first place that of the Vicar of Christ. Let theologians be aware of their heavy responsibility, both in the matter of seeking the truth — that they should do so with complete scientific integrity —
and in the communication of their conclusions, which they should
present in a way calculated to inspire in their fellow Christians love
and respect for the word of God and for the Church. Let bishops foster
collaboration among theologians, and especially exchange of views between theologians and the magisterium, particularly by means of
episcopal commissions for doctrine." (Synodus Episcoporum, *Relatio
Commissionis synodalis,* constitutae ad examen ulterius peragendum cir-
ca "opiniones periculosas hodiernas necnon atheismum," pars secunda,
n. 4: De theologorum opera et responsabilitate).
See also: Card. Colombo, "Obbedienza al magisterio ordinario,"
Seminarium, luglio-settembre, 1967, pp. 527-542.

CHAPTER VI   DIVISIONS AND DEPARTMENTS IN THEOLOGY

One can consider theology under different aspects (from the point of view of its end, its matter, or its method) and consequently divide it up in different ways, and recognize different departments in it.

1. *From the End Pursued*

One can consider theology from the point of view of the end to which it is directed, asking oneself what the purpose of theological work is, its fundamental intention. Is it a theoretical end or a practical end which shapes it? A practical science has as its end the regulation of our actions, the ordering of our mode of life. A science which is theoretical or speculative in the scholastic sense of the word is directed to the knowledge of truth. It applies itself to knowing for the sake of knowing. It is a question of ascertaining not whether theology can help to make us better (that is only too evident), but of whether theology pursues this end before everything else. To this question one can give four

theoretical answers, and they are at the same time the four answers
which have, historically, been made.

(a) For Alexander of Hales, Albert the Great and Duns
Scotus, theology is quite simply a practical science; for it re-
kindles devotion and stimulates the will to move towards its
ultimate good. Alexander of Hales calls theology an "affective
science." Albert the Great calls it "a knowledge which disposes
to piety." [1]

(b) For Henry of Ghent, on the other hand, theology is
purely and simply a theoretical science; for it aims at the knowledge and contemplation of God.

(c) For St. Bonaventure, theology is at the same time theoretical and practical, but principally practical; for it seeks first
to make us better. Its primary end is not to speculate but to
teach us to live as Christians. St. Bonaventure's question in the
Preface to the Commentary on the Sentences is typical in this
connection: "Does one engage in theology from the desire to
see or in order to become good?" [2] Theology is at the immediate service of Christian life. "For this knowledge," says St.
Bonaventure, "is an aid to faith; and faith is in the intellect in such
a way that the more it conforms to its own nature the more it
moves the heart. The thing is clear; for to know that Christ died for
us, and other truths of this kind, cannot but evoke love, unless a
man is a hardened sinner." [3]

It is obvious that Alexander of Hales, Albert the Great and
Bonaventure have a theology which stresses the aspect of salvation and the affective character of theology. They are in the line
of St. Augustine and St. Bernard. From this point of view it is

---

1. "Scientia secundum pietatem," "scibile secundum quod est inclinans ad
   pietatem" (*S. Th.*, 1:2).

2. "Utrum theologia sit contemplationis gratia an ut boni fiamus" (*1
   Sent.*, prooemium, q. 3.).

3. "Nam cognitio haec juvat fidem et fides sic est in intellectu, ut quantum
   est de sui ratione, nata sit movere affectum. Et hoc patet. Nam haec
   cognitio, quod Christus pro nobis mortuus est, et consimiles, nisi sit
   homo peccator et durus, movet ad amorem" (*1 Sent.*, prooemium, q. 3.).

not so much the truth in itself with which we are concerned in theology, as the value of the truth for life. This is a legitimate point of view and a sublime one.

(d) In St. Thomas the emphasis is differently placed. We engage in theology with the additional intention of becoming better and of leading others to sanctity, but theology is principally a theoretical science.[4] If, indeed we ask ourselves to what end theological work is first ordered, we are obliged to answer that theology seeks above all to know and understand the divine mystery. It wishes to understand first, and then to "edify," to build the mystery within us. It is by thinking about the truths of salvation that we discover their value for life; the truth of the mystery is its being ordered to our salvation. Theology is then first contemplation of the truth, and then the building up of Christ in us.

Normally a deeper knowledge of the word is bound to open out in a life conformed to this knowledge, just as faith flowers in charity and knowledge is fulfilled in love. A kind of fruitful reciprocity must exist between knowledge and life, the contemplation of truth bearing the fruit of holiness, and holiness in its turn arousing the desire to know more deeply. "Let not one believe," says St. Bonaventure, 'that learning will be enough for him without grace, speculation without devotion, research without wonder, observations without joy, work without religion, science without love, understanding without humility, zeal without the divine life, or reflection without the wisdom which comes from God." [5]

2. *From the Subject Matter Studied*

If one considers the matter which theology studies one can see it in a pattern of disciplines (apologetic theology, dogmatic

---

4. *S. Th.*, 1:1:4.
5. "Nemo credat quod sibi sufficiat lectio sine unctione, speculatio sine devotione, investigatio sine admiratione, circumspectio sine exultatione, industria sine pietate, scientia sine caritate, intelligentia sine humilitate, studium absque divina gratia, speculum absque sapientia, divinitus inspirata" (*Itinerarium mentis ad Deum*, Prol. n. 4, in S. Bonaventura, Opera Omnia, V [Quaracchi, 1891], p. 296).

theology, moral theology, spiritual theology, liturgical theology, patristic theology etc.) or in a pattern of treatises (on Revelation, on the Church, on God, one and triune, on creation, on the Incarnation, on redemption, on grace, on the virtues, on the sacraments, on the last things).

3. *From the Method Used*

If one looks at theology from the point of view of method one can speak of positive theology and speculative theology. Terminology here fluctuates. Some talk about historical theology (positive) and systematic theology (speculative). Others about the dogmatic part of theology (dealing with Scripture, the Fathers, the Church, the magisterium) and the systematic (or speculative) part.

The method of a science is determined by its object and its end. The object of theology is God in his inner life and in his design of salvation; the end of theology is the better understanding of the design of the God who saves, which is to introduce man into the inner life of God. This is the Mystery hidden in God from all eternity: the redemption of man and his return to the Father. It follows that the method of theology includes two essential and successive aspects, (a) the definition of the object of faith, or theology in its positive function, and (b) the understanding of the object of faith or theology in its properly reflective or speculative or systematic function.

For theology must first know the word of God, in a whole and precise way, and then understand what this word means. Just as in the experimental sciences one gathers together the facts in order afterwards to interpret them, so theology collates and systematizes the data of revelation (positive theology) in order to seek afterwards their intelligibility (speculative theology). The positive and the speculative are two essential functions, two complementary aspects, of theological work.

The second Vatican Council has in some measure given its blessing to this procedure in theology. The decree *Optatam totius* on the formation of priests, speaking of the place of theological studies in the life of those who are preparing for the priesthood, begins by saying: "The theological disciplines should be taught in such a way that, in the light of faith and under the guidance of the teaching authority of the Church, students may carefully derive Catholic doctrine from divine revelation" (the positive function), "understand it deeply" (the speculative function), "nourish their own spiritual lives with it, and be able to proclaim it, unfold it and defend it in their pastoral ministry." [6] A few lines further down, theological procedure is described as follows: "Dogmatic theology should be taught so that biblical themes are presented first. Students should be shown how the Fathers of the Eastern and Western Church contributed to the faithful transmission and illumination of each of the individual truths of revelation, and also given some account of the later history of dogma, without forgetting the relation of this to the general history of the Church." This first part of the decree's treatment of theology clearly describes its positive function. "Then," the text continues, "so that the mysteries of salvation may be known as fully and accurately as they can be, students should learn, under the tutelage of St. Thomas, to penetrate them more deeply by means of the speculative reason, and to see how they are inter-connected." Here it is obviously a matter of the speculative function of theology, of the understanding of faith.

---

6. Decree *Optatam totius,* n. 16.

PART II
THEOLOGICAL METHOD

CHAPTER I   THE POSITIVE FUNCTION OF THEOLOGY

1. *The nature of the positive function*

Theology, we have said, is making faith intelligible; it is the quest of the mind in its desire to understand. Into the mystery which it possesses through faith, theology seeks to penetrate more deeply, in order that it may have an understanding of it which is more and more living and more and more lived. The prospect is a never-ending one, for the mystery reveals new depths the further the mind ventures within. But if theology is the science of the object of faith, it must first, at its own level which is that of science, take possession of this object. Positive theology is precisely "the function by which theology enters into possession of the truth revealed." [1] It is the promotion to the scientific level of the *auditus fidei,* that is of "the faith which enters by the ears," which is effected in the believer pure and simple through preaching and catechism. Preaching and catechesis assure in us a sufficient knowledge of the object of faith, but theology, as the science of God and his mysteries, is not content with this minimum knowledge. It wishes to know the object of faith as it is expressed in

---

1. Y. Congar, art. "Théologie," *DTC* XV, 1:462.

tradition and Scripture, but in a manner at once methodical and exhaustive, in all its richness and all its implications.

What does this mean in concrete terms? Positive theology studies the way in which God reveals himself to us, the way in which he leads us to experience, through his action in history, his divinity and our humanity. This is why it studies the relationship of God with Israel, his manifestation in Jesus Christ, and in the witness of the apostles. It seeks to define what God has revealed, and how he has revealed it, clearly or in a hidden fashion, explicitly or implicitly. For instance, the divinity of Christ, the duality of natures in him, the Immaculate Conception and the Assumption of the Blessed Virgin are not all found in tradition and Scripture in the same way or with the same explicitness.

Positive theology must study also the progress of revelation in its historical and constitutive phase, up to the end of the apostolic age. For God did not reveal everything all at once from the very beginning, but gradually: "At various times and in various ways God spoke of old to our fathers through the prophets, but in these last days, in our own time, he has spoken to us through his Son" (Heb 1, 1). The revelation of Christianity was itself progressive, spreading out over the whole of the first century. Christ manifested himself to the Jews of his own time as the promised Messiah, as the transcendent Son of man and the suffering servant, as the Son of the Father, come into the world "to free us from the darkness of sin and death and bring to us a life which is everlasting." [2] These declarations Christ made progressively within the economy of a necessary discretion. After his death the apostles read again in the Holy Spirit the Master's words and actions. They understood then what was beyond their understanding before the passion and resurrection and pouring out of the Holy Spirit. What they now transmit to the Church are the words and actions of Christ, but with the understanding of them which came both from the illumination of the Spirit and the experience of the life of the Church. It is the whole, the words and actions of Christ and progressive understanding of them by the

---

2. Const. *Dei verbum,* n. 4.

apostles, which has for us the value of revelation and constitutes the object of our faith. The synoptic tradition, St. Paul, St. John, represent deeper and deeper moments in this relearning by the apostles of Christ's earthly life. It is then part of the duty of positive theology to distinguish the synoptic, the Pauline and the Johannine images of Christ.

It is also its task to determine what has been proposed for our belief by the magisterium of the Church (explicitly or implicitly), and what authority it has given to its pronouncements (whether they are those of the ordinary or of the extraordinary magisterium). An encyclical and an ecumenical council have obviously not the same authority; and in a council all its decisions do not carry the same weight. The second Vatican Council is an example of this. We should remember also that the documents produced by the magisterium are directed to a precise and limited end. Each arises in an historical context from which it derives its perspective, and takes its resonance. Often directed at some particular error it has, in its exposition of doctrine, its own particular emphasis, of which it is necessary to be aware; often also it leaves in some obscurity those aspects of truth which although they have not been attacked, are nonetheless part of the treasure of the faith. Finally, we should notice that in the promulgation of revealed truth, modern formulas are much more elaborate than primitive ones. For instance, the formulation by the first Vatican Council of the infallibility of the pope is much more elaborate and full of nuances than its expression in early documents of the Church.

It is all this labor of technical precision, of doctrinal and historical research, that theology in its positive function undertakes. It seeks to retrace the whole history of the object of faith, in its revelation, in its transmission, in its promulgation, in all the forms in which it has been expressed. Theology is the science of the whole content of revelation. It wishes to know revealed truth in its totality, in the characteristically methodical and exhaustive way which distinguishes science. It does not engage in this research out of a mere craving for erudition, but because its aim is to arrive at a deeper and more fruitful understanding of the word of God. In fact, to every renewal in the Church in the field of positive knowledge, there corresponds a renewal of theological reflection itself.

2. *Divisions of positive theology*

The one revelation of God, the one gospel, the one truth of salvation, has been transmitted to us under the form of tradition, and under the form of Scripture. Both express one and the same mystery, both are directed to one and the same end, the salvation of men; both are the word of God.[3] This one deposit of faith, which tradition and Scripture together constitute, has been entrusted to the Church as a whole in order that she may live by it. But it is to the magisterium of the Church that Christ has entrusted the function of interpreting the word of God, whether written or transmitted through tradition. The magisterium, by this mandate expressly received and with the help of the Holy Spirit, "listens to the word of God devoutly, guards it scrupulously, and expounds it faithfully, drawing from this one deposit of faith all that it proposes for belief as divinely revealed." [4] One can, therefore, distinguish in positive theology, three departments, the theology of scriptural documents, the theology of the witness of tradition, and the theology of the teaching of the magisterium. The whole of this constitutes what are called the sources, which theology explores in order to know revelaton in all its fullness and richness of life.

1. The theology of scriptural documents is based on exegesis. The aim of this is to understand the thoughts of the sacred author, what he wanted to say and intended to teach. Its object is first of all the literal sense. Its method is that of textual criticism, literary and historical, which establishes the text, discerns its sense, its literary form, and places it in the whole milieu in which it was composed and to which it was addressed, distinguishing

---

3. *Ibid.*, n. 9.
4. *Ibid.*, n. 10.

the importance and the limitations of the teaching which it contains. The exegete, says the constitution *Dei verbum*, "must try to find out what meaning the sacred writer intended to express and did in fact express, in the particular circumstances in which he wrote, in relation to his own time and culture, using the literary forms then in vogue." [5] It belongs also to exegesis to make a synthesis of the data of the scriptural texts.

2. The theology of tradition is concerned with the witness of the Fathers, the Doctors and the theologians of the Church, and with the witness of the liturgy, the history of the Church and Christian life as it is lived today.

(a) The Fathers of the Church are witnesses to her tradition. The value of their witness lies less in their proximity to the apostolic age than in the fact that they systematized in their writings revelation as it was received, believed and lived in the Church. In technical usage, the term "Father of the Church" implies four things: antiquity, orthodoxy of teaching, explicit or implicit approbation by the Church and sanctity. The patristic age is considered as coming to an end in the West with St. Gregory the Great (604) and St. Isidore (636), and in the East with St. John Damascene (749). Those who fail to fulfill one of the four requisite conditions, even men of great genius like Tertullian and Origen, are called simply ecclesiastical writers.

The term "Doctor of the Church" only partially coincides with "Father of the Church." When the general esteem in which the Church held the Fathers became explicit, she raised them to the rank of Doctors. In the East St. Basil the Great, St. Athanasius, St. Gregory of Nazianzus, St. John Chrysostom, are considered to be so; in the West, St. Ambrose, St. Jerome, St. Augustine and St. Gregory the Great. The list of Doctors however, is not like that of the Fathers, confined to antiquity. It includes, for example, St. Thomas Aquinas, St. Bonaventure, St. Albert the Great, St. John of the Cross, St. Peter Canisius, St. Robert

---

5. *Ibid.*, n. 12.

Bellarmine, St. Francis de Sales, and St. Alphonsus Liguori. The Doctor of the Church is distinguished not only by the sanctity of his own life, but also by the striking role he has played in the doctrinal life of the Church, and by the particular approbation of the magisterium. He is considered a true master of the Christian faith. The constitution *Munificentissimus Deus* of Pius XII enumerates theologians also among the witnesses of tradition. One can, in effect, hold to be the object of faith whatever theologians have unanimously held to be so.

(b) The liturgy also constitutes a privileged witness to tradition in all its richness, so that it would be hard to find a truth of faith which is not in some way expressed there. For the liturgy, lived by the whole ecclesial community, the Church teaching and the Church believing, in one continuous *credo,* is a more than normal manifestation of the faith of the Church. It is the faith proclaimed in worship; for the Church prays as she believes. In the proverb, *lex orandi lex credendi,* the emphasis must be put on the objective dogmatic reality which informs the liturgy. Piety does not create dogma; rather it is its manifestation. Through the sacramental life, through the preaching of the word, through the unfolding pattern of its feasts, with their center in Easter, the liturgy celebrates and actualizes unceasingly the Christian mystery, the object of its faith.

(c) Church history studies the development through the centuries of the institution founded by Christ and guided by the Holy Spirit. Hence its importance in the understanding of the mystery of salvation. By the history of the Church, we mean not only the history of councils and heresies, but also the history of particular institutions (like the episcopacy and the diaconate), the history of the foundation of religious communities, the history of sanctity, in short the history of the whole people of God.

(d) We are concerned also in the witness of tradition with the faith of Christians as it is expressed today. For the people of God does not cease to meditate upon the word of God and to live by it. The life of faith under the guidance of the Spirit,[6] with

---

6. Const. *Lumen Gentium,* n. 12 and *Dei verbum,* n. 8.

the understanding of spiritual realities which it brings, is itself a way of finding out about what is being lived, and is capable of making discoveries. The expressions of the Christian faith which have arisen through the inspiration of the Holy Spirit, given in new gifts to each new time, constitute an important theological source. So the growing awareness of the role of the laity in the world, the foundation of secular institutes, the orientation of the religious life towards new duties, the interest of the Church in Christian communities separated from it, and in the great non-Christian religions of salvation, all this which comes about through the action of the Spirit, is faith in its fruit-bearing, and the object of theological reflection.

3. The theology of the teaching of the magisterium applies itself to knowing the faith of the Church as it is expressed in the multiform interventions and declarations of the Church's teaching authority. The magisterium as the authorized interpreter of the word of salvation, operates in two ways, according to which it is divided into the ordinary and extraordinary magisterium. The extraordinary magisterium is exercised by ecumenical councils and by the pope speaking *ex cathedra,* that is as the shepherd and teacher of all men, in the exercise of his full authority and with the intention that his words should be binding upon all the faithful.[7] The ordinary magisterium is exercised by the bishops, individually (in preaching, in catechisms, in synodal letters and pastoral directives) or collegially (through interdiocesan synods and episcopal conferences) and by the pope, either directly (through encyclicals, addresses or letters), or indirectly through his auxiliaries (the Roman congregations and dicasteries). The encyclical has, since the nineteenth century, been one of the privileged forms of the ordinary magisterium of the pope. Each encyclical constitutes, on a given point, a broad explanation of Catholic doctrine, in which it is less a question of condemning, correcting or warning than of clarifying, teaching and illuminating for the whole Christian community, the unfathomable riches of

---

7. Const. *Lumen Gentium,* n. 25.

Christ. Canon law, which regulates the discipline of the Church, in so far as it is elaborated under the control of the magisterium and is officially promulgated by it, can be considered as forming part of its records.

3. *The aims of positive theology*

1. The first aim is the taking possession of and defining, at a scientific level, of the whole of revealed truth as it is expressed in tradition and Scripture.

2. This intellectual grasp of the whole content of the object of faith is already an incipient understanding of revealed truth. For we understand better a reality of which we know the origin and can follow the development. So the mere fact of gathering together the various images which represent the inner nature of the Church (a People, a Vine, a Temple, a City, a Body, a Bride), as the constitution *Lumen Gentium* has said, is already an enrichment of our understanding of the mystery. In the same way, the synoptic, Pauline and Johannine approaches to the mystery of Christ allow us to form from all of them a more adequate image of him and of his life as the Son in the deep mystery of the Trinity. In the same way again, new light is shed upon the knowledge we have of Christ's holiness through the Gospels, by the multiform expressions of his holiness in the lives of the saints and in the main currents of the Church's spirituality. Research of this sort gives firmness to our faith; for it reveals to us the splendor of the Christian mystery; it assures the soundness of theological procedure, and can often forearm speculation against the dangers of considerations which are not in accord with the texts or with the facts of history.

3. Positive theology can, on occasion, fill an apologetic role, that is it can show that Christian doctrine is original, and not a commodity borrowed from neighboring religions. It can show also that there is a continuity between what the Church preaches today and what was preached by the primitive Church. It is im-

portant to notice, however, that theology cannot, in the case of each Christian dogma, demonstrate a perfect material identity between the faith of the first centuries and the faith of the Church today, and this is so for two reasons. In the first place the historical records which would allow us to reconstruct a complete and exact picture of the faith of the primitive Church are quite simply lacking. In the second place there is in the Church a constant process by which the object of faith becomes more and more explicit. Consequently we can perceive often only a continuity of mind.

4. *Regressive procedure and genetic procedure*

Positive theology is not just a combination of philology and secular history. It does not content itself with studying the exterior facts which are the landmarks of the history of Israel, that is with factual history. Nor does it content itself with studying the current of religious thought represented by Israel, solely from the point of view of its place in the history of religions (*religionsgeschichte*). Positive theology makes use of philology and history, but in the perspective of faith. What it seeks in texts and facts is the revelation of God's mystery and of his saving purpose. It regards the books of the Old and New Testaments as sacred and inspired, and their authors as witnesses to divine truth. Its *a priori* is the recognition of the supernatural nature of its object and of the divine character of the foundation of the Church. It does not, therefore, operate under the guidance of reason only, but in the ambience of faith and under the guidance of the magisterium of the Church. At the basis of positive theology are a theology of revelation, a theology of inspiration, and a theology of the Church.

(a) A THEOLOGY OF REVELATION

The revelation of God to men is a unique and coherent whole, of which Christ is the keystone. If, therefore, we wish in positive theology to appreciate the exact significance and bearing of a particular text we must place it in this vast context. Each word of God's speech has to be seen in the context of paragraph, and in the context of what he has said in its entirety. The role of faith here [8] will be to orientate our inquiry and save our thought from proceeding along *cul-de-sacs*.

(b) A THEOLOGY OF INSPIRATION

Positive theology takes for granted that the books of the Old and New Testaments "having been written under the inspiration of the Holy Spirit, have God as their author." [9] On the other hand, if it is true that God has used the sacred writers as free and intelligent instruments, that he has respected their personalities and their artistic gifts, it is indispensible to study in Scripture all that reflects the personality of the writer, and to know the historical and literary context of each part of Scripture. [10]

(c) A THEOLOGY OF THE CHURCH

God has not deposited his revelation in Scripture for every man to interpret it in his own way. He has entrusted his word to the Church, so that the whole Church may live by it, but it belongs to the magisterium alone, as the servant of the word, to interpret it authentically in the name of Christ. [11] Only the Church, in its living tradition, can tell us which books are validly inspired and therefore valid witnesses of God. [12] If it is a question of the Doctors of the Church only the Church has authority to tell us which of its writers are authentic witnesses to the word of God.

All these things granted, the procedure of positive theology can still be conceived in two ways, either as a regressive pro-

---

8. Const. *Dei verbum*, n. 12.
9. *Ibid.*, n. 11.
10. *Ibid.*, nn. 11 & 12.
11. *Ibid.*, n. 10.
12. *Ibid.*, n. 8

cedure or as a genetic one. Historically both approaches have been used and in a representative way. Both can be justified from the documents of the magisterium [13] itself. Each, as we shall see, has its advantages and its inconveniences.

The regressive approach, described by A. Gardeil [14] and practiced during the whole of the last century in dictionaries and manuals of instruction, takes as its point of departure the doctrine of the Church as it exists today, and goes back to the sometimes obscure origins of this doctrine. It travels backwards from the present explicit doctrine which is expressed in the ordinary and extraordinary teaching of the magisterium, in order to find in the sources, sometimes explicitly, but sometimes also only implicitly, the foundation of the present day teaching. Basing itself thus on the present faith of the Church, which is more explicit and better formulated, positive theology may by this approach discover in texts a meaning which philology and history alone could not perhaps have discovered. But in the light of the Church's faith today it can catch in mere indications a continuous manifestation of the same awareness becoming more and more explicit as time goes on. For example in the light of the present dogmas of the Immaculate Conception and Assumption of the Blessed Virgin, positive theology will find in the indications of Scripture and the facts of Tradition an expression of the uninterrupted faith of the Church. All the more so because positive theology communicates with the Church's past which it questions as a family inheritance.

The obvious advantage of such an approach is the security which it gives to the theologian, but all the same it is not without dangers. The first is that of a false supernaturalism, which, in

---

13. The encyclical *Humani Generis* (*DS* 3886) favors the regressive procedure; the second Vatican Council on the other hand, in the constitution *Dei verbum*, n. 12, and in the decree *Optatam totius*, n. 16, favors the genetic.

14. A. Gardeil, "La réforme de la théologie catholique," *Revue thomiste*, 11 (1903): 5-19; 197-215, 428-547; E. Dublanchy, "Domatique," *DTC* 4: col. 1524, 1533; Pius XII, *Humani Generis* (*DS* 3886); Y. Congar, *La foi et la théologie*, p. 140.

order to safeguard Christian faith, eliminates those texts which cause difficulties, or forces the meaning of others which do not seem to it sufficiently favorable. An analogous danger is that of anachronism, which consists in reading into a word or expression which we encounter in a document from the past, the sense which it has for us today, after twenty centuries of Christianity. Connected with this error in method is the further error of those who want to find in the sources of revelation the doctrine of the Church in all its present clarity, for instance upon the Assumption of the Blessed Virgin or on the three sacraments which imprint an indelible character upon the soul. There are times when one will find nothing more in tradition and Scripture than indications. A final danger of the regressive approach is that of preserving only those aspects of revelation which have been emphasized by the magisterium. For if it is true that the documents of the magisterium are clearer and more explicit, there will always be more richness to be found in the data of revelation itself.

To avoid these dangers, other theologians — and they are today in the majority — prefer a genetic approach, more in accord with man's historical dimension, and with the economy of salvation. This approach takes as its point of departure revelation itself. It makes use of the data and techniques of literary and historical criticism, in order to determine the original import of the texts in their social, cultural and religious context, which has long since disappeared. It tries to trace the history of revelation authentically, as it unfolded stage by stage in the past, without prejudging the present explicit formulations of the magisterium. It tries to detect the themes of Scripture in order to follow their development and orchestration through the centuries, a coherent development, but a development compatible with pauses and even with partial regressions. The immediate objective of the genetic approach is the same as that of the historian without faith, although believer and unbeliever judge differently of the value of the facts which they find in the texts. The believer recognizes the history of divine revelation in a process where the unbeliever sees only the history of a religious ideal forged by a particular group of men. Theology has nothing to fear from this loyal pursuit, even if, on occasion, it has to rectify certain views inherited from past ages, when it finds on what slender foundations they are built. In this genetic procedure, bound up with the rhythm of revelation in its totality as in its partial manifestations, tradition and the magisterium of the Church are, for the theologian, a light which both purifies and gives life. If one of his conclusions seems to contradict the explicit teaching of the magisterium he should try to find, in a deepening of his understanding of the texts, a solution to this apparent incompatibility. But the results of his analysis cannot be dictated to him from outside, in defiance of the data provided by the texts.

Like the regressive approach, the genetic approach carries with it its own advantages and dangers. Among the advantages it is worth noting the following:

(a) It guarantees the exact reading of the texts in their original tenor, and so prepares the way for a theological and spiritual reading founded on the literal sense. For the mystery of salvation is revealed in history and through history, according to the language and experience of men at a particular time. The purely literary and historical reading of Scripture must therefore, precede the theological reading.

(b) The genetic approach allows us to follow the progress of revelation step by step through history, and in some sort to get to the very heart of that admirable teaching technique by which God brought the people of Israel to maturity and prepared it, little by little, for the fullness of himself in Christ.

(c) It means that we lose nothing of the riches of revealed truth. In no way prejudging the later explicit formulations of the magisterium, the genetic approach listens to the word of God as it is spoken, and tries to grasp all its themes and all its nuances. It can thus discover aspects of revelation which the teaching of the Church has not up to now stressed, or has stressed very little. In this way it prepares for and gives ripeness to the decisions of the magisterium.

(d) Finally, it enables us to purify the later stages of dogmatic formulation of the imperfections which could in the past have crept into them.

But like the regressive approach the genetic approach has its dangers:

(a) The first is that of becoming so bound up with the *epaphax* of revelation in its historical setting that we are entirely unconcerned about its later developments and about the immense labor accomplished by the Church in order to interpret and make ceaselessly contemporary the word spoken at a particular moment of history.

(b) The second danger, analogous to the first, is that of canonizing in some way the modes of expression we find in Scripture to the point of closing our minds against every other type of expression and systematization because it is not biblical. In its acute form, this attitude could become a contempt for all theology, patristic, medieval or modern. There is a return to sources which is like a sort of biblical romanticism. The pre-scientific language of Scripture must be submitted to the most rigorous analysis, so that science may recover, as far as possible, all the richness of meaning which it originally contained.

The description we have just given of these two approaches, the regressive and the genetic, is, of necessity, stylized. We have described types, from the point of view of methodology. But we know that types do not exist in a pure state. At the level of the consciousness of their activities in the minds of those engaged in research, there is probably not so great a difference between the two procedures. At this psychological level there are elements which rather bring the two ways together than set them apart.

The two approaches have, in fact, a common element, the faith of the believer as it is expressed in the living tradition of the Church and its present teaching. This faith is like a light in which the positive theologian lives and is purified. The presence in him of his living faith not only prevents deviations which would carry him outside his faith, but, also places his research within the current of the living tradition of the Church, orientates it (by the analogy of faith), and fosters it (after the manner of a catalyst); beyond that, it presents itself to him as a working hypothesis, certainly always to be verified, so that he will affirm nothing that is not warranted by the texts, but as an hypothesis which attracts him, which has probability on its side.

In this way, the methodological difference between the two approaches is often reduced in practice to a difference of emphasis, some being more attentive to revelation in its historical setting [15] (*terminus a quo*) others, on the contrary, being more sensitive to its realization in the Church of today (*terminus ad quem*).

It is more or less inevitable that the theologian applying himself to positive scientific research, and bound by a twofold loyalty, loyalty to the Church and its living magisterium, loyalty to the demands of literary and historical criticism, will sometimes experience painful tensions, especially at times when the rhythm of discovery having been suddenly accelerated, he no longer sees how to reconcile the data of faith with those of science. We must remember Loisy and Lagrange. At these times he must recognize that his status in research depends only partly upon the judgment of pure savants. His procedure has its adequate justification only within the Church, of whom he is the humble servant.

---

15. On the genetic procedure in exegesis, see P. Grelot, *La Bible, Parole de Dieu* (Paris, 1965), ch. VII, pp. 311-391.

CHAPTER II   THE SPECULATIVE FUNCTION OF THEOLOGY

1. *Understanding the Mystery*

Theology in its positive function collates and systematizes the data of revelation contained in Scripture and tradition and interpreted by the magisterium. This appropriation of what is given by faith is already an initial experience of the Mystery, but theology in its speculative function intends to pursue and deepen it. Since he is a Christian, the theologian knows that the Mystery, at its center, remains impenetrable during our earthly life, but he knows also that the Mystery is inexhaustible in its intelligibility, and that this intelligibility throws more light upon the mystery of man than man can produce by himself. The Mystery is not so much darkness as superabundance of light. To the movement of the *auditus fidei,* which positive theology realizes in its definition of what God has revealed and what the Church proposes for our belief, there succeeds then the movement of the *intellectus fidei,* which is properly a methodical, discursive exercise of the mind seeking to clarify the Mystery.

This intellectual understanding of the faith existed already in the primitive Church and in the patristic period, with Irenaeus, Clement, Origen and Augustine for instance. But it was exercised only in an occasional fashion, that is in the rhythm of solving problems, or under the shock of heresies. In order to solve these problems and combat these heresies the more cultivated Christians of the time explained, argued, or refuted their adversaries (the Gnostics, the Arians, the Nestorians, the Pelagians and so forth). What in the early Church and in the patristic era was distinguished by being an occasional activity, the theologians of the Middle Ages undertook systematically, as a task of the Church. The importance of Abelard's *Sic et Non* lies precisely in its showing that quotations from the Scriptures and from the Fathers are not always enough to solve a problem: there is also a different and patient process of reasoning required. From then onwards a new field of inquiry was open to the medieval theologian. This process of systematic rational reflection was pursued and shaped by St. Anselm and Peter Lombard in the twelfth century and by St. Bonaventure and St. Thomas in the thirteenth.[1]

2. *The medieval idea of theology*

Heir to the Aristotelian idea of science as certain and deductive knowledge, the Middle Ages defined theology according to its speculative function, its role being to deduce certain conclusions from the truths revealed. It immediately follows that, since the positive function is not deductive, it could be assigned only a subsidiary role. In the Middle Ages therefore, talking about theology as a science meant talking about speculative theology. Today, authors and manuals speak indifferently of speculative theology or scholastic theology.

It is not surprising that the theologians of the time should thus define theology by its speculative function. Their inspiration and guide was Aristotle; moreover the speculative function was more fully elaborated among them, and enjoyed an authentic scientific

---

1. B. Lonergan, *De intellectu et methodo* (ad usum auditorum, Romae, PUG, 1959), p. 49.

status, while the historical method was, on the contrary, in its infancy; indeed the recourse to history, when it was made, was accompanied by such a lack of critical sense that it would have been difficult to apply the term science to it at all. However that may be, it was certainly to be feared that in thus defining theology by its speculative function theologians would come to underestimate the value of positive work, and so lose the precious fruits of research. The wider notion which we have of science today enables us to understand better that the positive and speculative functions are equally necessary to theology and that both are of its essence.

Fortunately, there is more to theology as practiced in the Middle Ages than in its definition. The process of deduction which the medieval doctors assigned to theology as its principal duty can, in fact, be conceived and put into practice in three different ways.

(a) Theology may be said to be deductive in the sense that it argues to a new conclusion either from revealed premises (for example: Christ is truly man; but every man is endowed with intelligence and will; therefore Christ has a human intelligence and will) or from a premise of faith, and a premise of reason (for example: Christ is a king — truth revealed in John 18, 37; but every king has the right to judge and punish his subjects — truth of the natural order; therefore Christ has the right to judge and punish men). That this sort of deductive process is legitimate in theology no one would dream of denying. But to make of theology a science of conclusions is to remain at the periphery of theological activity in the proper sense. This conception of theology, which was that of the decadent scholasticism in the work of John of St. Thomas, Gotti and Billuart, progressively invaded men's minds from the fourteenth to the sixteenth centuries, but it cannot be said to be that of the great doctors of the thirteenth century, like St. Thomas and St. Bonaventure.

(b) Theology may be said to be deductive in the wider sense that it clarifies one truth of faith by another. A truth of faith which clarifies another is called the principle; and that which is clarified is called the conclusion. Thus the mystery of Christ's resurrection clarifies the mystery of our resurrection.[2] From this point of view the deductive work of theology consists in searching out the ways in which one mystery depends on another and explaining the truths of salvation by showing their inner coherence. This recalls the second way of understanding the mysteries suggested by the first Vatican Council.[3] And this way of looking at things represent the practice of St. Thomas and St. Bonaventure.

(c) Theology may be said to be deductive in the still wider sense that it seeks to draw from the revealed datum all the richness of intelligibility which it contains, going from a general understanding of the mystery to a deeper and deeper understanding, and making use for this purpose of all the tools of rational reflection, that is to say not only deduction in the strict sense, in the form of syllogism, but also all the procedures revealed by modern science, phenomenological analysis for instance, the argument from convergence and genetic explanation. One might define the object of theology in its speculative function as deeper and deeper penetration into the heart of the Mystery.

3. *The main tasks of theology in its speculative function*

The essential tasks of speculative theology can be reduced to three: to understand, by appealing to every form of intellection which the human mind has devised; to systematize, or order in a coherent synthesis the results of this reflection; to judge, or assess the value of the reflection made and the synthesis obtained.

1. UNDERSTANDING

Without making any pretense of being exhaustive let us enu-

---

2. St. Thomas observes: "Fides est manifestativa alterius... in quantum unus articulus manifestat alium, sicut resurrectio Christi resurrectionem futuram" (*S. Th.*, 1:1:8). He adds: "Haec doctrina non argumentatur ad sua principia probanda quae sunt articuli fidei sed ex eis procedit ad aliquid aliud ostendendum" (*Ibid.*, 1:8).

3. Denzinger - Schönmetzer, 3016.

merate and describe some of the forms which theological reflection takes.

(a) *Definition* — Theology tries to make more precise and define in technical language, the ideas expressed in tradition and Scripture in pre-scientific categories, by means of images, metaphors and symbols, thus enabling a better grasp of the exact sense and bearing of revealed truth. This analytic and semantic work prepares the way for dogmatic definitions and prevents false interpretations. For instance what do the expressions "kingdom of heaven," "Son of Man," "mystical Body" mean? In what sense is Christ the Son of God? What does this generation mean in God? In order to understand the mystery of the Trinity, it is not without importance to define the terms, nature, procession, mission, relation. In the fourth century the introduction of the word ομοούσιος, consubstantial (Christ is consubstantial with the Father) was not made without dispute. And yet thanks to this more precise terminology important progress was made in Christology. In the twelfth century, when it was agreed to define sacraments as efficacious signs of grace, agreement was also reached on the number of sacraments.

(b) *Syllogistic deduction* — The deductive process can take different forms and consequently lead to different types of conclusion. The conclusion may be based on two revealed premises, or on one revealed premise and another not revealed. The conclusion drawn may be a truth already revealed elsewhere (explicitly or implicitly), or a truth virtually contained in revelation.

(c) *The argument from fitness* — When it is a question of God's inner life and his saving purposes, human intelligence cannot adduce necessary and demonstrable reasons. However, the mystery being already known by faith, it can show the sovereign fitness of the divine action, that is, manifest its profound intelligibility. So, in order to explain the delay in the coming of Christ. Irenaeus, Clement of Alexandria and Origen say that God had first to prepare humanity to receive the plenitude of the Incarnation. The epistle to Diognetus considers that men had to experience their own weakness before knowing the fullness of salvation. In the same way, if we cannot, properly speaking, demonstrate the necessity, for revelation, of an economy of Incarnation, we can at least understand that it was fitting that, in speaking to man who is being of flesh and spirit, God should meet him on his own level and speak to him in bodily form.

(d) *Genetic explanation* — This consists in following the evolution of a theme through the whole history of revelation. It does not consist merely in gathering together the fragments of a revealed truth dispersed through the centuries, but in explaining it from a consideration of the circumstances in which it was communicated to us. So the genetic explanation of Christ's messianic titles (Prophet, King, Son of Man, Suffering Servant) undeniably enriches our understanding of his mission and Person.

(e) *The analogy between divine realities and human realities* — Since it was God's will to use the whole pattern of human reality as a means of making himself known to man, it is part of theological understanding of revelation to scrutinize the meaning and bearing of the analogies set up. It is because God made all things, and man in particular as an image of his own perfection, and because all things have their primary source in him, that a revelation of the divine life is possible. If human realities, deficient as they are, had no connection with the mystery of the Being of God, a dialogue between God and man would be quite simply impossible. If Christ can make use of all the resources of the created universe in order to help us to know God and his purpose, it is because the creating word has preceded the revealing word, and because both have their source in the same inner Word of God. On the basis of analogy, Christ sees in the human relationship of paternity and worship an image of his relationship to the Father. The analogy of father and son is a revealed analogy, chosen by Christ, and has therefore the normative character of an analogy proposed by God himself. The revealed analogies arouse the reflection of the human mind, which devotes itself to purifying them and transfiguring them in order to see in them something of the depths of the divine life. The theologian can also discover and himself propose new analogies: So St. Augustine and St. Thomas threw light on the mystery of the Trinity by the analogy of the operation of intellect and will in the human soul. This understanding by way of analogy is obviously a process which must be followed with discretion, and under the direction of the Church, especially in the case of analogies which are not revealed. Here, more than anywhere else, the statement of the fourth Lateran Council proves true: "Between the Creator and the creature it is not possible so to trace a likeness that the difference between them does not remain greater still." [4]

(f) *Phenomenological analysis* — Phenomenology is, as a method, the attempt to read reality and describe it faithfully; it is an attempt to apprehend, in particular existential situations concretely and rigorously analyzed, the greater realities of which they are the manifestation. Phenomenological analysis bears fruit, both in deepening our awareness in the analogies of faith (as for example the analysis of *the word* of *witness* and of *encounter* as human experiences deepens our awareness of the mystery of revelation), and in helping us to understand better those experiences which issue from divine action wedded to human freedom (in the phenomenon of conversion, for instance, the play of factors which result in faith and the new ways of acting which it creates). There is certainly never a perfect correspondence between the observations made and the supernatural life of faith, but phenomenological analysis remains nevertheless a useful and valuable approach.

(g) *The interconnection of the mysteries of faith* — This type of theological reflection, outlined by the first Vatican Council, consists in discovering and illustrating the multiple ways in which the truths of faith are linked with one another, in order to recognize the harmony of the total mystery, as it exists in the wisdom of God. For God himself has revealed the mysteries of faith to us, not as disparate elements, but as parts of a wonderful economy directed towards man's salvation. The mysteries of faith evoke and answer one another, serve one another and fall into a synthesis which reflects the unity of the one mystery which is in God. The Church has always considered the exploration of

---

4. Denzinger - Schönmetzer, 806.

the multiple ways in which the mysteries are united to one another
to be one of theology's most important and most fruitful tasks.
"So that the mysteries of salvation may be understood as fully as
possible," says the decree *Optatam totius,* "let students learn . . . to
penetrate them more deeply and to discover their interconnection." [5] The doctrinal splendor of the Fathers of the Church, of
Irenaeus, for instance, and of Origen and Augustine, proceeds in
great part from the fact that they could habitually illustrate this
connection and harmony of the mysteries among themselves. In
the same way, the magnificent structure of the medieval *summae*
is simply a reflection of the wonderful unity which the economy
of the mysteries presents. Scheeben, in the nineteenth century,
recovered this comparative interpretation of the mysteries. So,
to throw light upon the mystery of revelation, we can compare
the three ways in which God has manifested himself to men,
through creation, through the spoken word, and through vision.
To throw light upon the mystery of the Trinity we can stress that
in the economy of salvation the Father is first manifest, in the
creation of man and his elevation to the divine life; then the Son,
in the restoration of man through the Incarnation, in his redemption, and in the founding of the Church; and then the Spirit in
the sanctification of man and the formation of the mystical Body.

(h) *The connection between the mysteries, and man's last end*
— God has made man for salvation, that is for a life which is
one with the life of the divine Persons. Hence, if God reveals
something, it is not in order to satisfy our curiosity but in order
to show us the way of salvation. In point of fact, all the Christian
mysteries are connected with the double mystery of our end and
the means to it. Creation, elevation to supernatural life, and
redemption are concerned with our vocation to salvation. The
Incarnation, the Church, grace, the virtues, the sacraments, are
all concerned with the economy of means to salvation. It is then,
part of the business of theology to bring out this value for salvation which is inherent in each truth revealed.

---

5. Decree *Optatam totius* on priestly formation, n. 16. See also Vatican
   I. (*DS* 3016).

(i) *The argument from convergence* — The argument from convergence, which is often used in the historical sciences, is equally cogent in theology, especially in fundamental theology. The fact of revelation is established from signs and from the convergence of these signs. Our certainty, in this case, rests upon a convergence of signs which all function in the same sense.

2. SYSTEMATIZATION

One cannot discuss theological science without talking about systematization, that is the organic structuring of the results of theological reflection and their reduction to a unity. Systematization will vary according to the principle of unity chosen; it will vary also according to the basic assumptions (philosophic or other) which preside over theological work. Hence the number of theological syntheses possible. Thomist theology is theocentric while kerygmatic theology is Christocentric. Hence also the number of theological systems. This plurality is due to several factors: the use for instance of different philosophies (Aristotelian, Platonic, existential for example); different initial preoccupations (with the aspect of salvation for instance in St. Bonaventure or the aspect of truth in St. Thomas); a different mentality, or a different cultural milieu (in the East and in the West for example). Each system represents an approach to the mystery, an effort to interpret the reality. No one system is reducible to another, except on the plane of the reality which all seek to understand, or on that of the Church which recognizes all as valuable. But just as photographs of one cathedral, taken individually, could not exhaust the whole reality of the cathedral, so no system could exhaust the reality of the mystery. Each, of its nature, is imperfect and susceptible of improvement. The different systems are not, however, all of the same value. One system will be judged superior to another, if it neglects none of the essential aspects of the reality, and if it shows itself capable of assimilating new points of view within an organic and harmonious synthesis. In this respect the Thomist synthesis, whose vitality and power of assimilation have been manifest for centuries, represents a particularly happy historical success.

3. JUDGMENT

In the course of his work, the theologian has constantly to make personal judgments. For theology is not a simple repetition of the past: it grows as the rhythm of the understanding of revelation quickens. The theologian must be an initiator, a creator. Each new understanding of the revealed fact confronts him, therefore, with the responsibility of making a critical judgment upon the value of his own intuition. He is, as a man of science however, in a special position. In the human sciences, truth is an ideal, still to be discovered. In theology, on the other hand, truth in a sense, is already given at the point of departure. Moreover the authentic interpretation of this truth has been entrusted to the magisterium of the Church. So in one sense the theologian has to take the responsibility of judging his own intuitions, in another he works in the ambience of faith and under the constant direction of the magisterium of the Church. He accepts that, in the last analysis, his personal judgment must be submitted to the superior judgment of the magisterium, which has received a mission from Christ and a gift of the Spirit to interpret the word of God. Hence the necessity in the theologian of an attitude of deep humility. St. Thomas remains the example *par excellence* of this attitude of daring and responsibility in theological inquiry and at the same time of humility and submission to the Church.

CHAPTER III THE ORGANIC UNITY OF THE POSITIVE AND SPECULATIVE FUNCTIONS

1. *Two functions, not two theologies*

The positive and the speculative functions together express the essence of the theological *discursus*. They are not two theological disciplines, opposed or juxtaposed, but two functions of one and the same theological science organically bound together in a mutual and incessant collaboration. The theological process in its totality implies a double movement, a double operation, in which each part is equally necessary: the *auditus fidei* and the *intellectus fidei,* determination of the object of faith, and the understanding of faith. The positive function is the assumption of the *auditus fidei* at a scientific level; the speculative function is the mind's reflection upon the truth of faith methodically and systematically possessed. The total theological process is a quest of revealed truth and a quest of the mind on the subject of revealed truth. It is under the very pressure of the *auditus fidei* (of which positive theology is the scientific state) that the *intellectus fidei* (of which speculative theology is a scientific state) begins and continues.[1]

---

1. M. D. Chenu, *Toward Understanding St. Thomas* (Regnery, Chicago, 1955).

Between the two functions there is a constant *osmosis,* a reciprocal fecundation, a veritable "circumincession." Strictly speaking, the positive and speculative functions are not distinguished as two successive stages of theological work. For the speculative function begins already within the positive: the positive is the speculative coming to be, while the speculative is the positive at the termination of its movement (*in facto esse*). Doubtless in certain disciplines, from the immensity of the theological labor required, the positive function will predominate; in others on the contrary, the speculative will prevail. But the speculative function is never absent from positive work, just as the speculative activity itself is never exercised without constant reference to the positive facts upon which it is built. The positive and speculative functions are two aspects of the same process interpenetrating each other, and lending each other mutual support.[2]

This distinction between the positive and speculative functions is, to tell the truth, only an application to theology of a *processus* which takes place in all human knowledge. In all knowledge one can in fact distinguish as it were three levels, experience, understanding and judgment. Knowledge implies first a fact of experience which is the matter upon which the intelligence is exercised. This is followed by the process of intellection, the understanding of the fact thus received by the mind. Finally there is judgment which may be true or false, certain or probable (these being the qualifications of judgment).[3]

These three levels are found analogically in theological knowledge. In its positive function theology receives and appropriates revealed truth. In its speculative function it seeks to understand the truth which it has received and systematized. Finally, as in all human knowledge, the theological process ends in a judgment. Two differences, however, distinguish theology from the human sciences: the fact, or thing given, in theology is not given by experience but by revelation, and the judgment of the theologian,

---

2. P. Fransen, "Three Ways of Dogmatic Thought," *The Heythrop Journal,* 4 (1963), p. 4.
3. B. Lonergan, *Insight* (London, New York & Toronto, 1957), pp. 272-278.

though it is a personal judgment, remains subject to the supreme judgment of the Church.

The positive and speculative functions are so bound together that the one cannot subsist without the other. If we try to make of them separate disciplines rather than aspects or functions of the same process of knowledge, this will result in grave inconveniences for both.

2. *No speculative function without the positive*

1. The doctrine to be found in Scripture and in some at least of the Fathers of the Church is theology in a pre-scientific state, that is un-systematized and expressed in the form of images. But theology is bound to know and deepen its understanding of the object of faith in this pre-scientific form; for revelation, which is the object of both faith and theology, has been communicated to us so. If therefore theology wishes to be faithful to the demands of the object of faith and to its own proposal to understand faith, it must remain in contact with faith in the form in which it is given.

2. There are, in revelation, not only clear and explicit statements, which theological reflection can secure immediately in order to make them the premises of its demonstrations; there are also latent layers of meaning, which exist only at the level of indications and suggestions. This is why theological reflection must remain in intimate and continuous contact with the modes of expression in which truth is revealed, so that it may be sensitive to all these suggestions, and grasp the elements of doctrinal synthesis which begin in the form of simple orientations.

3. Without the positive, the speculative function, cut off from its source, is exposed to the danger of anachronism. For all the theological categories, such as revelation, tradition, inspiration, grace, sacrament, nature, person, supernatural, mystery, have been elaborated in the course of the centuries in precise historical contexts, and in a continuous relationship with the life of the Church. Consequently, without a history of dogma and a history

of the Church, theological reflection cannot escape the risk of doctrinal anachronism.

4. Indeed, without the positive function theology is no longer theology, but philosophy: it is understanding, but it is not understanding of the faith. A theology which ceases to draw its life from contact with revelation at source, becomes desiccated and sterile.[4]

3. *No positive function without the speculative*

1. The history of a science, (medicine for example) can be made only by an expert in that science, who is perfectly conversant with its present state. Similarly the history of theology can be written only by an expert in theology. For to appreciate the pre-scientific state of theology in Scripture and the Fathers correctly, it is important to be well acquainted with the later developments of theological reflection upon the deposit of faith. How indeed could the positive theologian judge of the progress, the deviations, the partial regressions, the novelties of a process if he did not know the point at which it had arrived and its orientations today? Without the speculative function the positive has no criterion for its specific judgments or its general appreciation.

2. The positive function is constantly confronted with difficult questions of dogma, questions of the Trinity, of Christology, of original sin, of grace, of the sacraments, of eschatology and the rest. The inquirer who attacks these questions without a sound theological formation is in danger at every moment of making grave mistakes, or of regarding as a novelty something that theological thought discovered long ago. The positive theologian cannot becomingly ignore the reflection pursued throughout the centuries by the Church.

---

4. Sacrorum fontium studio sacrae disciplinae semper iuvenescunt; dum contra speculatio quae ulteriorem sacri depositi inquisitionem neglegit, ut experiundo novimus, sterilis evadit (Pius XII, *Humani Generis, DS* 3886).

PART III
THE THEOLOGICAL DISCIPLINES

THE THEOLOGICAL DISCIPLINES

Theology, as a science, is one. It has its own object, its own finality, its own method. This unity is, however, compatible with a plurality of theological disciplines. Specialization, in theology as in all sciences, is a necessity imposed by the extent of knowledge, by teaching requirements, by a parallel evolution in the human sciences (philology, history, and literary criticism), by the appearance of new problems (in pastoral, missionary and ecumenical theology) and even of new objects (in the theology of terrestrial reality).

This division of theology into specialized departments is quite legitimate and constitutes a real progress, but only on condition that we remember that it is of an entirely different kind from the methodological distinction between positive theology and speculative or systematic theology. While this latter distinction permeates the whole of theology and each of its special departments, the division of theology into particular disciplines arises from the diversity of matters treated or from mere teaching convenience (as in dogma and moral theology for instance). Nor must one ever lose sight of the fact that the different theological disciplines are all at the service of one science, whose end is to understand and contemplate the saving mystery of the living God in his manifold and infinite wisdom. That is why they are intimately connected with one another and support one another, each contributing in its own way to an understanding of the one design of God.

The theological disciplines can be grouped in different ways. The order we have adopted is this.

God has intervened in human history and manifested himself to man to reveal to him the plan of salvation. The Word of God in Jesus Christ and through Jesus Christ: that is the first reality of Christianity. Apologetic theology and fundamental theology are the basic disciplines which have for their object the fact and the mystery of this Word in the world.

The contents of the Word spoken by God and received in faith are infinite. Dogmatic theology (ch. 2), supported by the results of specialized research, tries to understand the design of God in its totality; its object is the Mystery and the mysteries. It is presented in the description which we give of it, in the same way as a course in "general science" as compared with the special departments of the same science. It prepares the way for the particular disciplines and at the same time unifies them in a higher synthesis. In theology taken as a whole, it is at once the point of departure and the point of arrival.

The word in its first and original form of expression (in Scripture, in the Fathers, in the liturgy) is the object of biblical theology, patristic theology and liturgical theology (ch. 3). On the foundation of this word two disciplines study how the Christianity of the "new man" works in practice (ch. 4), in its universal structure (moral theology), or in its personal dimension in both an historical and an experimental sense (spiritual theology). The other disciplines concern the Church as a community or as an institution. Pastoral theology, missionary theology and ecumenical theology (ch. 5) deal with the apostolic activity of the Church, as she speaks to the faithful (pastoral theology), to the separated brethren (ecumenical theology) or to non-Christians at large (missionary theology). Canon Law (ch. 6), in a special relationship with dogma and moral theology, governs the institutional life of the Church, the divine-human society founded by Christ, and penetrates into a large part of its liturgical, pastoral and missionary activity. Finally, the history of the Church (ch. 7), which is not merely a description but an understanding of the life of the Church through the centuries, is a discipline, and at the same time a dimension, which affects every department of theology.

CHAPTER I APOLOGETIC AND FUNDAMENTAL THEOLOGY

I. FUNDAMENTAL THEOLOGY

1. *The theology of the word of God*

Fundamental theology is so called because it studies the first fundamental reality of Christianity, that is revelation, or the word of God spoken to men. In the order of our knowledge (*quoad nos*), the whole economy of salvation rests upon this intervention of God in history, this dialogue of love to which God calls man, inviting him to a community of life with the Father, the Son and the Spirit.[1]

But this reality, like other Christian realities (the Church and the resurrection of Christ for instance) has a double aspect: it is at the same time an event in history, assignable to a particular point in time, and a mystery of faith. It is the primordial mystery, the vehicle of all the rest, for it is the manifestation of the saving purpose which was in the mind of God from all eternity and which was realized in Jesus Christ. And, on the other hand, it is the first, determinative event of Christianity, which conditions

---

1. Const. *Dei verbum*, n. 2.

and justifies the choice of faith; for if God has spoken, the choice of faith is not a blind choice, but a human choice in conformity with the nature of man as a free and intelligent being. Revelation indeed owes some of its wealth of meaning to its two-fold aspect as mystery and event.

Like all true theology, fundamental theology sets out to understand its object, revelation, in its totality, that is to say in its mysterious entity, in its emergence in history, in the signs of this emergence, in the society which received the mission to transmit it, the Church, and in the objective forms in which it has been expressed and has endured through the centuries (Scripture and tradition). Fundamental theology speaks in a dogmatic sense of the mystery, and in an apologetic sense of the event. It derives its unity from its object of study, revelation, and from the profound purpose of all theological work, the desire to understand; its method therefore is, as it should be, at the service of this object and this end.

Looked at from this point of view, apologetic treatment and dogmatic treatment are complementary, both contributing to a better understanding of the object studied. "The Catholic synthesis is so sound and coherent" says H. Holstein, "that it seems to us more and more impossible to take to pieces what is, in the statement of Christianity as in our lives, an indissoluble whole." [2] H. de Lubac notes in his turn: "The interpenetration of apologetics and theology (i.e. dogmatics in this context), which in practice often seems necessary, is completely justified and justified of right. It is sterile prejudice and a false idea of their nature which opposes the one to the other. They are complementary and live in a mutual exchange. The terrain where they meet and where their collaboration bears most fruit, is fundamental theology." [3]

The dogmatic vision of revelation which must, in our opinion,

2. H. Holstein, "La théologie fondamentale depuis 1945," *L'année théologique*, 11 (1950):161.

3. H. de Lubac, "Apologétique et théologie," *Nouvelle Revue théologique*, 57 (1930): 378. H. U. Balthasar observes on his part in *La Gloire et la Croix*: "We shall have to talk about many things which are usually the

precede the apologetic vision,[4] sees revelation from the point of view of faith, as it does all the other Christian mysteries (creation, Incarnation, redemption for instance). It goes from faith to the understanding of faith, basing itself on Scripture as an inspired source and on the Church as a divine institution. It studies revelation as Trinitarian action and as structure of salvation: in its nature, its object, its properties, its finality.[5] The first effect of this dogmatic way of looking at revelation is that the reality which apologetics will afterwards survey critically from its own point of view, is presented accurately. If it is true that it is the credibility of revelation which is the object of apologetics, it is not unimportant to stress that the revelation in question is not revelation of a philosophic sort, a kind of gnosis, but an exceedingly specific revelation, which comes to us by way of history and the Incarnation. To construct an apologetic of revelation upon the slender foundations of a quasi-nominal definition, without solid biblical and patristic support, is surely to risk missing the real problems. How can we pretend to establish the fact of revelation, asks K. Rahner, without trying to be exact about its content?[6]

The dogmatic presentation of revelation at once places the student in the presence of the reality which controls his whole life, the living God who emerges from his mystery, enters history,

---

concern of what is called fundamental theology. But that should not lead anyone to imagine that we are proposing to develop here a fundamental theology distinct from dogmatic theology and in opposition to it. Our train of thought is rather the attempt to convince the reader that these two aspects of theology are inseparable" (*La Gloire et la Croix,* vol. 1, Paris, 1965, pp. 11-12).

---

4. We possess revelation and live by it before we even ask ourselves questions in a methodical way about its entry on the scene of history. Historically, moreover, apologetics is the fruit of dogmatics: it is on second thoughts that theology has been led to make a special treatise on Catholic dogmas' titles to credibility. Apologetics is the last stage of dogmatic reflection.

5. R. Latourelle, *Theology of Revelation* (Alba House, New York, 1966).

6. K. Rahner, "A propos de la réforme des études ecclésiastiques" in *Est-il possible aujourd'hui de croire?* (Paris, 1966), p. 203.

is made flesh and becomes Gospel, the good news of the design of love which he has followed from all eternity. The unheard of news is that man is saved, and that through faith in Jesus Christ we enter into life, the life itself of the Father and the Son and the Spirit. This confrontation with the living word of the living God, besides attracting the soul of the Christian, arouses in his intelligence the desire to understand. For revelation, by the wealth of its content, and the multiplicity of its aspects and paradoxes, provokes theological understanding. It is not a negligible matter from the educational and pastoral point of view, that we should begin theology by the study of a reality whose wealth and splendor overwhelm the student and arouse in him an overmastering intellectual curiosity. One might add that this dogmatic presentation of revelation constitutes at the same time a stepping-stone to an engagement of faith, the response to the Word which has been spoken.

The Church claims that this reality which we call revelation, which we possess in faith and by which we live, is not a purely subjective possession, but an event of history, reaching its most concentrated point in the appearance of Jesus Christ. It is here that the apologetic problem is, properly speaking, situated. God has spoken to man and the fact of his Word can be solidly established. The task of apologetics is, therefore, to establish the fact of revelation, that is the fact of God's intervention in human history, the fact of a Word which men can understand, the fact of the invitation to decide in faith. In short, the task of apologetics is to establish the fact of the Word in history, and the fact of the Church as the trustee and mediatrix of this Word through the centuries. It studies the fact of "The Word coming into this world." It confronts the Word with the demands of reason and science; and it confronts reason and science with the demands of the Word. It is the meeting place of eternity and time, of the human and the divine. In thus establishing the fact that God has spoken to men, and the fact of the Church as mediating what he has said, apologetics fulfills an indispensable task. In speaking to all men, the Church has to give firm grounds for believing that the word she speaks and lives by is not a human word but *the* word of God which needs to be heard within the one Church founded by Christ.[7]

2. *The first categories of Christianity*

The first year of theological studies can be called fundamental in another, and no less important, sense. Every science begins by defining and explaining its basic notions, its first categories. These may become more precise and richer in meaning later, after the experience of using them; but they have to be stated in some form at the beginning of every science. Philosophy has to define the first categories of its thought: the ideas of being, truth, certainty, evidence, objectivity. Theology, or sacred science, has also to define and elaborate the ideas which it constantly uses. The concepts of revelation, inspiration, credibility, faith, mystery, dogma, magisterium, tradition are first categories, implied in every theological process, categories, therefore, which need to be identified and made precise. It is a question of a sort of theological semantics.[8]

Although fundamental, this is none too easy. Let one example suffice. *Homo spontaneus,* that is to say the prophet-writer, lived and described revelation in the symbolic language of pre-scientific man; *homo speculativus,* in the Middle Ages, afterwards elaborated a theory of prophetic knowledge; finally *homo criticus* reflected upon the experience of *homo spontaneus* and the elaboration of *homo speculativus.* But his critical reflection is far from being finished. Throughout the whole course of theology other concepts will be elaborated in the same way (grace, sacrament, supernatural, and so on), but it belongs to fundamental theology to elaborate and define the very first categories of Christianity and of theological language.[9]

---

7. The complementary nature of dogmatic and apologetic treatment, is a truth which should be applied not only to revelation as such, but also to the signs of revelation. Cf. R. Latourelle, "Apologétique et Fondamentale," *Salesianum,* 28 (1965), pp. 270-271.

8. G. Söhngen, "Fundamentaltheologie," *Lexikon für Theologie und Kirche,* 4, pp. 456-457.

9. Fundamental theology in the usual sense of the word should not be

II. APOLOGETIC THEOLOGY

Apologetics corresponds to only a part of fundamental theology as we have just described it. It is the part which studies the fact of revelation and the ensemble of signs which allow us to conclude with certainty that the fact exists. In so doing, it establishes the reasonable character of the decision of faith. But before any further explanation of the nature and purpose of apologetics, it is not without point to attempt to define its character by negation.

1. *Definition by negation*

1. Apologetics is not a technique of conversion. A great many of the ambiguities which hover about it arise from the persuasion, more or less open, that its task is to convert. G. Rabeau, for instance, in the encyclopedia *Catholicisme,* writes that "the end of apologetics is to lead to faith." [10] Now as thousands of readers have closed our works of apologetics without being converted, one might well heap opprobrium upon a science unfaithful to its task.

It is important, therefore, to distinguish apologetics as a technique and apologetics as a science. There does exist a technique of conversion, or better a pastoral method of conversion, which depends on psychological and educational principles, and

---

confused with fundamental theology as proposed by Karl Rahner. The fundamental theology, or basic course, which he describes contains both more and less than fundamental theology in the classical sense. It contains more; for it studies not only the fact but also the content of revelation, that is the different mysteries of Christianity. It contains less; for it makes a choice among the problems of fundamental theology as classically conceived. The criterion of its selection is this: it studies the mysteries and grounds of faith which have an existential echo in the life of men today. To tell the truth, it is rather a fundamental dogmatics, of a synthetic and existential sort.

Cf. K. Rahner, "A propos de la réforme des études ecclésiastiques," in *Est-il possible aujourd'hui de croire?* (Paris, 1966), pp. 175-225.

10. G. Rabeau, "Apologétique," *Catholicisme,* I, p. 717.

is practiced by missionaries and centers devoted to conversions problems. It consists in presenting a conspectus of Christian doctrine to an individual or group and inviting belief. It takes very varied forms, as varied, to tell the truth, as the individuals themselves, simple arguments for the simple, elaborate and learned ones for the more cultivated. This pastoral method of conversion is necessary in the Church; it may even take a quasi-scientific form, but it is not what we call apologetic theology. That is properly a science, which has its own object, its own finality and its own method.

Need one add that an apologetic demonstration, even if it is perfectly administered, cannot produce faith *ex opere operato?* Apologetic demonstration seeks to establish the fact of revelation from the signs of this revelation in history. Its argument concludes in the credibility of Christian truth and the rational character of our faith. It develops a process of reasoning and ends in a kind of certainty which are of the same order as itself. In itself, it does not tend to faith. While apologetics is a science, faith is a religious and saving act, a personal and total adherence to God and to his word. While the judgment of apologetics is in the speculative and scientific order, the assent of faith is in the existential order and is a gift of grace. It is very possible that on the road to conversion, the manifestation of Christianity as value, as it is revealed in an encounter with authentic holiness, is more attractive than the most complete and learned demonstration that the most rigorous apologetic can produce.

2. Although its origins may suggest the contrary, apologetics is not a system of defense against adversaries. Its attitude is not the exterior opportunist attitude of an orthodoxy with its claws out, always in a state of aggressiveness, wasting its time and strength in dealing or parrying blows. For three centuries apologetics devoted the best of its resources to sword-crossing, but very happily it ended by losing the polemic and strident tone which had discredited it. Apologetics is, first and before all, a positive science, which would have existed even if no enemy had ever existed. Moreover, students today, who live in an ecumenical

climate, reject violently the sort of apologetics which is bristling with points barbed with iron. It is indeed significant of the change which has taken place in men's minds that Protestant or Muslim students can attend courses in apologetics given in Catholic universities without experiencing the least embarrassment or constraint.

3. Apologetics is not, as certain writers such as Dieckmann have believed, a simple philosophic-historical dissertation. Although apologetics makes use of history and philosophy it does not follow that for that reason it avoids theology. Theological understanding does not cease to be theological because it becomes critical. Apologetic theology is true theology: inside the faith, it is always, in the believer, the quest of the intelligence applied to the content of revelation. Theological reflection applies itself to understand the property of the object of faith which is its credibility, and the property of faith itself which is its reasonableness. The fact that reflection here, because of the immediate end it pursues, must make use of the data of history, philology and philosophy, detracts nothing at all from its essential purpose, which is to understand revealed truth, here, as a fact of history, in dogmatics, as a mystery of faith. Indeed, because of a false conception of the theological process the distinction between apologetics and dogmatics has been pushed to excess.

4. Apologetics is not philosophy of religion. The essential aim of the philosophy of religion is the aim of a philosopher pure and simple, not of a Christian as such. It does not study the mysteries as objects of faith, as dogma does, or as worthy of faith as apologetics does; it studies religion as an activity of man and as activity of consciousness. It studies the phenomena which religion unlocks there, the categories which it brings into play. For the philosophy of religion, revelation is never anything but a negative criterion. Apologetics on the other hand works always under the direction of the Church, and under the pressure of faith in search of understanding. As Y. Congar puts it, the philosophy of religion studies the religious act, the Christian faith, but superficially. "Its

level of operation and its method prevent it from making a final judgment upon the whole, either of the existential conditions of faith, or of its object." [11] This judgment belongs to theology.

5. Finally it is perhaps not without point to stress that apologetics is not a kind of know-all or jack-of-all-trades. There is a real temptation for apologetics to develop an annexing spirit, and to become a sort of encyclopedia of sciences. Under the pretext of being open to the problems of the time it risks becoming a slave to them. It is in constant danger of being submerged by an avalanche of disciplines, all excellent in themselves but coming between it and its main object, and producing in the student a disastrous dissipation of mind. Philosophy of religion, sociology of religion, psychology of religion, history of religion, ecumenism — apologetics sometimes gives the impression in Lang's phrase of being a pantology. It talks about everything except the true religion. Not to mince matters — and since everything which is good in itself should not be introduced into every programme — it seems to us that the task of apologetics begins only when it is a question of supernatural revelation. Research upon the nature of religion as such, and upon its necessity is not directly the object of apologetics or of fundamental theology.[12]

2. *The nature of apologetics*

After recalling in this way what apologetics is not, let us look at what it is.

1. Theologians today (for example: de Lubac, Congar, K.

---

11. Y. Congar, *La foi et la théologie* (Bruges & Paris, 1962), p. 190. For the relation between philosophy of religion and theology, see R. Virgoulay, "Foi et critique. La philosophie de la religion et la théologie," *Recherches de science religieuse*, 54, (1966), pp. 497-529.

12. This is obviously not to deny that universities and faculties of theology may and should offer courses in the history of religions and in the psychology and philosophy of religion, nor that seminaries should "introduce their students to a knowledge of other religions" (Decree *Optatam totius*, n. 16). We merely suggest that these disciplines are not directly the concern of apologetics.

Rahner, H. U. Balthasar, Bouillard, Torrell, Liégé, de Bovis, Holstein, Lang, Garrigou-Lagrange, Tromp, Nicolau) recognize that apologetics is true theology. It depends on the theological habit, in being an exercise in understanding revealed truth. It sets out to understand this precisely in so far as it is revealed, and consequently in so far as it is deserving of faith. Or, if one likes to put it that way, it seeks to show the rightness, from a human point of view, of the choice of faith which is the source of all Christian theology. For if faith is a free and reasonable act, reason should be able to demonstrate that it is such. This reflection which is quite primary, is analogous to ontology and epistemology in philosophy.

2. There are different formulations in different authors of the primary purpose of apologetics, but in substance all these formulations are identical. If we look at apologetics from the point of view of revelation, we shall say that it is the science of the human credibility of revelation. It sets out to establish in a methodical manner (in conformity with the exigencies of science), by means of discursive reasoning which is speculatively valid (complying not only with the demands of practical life but also with those of the critical intellect), and universally valid (by reason of the objective value of the arguments and not only because of the authority of the person speaking or the slender ability of the person listening) that the Christian religion is deserving of faith because it is divine in origin. In other words, it is the scientific exposition of the signs which witness to the fact of revelation and, consequently, to the credibility of the Christian religion. If we look at apologetics from the point of view of faith, we shall say that it sets out to "demonstrate by reasoning valid in the eyes of an unbeliever what the believer considers to be the rational foundations of the decision of faith." [13]

3. Apologetics must concern itself not only with the object

---

13. H. Bouillard, "L'expérience humaine et le point de départ de la théologie fondamentale," *Salesianum*, 28 (1965), p. 276. Several theologians are asking at the moment whether it is better to put apologetic theo-

of its study (the witness to Christ, the signs of his mission, the foundation of the Church), but also with the human subject to whom revelation and the signs of revelation are addressed. By the human subject is understood man with his aspirations, his passions and his deep needs, those of which Pascal and Blondel for instance have written. If apologetics has as its object the human credibility of revelation it cannot content itself with studying revelation and the signs of revelation in themselves; it must be equally interested in the conditions which determine, *ex parte subjecti,* their efficacious reception.[14] What is needed is an integral apologetic which takes account of both subject and object. For it is of its essence that apologetics should be equally concerned with the problem of the adequate statement of revelation (its objective pole), and with the problem of the receptive capacities of the subject and the conditions of his receptivity (its subjective pole). If apologetics neglected the subject, "it would fall before

logy's critical reflection upon the object of faith at the beginning of the theology course, as it now generally is, or at the end, as has been proposed in certain quarters. See for instance C. Vagaggini, "La teologia dogmatica nell' art. 16 del Decreto sulla formazione sacerdotale," *Seminarium,* 18 (1966), p. 826; A. Locatelli, "L'insegnamento della teologia fondamentale nel rinnovamento degli studi teologici," *La Scuola Cattolica,* 95 (1967), pp. 85-123. Logically and ideally, it is true that this critical reflection upon the whole problem of the object of faith and its credibility comes better after the complete exposition of what faith teaches, particularly after Christology and ecclesiology. Nevertheless experiments made here and there, in divers countries, have shown this ideal order is psychologically and educationally amiss. By the end of dogmatics the student's interest in apologetic problems (in the historical study of the witness to Christ, and of its signs, and of the foundation of the Church) is for the most part blunted. The historical study of the Gospels, centered upon the Person of Christ and on the signs of his glory comes much better at the beginning of theological studies. There is a place, however, at the level of specialization in fundamental theology for a teaching degree, for a course which would take up again at a deeper level this critical reflection upon the fact of revelation begun upon the threshold of theological work.

14. N. Dunas, "Les problèmes et le statut de l'apologétique," *Revue des sciences philosophiques et théologiques,* 43 (1959), p. 658.

long into a dry-as-dust extrinsicism." If it ignored the *facta divina* and "presumed to shut itself up in the subject" [15] it would dissolve in words without meaning. Objective and subjective apologetics are not therefore, two different modes of attack, designed at conversion, or two different methods successive in time, but two aspects of one, integral apologetics. From this angle the consideration of its subjective reception is not merely parallel to the demonstration of truth, but co-extensive with it in every part, entering into the texture of every argument. It is particularly important at two privileged moments; first, at the outset, to show that if man is attentive to the facts of his own interior universe, he cannot refuse at least to entertain as an hypothesis a conclusion which would come to him from God, as a gift, and to study the conditions of his acceptance of the word of God which would eventually signify to him this conclusion and this gift; and then in the treatment of the signs of revelation, in order to show that in the concrete the signs cannot be deciphered without certain dispositions, in the absence of which they remain enigmas, phenomena not merely abnormal but exasperating. True apologetics thus keeps a middle way between an apologetics pre-occupied with the object and a pastoral apologetics pre-occupied immediately with conversion.

4. Apologetic reflection upon the fact of revelation is an ecclesial function: it is that by which the Church takes cognizance, for herself, and for those who question her, of the rightness from a human point of view of the engagement of faith. If the Church ceased to reflect upon the intervention of God in history and on the signs of this intervention, she would in the end be exposed to the danger of fideism: engaged in the adventure of faith, she would no longer know why or how she was engaged. This apologetic reflection is addressed first of all to her own sons and daughters, whom she wishes to strengthen in their faith, after the man-

---

15. A. de Bovis, "Bulletin d'apologétique," *Recherches de science religieuse,* 43 (1955), p. 624.

ner of St. Luke writing to Theophilus to reassure him of the validity of the teachings he had received (Luke 1, 1-4). In our time particularly, the Church must help the Christian to see where he stands in relation to the atheism which is all about him, and in relation to non-Christian religions. Apologetic reflection belongs also to the missionary function of the Church, for she must normally be able to present, to those moving towards faith not only Christ's teaching but also the signs which accredit him as the Father's Son. She must be able to meet the unbeliever and hold rational discourse with him, in a way which will be valid even in his eyes.

5. Apologetic demonstration ends in a high degree of certainty, of the same order as is obtained in the human sciences, but this certainty remains a moral certainty. For apologetic demonstration draws its support from signs, that is from particular contingent realities to which it has access only by way of human witness through documents which remain critically hard to assess. To this doubly mediate character of a demonstration made by way of signs and human witness is added a conclusion obtained by means of convergence, the convergence of indications of the intervention of God in human history. There is a certainty proper, respectively, to mathematics, to metaphysics, to history, to psychology, to sense perception. Where it is a question of signs and historical witness to them, we are moving on the plane of history, and psychology and sense perception. The certainty we obtain is moral certainty.[16]

6. Apologetic science as a whole is a collective possession of the Church as a social body. Just as a doctor could not possess in his individual capacity the whole of medical science, so no Christian, no theologian, could exhaust the intelligibility of each

16. N. Dunas, "Les problèmes et le statut de l'apologétique," *Revue des sciences philosophiques et théologiques*, 43 (1959), p. 657; G. Thils, *Orientations de la théologie* (Louvain, 1958), pp. 79-82.

and every sign of the Christian revelation. Apologetic science presupposes among other things a profound knowledge of Scripture, tradition, the history of Israel, the history of religions and so on. As with the human sciences, its possession is a collegial possession. And the faithful, in different degrees, according to the intelligence and cultivation and grace of each, participate in the science of the Church. This sharing of apologetic science and of its collective certainty is important, particularly when it is a question of signs rich in meaning but exceedingly complex, and therefore difficult to interpret — the sign we see in the fulfillment of messianic prophecies for instance. Nevertheless, a good many individual Christians can arrive at an understanding of Christianity's titles to credibility which constitutes a coherent and valid body of knowledge even for the unbeliever.

3. *Apologetics and dogmatics*

Apologetic reflection has as its object the first and fundamental facts of Christianity, that is the fact of revelation and the fact of the Church. It cannot therefore, in its demonstration derive support from the inspired character of Scripture or the divine character of the Church; for these are precisely the things in question. It refuses to introduce into the course of its arguments any affirmation of faith, and sets out to be a rational dissertation which has sense and validity even in the eyes of the unbeliever. It considers the texts of Scripture as historical documents, whose value is to be established according to the exigencies of historical criticism. In the same way the arguments which it derives from philosophy have to convince the critical reason because of their intrinsic value and not because of the authority of the Church. Its historical or philosophic reasoning has to carry its justification within itself. It is not a matter, for the theologian, of suspending his faith, but of adapting his procedure to the end in view, the end of establishing in critical terms the fact of God's intervention in history and his word to men, by showing that the signs of revelation belong to an historical train of events which are really there. Because this critical reflection is that of a believing theologian, it arises under the pressure of faith seeking to understand its object, and it is exercised under the direction of the Church, which gives to apologetics the object of its reflection, the categories it uses (revelation, miracle, mystery and so on) and even indications as to method.

BIBLIOGRAPHY I

ALAND, K., *Die Apologie der Apologetik*, Berlin, 1948.

BOUILLARD, H., « Le sens de l'apologétique », dans : *Bulletin du Comité des études*, n. 35, Paris, 1961, pp. 311-327.

BOUILLARD, H., *Logique de la foi*, Paris, 1964.

BOUILLARD, H., « L'expérience humaine et le point de départ de la théologie fondamentale », *Concilium*, n. 6 (1965) : 83-92.

CAHILL, P. J., « Apologetics », *New Catholic Encyclopedia*, I : 669-674.

CONGAR, Y., *La foi et la théologie*, Paris, 1962.

COPPENS, J., « Un essai de synthèse apologétique », *Ephemerides theologicae lovanienses*, 1937, pp. 447-466.

CREHAN, J. H., « Apologetics », *A Catholic Dictionary of Theology*, I : 113-122.

DE BOVIS, A., « Bulletin d'apologétique », *Recherches de science religieuse*, 43 (1955) : 599-624.

DE LUBAC, H., « Apologétique et théologie », *Nouvelle Revue théologique*, 57 (1930) : 361-378.

DULLES, A., *Apologetics and the Biblical Christ*, Woodstock, 1964.

DUNAS, N., « Les problèmes et le statut de l'apologétique », *Revue des sciences philosophiques et théologiques*, 43 (1959) : 643-680.

GABOARDI, A., « Teologia fondamentale. Il metodo apologetico », in : *Problemi e Orientamenti di Teologia dommatica* I, Milano, 1957, pp. 56-103.

GARDEIL, A., *La crédibilité et l'apologétique*, Paris, 1908.

GARDEIL, A., « Crédibilité », *Dictionnaire de théologie catholique*, III, 2 : 2201-2310.

GARRIGOU-LAGRANGE, R., « L'apologétique dirigée par la foi », *Revue thomiste*, 24 (1919) : 193-213.

GARRIGOU-LAGRANGE, R., « L'Apologétique et la théologie fondamentale », *Revue des sciences philosophiques et théologiques*, 9 (1920) : 352-359.

Gössmann, E., « Fundamentaltheologie und Apologetik », in :
E. Neuhäusler und E. Gössmann, *Was ist Theologie*, München,
1966, pp. 25-52.

Holstein, H., « La théologie fondamentale depuis 1945 », *L'année
théologique*, 11 (1950) : 133-161.

Kolping, A., « Fundamentaltheologie im heutigen Hochschul-
unterricht », *Theologie und Glaube*, 54 (1964) : 115-126.

Kolping, A., « Zehn Jahre einer neuen Fundamentaltheologie »,
Münch. Theologische Zeitschrift, 15 (1964) : 62-69.

Lais, A., « Apologetik », *Lexikon für Theologie und Kirche*, 1 :
723-731.

Lang, A., *Fundamentaltheologie. Die Sendung Christi*, München,
1945, pp. 1-32.

Latourelle, R., « Apologétique et Fondamentale. Problèmes de
nature et de méthode », *Salesianum*, 28 (1965) : 256-273.

Le Bachelet, X.-M., « Apologétique », *Dictionnaire apologétique de
la foi catholique*, 1 : 189-251.

Liégé, A. et Congar, Y., « Bulletin d'apologétique », *Revue des
sciences philosophiques et théologiques*, 33 (1949) : 53-74.

Locatelli, A., « L'insegnamento della Teologia fondamentale nel
rinnovamento degli studi teologici », *La Scuola Cattolica*, 95
(1967) : 95-123.

Maisonneuve, L., « Apologétique », *Dictionnaire de théologie
catholique*, I, 2 (1923) : 1511-1580.

Malmberg, F., « Apologetica als theologische Wetenschap »,
Bijdragen, 1958, pp. 104-145.

Metz, J.-B., « Apologetik », *Sacramentum mundi*, 1 : 266-276.

Saint-Jean, R., *L'Apologétique philosophique. Blondel 1893-1913*,
Paris, 1966.

Saunders, D. J., « A definition of Scientific Apologetics », *Theological
Studies*, 5 (1944) : 159-183.

Söhngen, G., « Fundamentaltheologie », *Lexikon für Theologie und
Kirche*, 4 : 452-459.

Straubinger, H., « Die Apologetik als theologische Disziplin »,
Theologische Quartalschrift, 121 (1940) : 14-25.

Torrell, J.-P., « Chronique de théologie fondamentale », *Revue
thomiste*, 64 (1964) : 97-103.

Torrell, J.-P., « Théologie fondamentale », *Revue thomiste*, 67
(1967) : 439-442.

CHAPTER II   DOGMATIC THEOLOGY

The expression dogmatic theology is not without ambiguity; for it is used today in slightly different senses.

In the first sense dogmatic theology is opposed to moral theology, and to the other theological disciplines. While dogmatics tries to see more deeply into the great Christian mysteries in themselves and for themselves (into the Trinity, the Incarnation, grace and so on), moral theology is concerned above all with man's behavior; it is interested in the practical aspect of dogma, and gives a good deal of space to ethics in the philosophical sense.

In a stricter sense, dogmatic theology is the exposition and scientific investigation of the word of God as it is preached and taught by the Church. The aim of dogmatics is to penetrate more deeply into the meaning of each of the mysteries of salvation and to show how what the Church preaches today is homogenous with the facts of Scripture and tradition.[1] Its procedure is at once genetic and regressive, in a complementary way. It is genetic in that what the Church preaches today can be understood only by knowing its genesis in revelation; it is regressive in that what the Church preaches today, on the culmination of dogmatic development, constantly throws light upon what we read in the past.

---

1. Denzinger - Schönmetzer, 3886.

The second Vatican Council's decree *Optatam totius* has re-
tained the current terminology which distinguishes dogmatics
from moral theology, but, in the description which it gives of it,
dogmatics is not opposed to the other theological disciplines as
a particular discipline in relation to other particular disciplines,
but rather as a general science (integral and synthetic) in relation
to specializations of this science. Dogmatics assumes the conclusions of the particular disciplines and makes an organic synthesis of theological knowledge.[2]

1. *Dogmatics according to "Optatam totius"*

In the sixteenth section of the decree on the formation of
priests, the second Vatican Council has expressed its conception
of the nature and procedure of dogmatic theology. To understand
the text it is necessary to read it in the context of the Council's
presence and work in the world, and to take into account the
concrete theological method adopted by the Council in its treatment of the great problems to which it addresses itself in the Constitutions on revelation, the Church, the liturgy, and the Church
in the world. In these Constitutions its procedure is based on
Scripture, with constant attention to showing the relevance of
each mystery to the spiritual and pastoral life of the Church in
an attitude of dialogue with the world and with other Christian
communities.[3] The text of the decree stresses five points or aspects of theological procedure.

1. "Biblical themes should come first." By biblical themes
we are to understand those aspects of religious experience in the
Old Testament which find their fulfillment in Jesus Christ, and
which have been assumed into subsequent Christian experience
and lived there — the covenant, the law, the word of God, the
messianic expectation, sin, the remnant of Israel, the desert, the

---

2. C. Vagaggini, "La teologia dogmatica nell' art. 16 del Decreto sulla
  formazione sacerdotale," *Seminarium*, 6 (1966), p. 822.
3. *Ibid.*, p. 820.

vine, for instance. The notion of a biblical theme, therefore, suggests the genesis of revelation, the concrete way in which the great categories in which the Christian revelation has been proposed to us were stated and developed and given depth. Analytic study of the scriptural books enables us to grasp these themes at different stages of their development. The mystery of Christ is the focus where they all meet in convergence and where they take their definitive dimension. The exposition of biblical themes is the final fruit of exegesis and of biblical theology.[4]

In thus founding the whole theological procedure on the great scriptural themes, we guarantee the unity of theology, whose task is precisely that of exploring the history of salvation, whose center and summit is Christ. And in this way too, we stress that Scripture is not, in theology, simply an authority to which we can appeal to defend our position or to refute the contrary position, or simply a theological ground for a proposition already authenticated elsewhere. Scripture is the revealed fact itself, in its living historical form, the fact we are to investigate, the matter on which theological reflection has to be made. This unique word of God is the object of faith, which has to be entered into and understood, in itself, and in all its spiritual and pastoral implications. Scripture in this way "is, as it were, the soul of theology." [5]

This biblical basis, which, at the very outset, places the student in contact with the word of God, has many other advantages to offer, besides that of being the nursing ground of theological work. It sensitizes the mind to the historical and pedagogical dimension of revelation; it guarantees the christological orientation of theology; it enables us to avoid the danger of anachronism, which consists in forcing the text, in order to make it say more than it does; it constitutes a first grasp of the intelligibility which, as it were, emanates from biblical data when they are gathered together and systematized; and it fosters the present *rapprochement* between Catholics and the separated Christian

4. P. Grelot, "L'enseignement de la Sainte Ecriture," *Seminarium*, 6 (1966), pp. 873-874.
5. Const. *Dei verbum*, n. 24.

communities, especially Protestants, for whom Scripture is in a privileged position.

2. "Students should be shown also . . . what the Fathers of the Eastern and Western Church contributed to the faithful transmission and illumination of the individual truths of revelation, and the rest of the history of dogma should be treated in the same way." The Fathers of the Church are the witnesses to tradition, and, after the apostles, the first theologians of revelation. Some are witnesses to the apostolic tradition; others are witnesses to tradition in the sense that they express, through their writings and their lives, the faith which the Church perpetuates and transmits through the centuries. To understand the Fathers of the Church we must, as in the case of Scripture, take into account the literary form in which they chose to write, and see them in the historical framework of their time. We must distinguish also between their witness to the Christian faith, and their personal exploration of its depths. For the Fathers are also the first research workers and theologians. Their writings certainly have not the methodical and "structured" character of the great medieval *summae;* as a compensation they are more sensitive than the scholastics to the dynamic and historical aspects of revelation. They stress its progress and its deep unity. They insist on its essentially salvific character. With them again, the life of faith and the science of faith are in constant communication. To the study of the Fathers of the Eastern and Western Church, the decree adds the later history of dogma, to be viewed in the light of the history of the Church. For we could not understand the decisions of the magisterium, if we were to ignore the context in which they were made.

The first two points mentioned (embracing Scripture, the Fathers of the Church and the history of dogma) are obviously connected with the positive function of theology. The three which follow, introduced by *deinde,* and bound together by co-ordinating conjunctions (*ea . . . eademque . . . atque*), deal with the speculative function. This is described as a methodical effort "to illuminate as fully as possible (*integrare quantum fieri potest*) the mysteries of salvation" set before us in the biblical themes and in the witness of the Fathers of the Church. Not only must theology gather together the data of revelation, but it must also understand these data in as integral a way as possible, and systematize the results of its reflections. A theology which scarcely passed beyond the positive phase and attached little value to the speculative function, would therefore be unfaithful to both the spirit and the letter of the decree.

3. "Students should," says the decree, "try to penetrate more and more deeply into the mysteries of salvation, and see how they are interconnected." This is to be done "with St. Thomas as master." In explicitly mentioning St. Thomas the Council obviously does not intend to exclude the other Doctors of the Church, to whom St. Thomas himself owes a great deal. Nor does it intend to reduce our understanding of the mysteries to the light shed upon them by St. Thomas. The decree proposes him, not as the master of all but as a master and an example for all, as a specially distinguished master, who commends himself to us by his inquiring and creative disposition, his intellectual vigor, his willingness to confront faith with reason, his love of truth, the fruitfulness of his intuitions, the soundness of his systematization, the synthesis in him of the science of God and life in God.[6]

4. "Let them learn," the decree goes on, "to recognize these same mysteries always present and operative in liturgical actions and in the whole life of the Church." This passage is to be understood in the context of the Constitution on the liturgy, to which it refers explicitly. The salvation Christ announced and accomplished during his earthly life is ceaselessly proclaimed and actualized in the liturgical life of the Church. The mysteries which are the object of faith and of theology are lived and celebrated by the Church every day; every day Christ is present in the Mass, present in the administration of the sacraments, present in the preaching and prayer of the Church. That is why the liturgy constantly

---

6. The texts of Pius XII and Paul VI cited by the decree in note 36 show plainly that this is the tenor of the Council's thought.

repeats: today, Christ is born, today he dies for our sins, today
he rises again. Through the liturgy of the Church, God calls every
man, and invites him to make the choice of faith, which will lead
him into the mystery of salvation. It is then for theological understanding to show how the mysteries of salvation are always present
and always active in the liturgy. But the life of the Church over-
flows what can properly be called her liturgical activity. The
mysteries of salvation permeate the whole life of the Church;
it is through them that she lives in all her manifestations, in
preaching, in the apostolate, in works of charity, in personal
prayer. They inspire the response which she makes to the problems of men. *Gaudium et Spes* is an example of the light which
they throw upon man's origin and destiny (n. 12), upon sin (n.
13), upon the dignity of man (nn. 14-17), upon the meaning of
death (n. 18) and upon the new Man, Christ (n. 22).

5. Finally, let students "learn to look for solutions to human
problems in the light of revelation, to apply eternal truths to the
changing conditions of human affairs, and to communicate these
truths in a way which the contemporary world can understand."
This statement returns to the preoccupations of *Ecclesiam suam*
and *Gaudium et Spes*. While she must be faithful to the truth received from Christ, the Church must also attend to the contemporary conditions. She must "put Christianity into circulation, in the
forms of thought and language and culture, and according to the
usages and tendencies of men as they live and move on the face
of the earth today." [7] "It is her duty," says *Gaudium et Spes,* in
order the better to accomplish her task, "to scrutinize the signs
of the times and interpret them in the light of the gospel, so that
she can answer in language intelligible to each generation, the
perennial questions which men ask about this present life and
the life to come, and about the relationship of the one to the
other." [8] Theology, like the Church, must be an active encounter
between the spirit of faith and the spirit of the age. The word of

7. Paul VI, Encyclical *Ecclesiam suam,* AAS 56 (1964), pp. 640-641.
8. Const. *Gaudium et Spes,* n. 4.

God must be constantly put in touch with the spiritual situation of men today. Consequently theology needs to be provided with antennae, sensitive to the agonies as well as the aspirations of the contemporary world.[9] For the word of God demands always to be relived and rethought in order to solve the problems of each new time. Progress of all sorts, economic, social, political, biological, psychological, gives rise to new problems which call for answers adapted to them, made to the measure of the problems themselves. It is equally necessary that theology should be sensitive to the language of the contemporary world, so that it may formulate its answers in terms which are intelligible to man today.[10] The Council has given an initial example of this sensitiveness, both to present problems and to present modes of expression. In this respect it would seem that a sound knowledge of contemporary literature and contemporary philosophy are indispensable to any serious theological culture. To be intensely present in the world is the necessary condition of a theology which wishes to have any influence on the human and religious life of our time.

The Council's exposition of dogmatic procedure is obviously not presented as a schema *ne varietur,* in which the five points indicated would have to be found in the treatment of every mystery, and to follow these in the same order. Certainly there is the intention to stress in theological procedure a double momentum: the positive momentum of the *auditus fidei,* and the reflective momentum of the *intellectus fidei.* But within this double momentum there is room for a good deal of freedom. The points mentioned are not necessary stages in an always identical itinerary, but rather aspects of theological dissertation taken as a whole. There are problems where positive exposition will take a larger place (on the subject of penance for instance), and others where the speculative element will predominate (on the subject of grace and freedom, or of the consciousness of Christ). In sacramental theology liturgical implications will be more marked. The theme of grace and the theological virtues will lend itself to a more acute

---

9. *Ibid.,* n. 4.
10. *Ibid.,* nn. 44 & 62.

perception of the spiritual life, that of the Church to pastoral considerations. Sometimes even, some aspect may be omitted, for lack of sufficient monographs on the subject.

Dogmatic theology as described by the Council rests on the results of specialized research, and sets out to make an organic synthesis of these results and arrive at an understanding of the mystery in its totality, that is in its internal unity, in the multiplicity of its expressions, and in its implications for spiritual, liturgical and pastoral life. It is not only understanding of the mystery in itself, but also understanding of the values contained in it for Christian life today. If this is the reality designated by the term dogmatic theology, would not some other term, such as general theology, be more suitable to describe it? For if the Council makes no change in the traditional terminology, which places dogmatic among the particular theological disciplines (in the same category as moral theology, spiritual theology, and pastoral theology), the description which it gives of it, and also the use which it makes of it, is orientated towards a richer meaning, towards, as it were, a plenary sense. In the spirit, if not in the letter, of the Council, dogmatics harks back to the notion of theological wisdom, or the higher knowledge which unifies in an apex different kinds of special knowledge. Could we not see this rediscovery of the plenary sense of dogmatics as one of the fruits of the Spirit? It is through dogmatics understood in this way, that the continuity of what the Church preaches, and of the development of dogma is assured. This integral science of the faith is indispensible to the specialist (to the exegete, to the liturgist, or to the expert in patrology), who can find there, if not premises, at least indications which will orientate his research and prevent it from taking wrong directions.[11]

2. *New Orientations*

The decree on the formation of priests invites theology to

11. Z. Alszeghy and F. Flick, "Il movimento teologico italiano," *Gregorianum*, 48 (1967), p. 322.

find its center in the mystery of Christ and the history of salvation. The whole Council, besides, revolves as it were upon the personal relations of God with Israel, with the Church, with the contemporary world, with each of the faithful. This orientation itself corresponds to the general orientation of theology in the last few decades.

Scholastic theology was a theology of the mystery in itself rather than a theology of history, and the order adopted in the *summae* is a logical order rather than an order founded upon the economy of salvation. Twentieth century theology, on the other hand, arising as it does from the renewal of biblical and patristic studies, finds its axis in the history of salvation. It is interested not only in understanding the mysteries in themselves, but in salvation as it appears in human history and in the life of each individual human being. This attention to the history of salvation affects theology in three ways.

If theology's primary source is this history of salvation its first attention will be given to revelation as it is communicated by tradition and Scripture. But the salvation, which was once proclaimed and accomplished by Christ, lives, perpetually contemporary, in the liturgical life of the Church, through her preaching and her sacraments. It follows that the biblical, patristic and liturgical strata of theology are much wider and deeper than they were formerly.

In this history of salvation, the object of the divine intervention, and of salvation itself, is man: it is he who is called, he who is saved. After God, therefore, man becomes the center of theological attention. In fact present day theology has a phenomenological and existential character in contrast to the essentialist tendency of the period which precedes it. If theology thinks of man as a social entity, it becomes ecclesiology and pastoral theology. If it thinks of him as an individual, in terms of his personal salvation and movement towards perfection, it becomes spiritual theology.

A theology which takes the history of salvation as its axis is therefore called upon to renew its life both in its source and in its implications; in its source, through biblical, patristic and liturgical theology, in its implications through pastoral and spiritual theology. The way in which each mystery of faith impinges upon spiritual and pastoral life — rather an *hors d'oeuvre* in the eyes of theologians in the past — is from now on an essential part of their task. One must confess that in this matter theology is still in a period of trial and error.[12]

It is right and fitting, therefore, in teaching dogmatics, that we should introduce each mystery from the point of view of the history of salvation, insisting in so doing, on the freedom of God's action and the wisdom and love of his design. To sum up, it is a matter of going back to an old perspective, the perspective of the first Fathers of the Church (St. Irenaeus for instance), which has been preserved by the masters and theologians of the spiritual life (so that the exercises of St. Ignatius of Loyola apply to the journey of each soul to God, the itinerary of the history of salvation), but which later theology has abandoned. Through the history of salvation the word of God is addressed to all men of all times, and addressed personally to each. Biblical theology, pastoral theology and spiritual theology are thus closely linked. The ideal certainly would be to reconcile in one and the same theology, the historical perspective and the ontological perspective of St. Thomas, to keep both the sense of economy and the sense of mystery.[13]

---

12. This threefold renewal of theology is provided for in the conciliar decree: (a) in reference to the theology of the history of salvation, "Let students be careful to derive Catholic doctrine from divine revelation," "in the teaching of dogmatic theology . . . biblical themes should come first," and ". . . other theological disciplines should be renewed by a more living contact with the mystery of Christ and the history of salvation"; (b) in reference to pastoral theology, "Let them learn to look for solutions to human problems in the light of revelation, to apply eternal truths to the changing conditions of human affairs, and to communicate these truths in a way which the contemporary world can understand"; (c) in reference to spiritual theology, "Let them nourish their own spiritual lives with the doctrine they have derived from revelation."

13. F. Bourassa, "Sur la Traité de la Trinité," *Gregorianum,* 47 (1966), pp. 254-285.

BIBLIOGRAPHY II

BALDANZA, G., BROCARDO, P., etc., *Il Decreto sulla formazione sacerdotale* (Ed. Elle di Ci, Torino, 1967), pp. 441-471.

COLOMBO, G., « L'insegnamento della teologia dogmatica alla luce del Concilio Vaticano II », *La Scuola Cattolica*, 95 (1967) : 3-33.

GILLON, L.-B., « Le programme des études ecclésiastiques », *Seminarium*, 18 (1966) : 327-338.

VAGAGGINI, C., « La teologia dogmatica nell'art. 16 del Decreto sulla formazione sacerdotale », *Seminarium*, 18 (1966) : 819-841.

SCHEFFCZYK, L., *Dogmatik*, in : E. NEUHÄUSLER, und E. GÖSSMANN, *Was ist Theologie*, pp. 190-213.

CHAPTER III   BIBLICAL THEOLOGY, PATRISTIC THEOLOGY AND LITURGICAL THEOLOGY

I. BIBLICAL THEOLOGY

For a long time biblical theology scarcely existed in the Church outside "the argument from Scripture," which was developed in dogmatic theology as a basis or a defense for the statements of the Catholic faith. Though in itself perfectly legitimate, such a use of Scripture is not without its dangers, notably the danger of applying to biblical categories the sense given to modern theological categories, without taking into account that there is not a perfect correspondence between them. There is the danger also of falsifying the ratio of the elements which compose the biblical synthesis, or of omitting one or another important element entirely.

Biblical theology, in its modern sense, arose against a Protestant background in the seventeenth century, in reaction to Catholic dogmatic theology, and for long it remained a Protestant possession. Because of its origin it was slow in making its way into Catholic circles and being fully accepted there. Even today the notion of biblical theology is vague enough, and it is not always easy to define where what goes by that name begins and ends. In actual usage two main senses of the term are distinguishable, corresponding to the two different types of work which are presented under its label.

1. *Senses in which the term is used*

1. Taken in its first sense, biblical theology sets out to organize in a coherent, harmonious and intelligible synthesis, the "message" of Scripture, either in part or in whole, perhaps in a particular book or a particular author. The emphasis is always on undertaking a theological synthesis, and this work is accomplished in faith and in a spirit of loyalty to the Church's norms of interpretation (Scripture, tradition and the magisterium).

Thus understood, biblical theology holds a middle way between speculative theology and exegesis. It is not just exegesis, which has as its end determining the exact sense of the sacred text. On the other hand it is not quite speculative theology; for the synthesis which it makes does not go beyond the biblical categories, and makes no appeal to theological reasoning as such. Nor does work of this sort ask what light such a synthesis can throw on the problems of men today, or what truths ecclesiastical tradition has been able, in the course of the centuries, to find virtually contained in it. Basing itself upon exegesis, biblical theology of this kind collects and systematizes biblical data and presents them to theological reflection no longer in a dispersed, but in a unified state. In this way it can grasp the partial syntheses which distinguish the main stages of revelation (Yahwistic history, Deuteronomist history, the priestly tradition, the wisdom tradition, the synoptic tradition for instance); it can concentrate on the teaching of a particular author (St. Paul, or St. John for example), or of a particular book (like *Job,* or *The Song of Songs*); it can trace a particular theme throughout Scripture, from its appearance onwards (the theme of the desert, or of water, or of sin); finally, it can expound the "message" of the Old, or of the New Testament as a whole. It will be obvious that biblical theology of this type scarcely differs from an exegetic synthesis or a systematization of biblical ideas. The works of Van Imschoot on the Old Testament and of Meinertz on the New are biblical theology in this sense.

Needless to say, biblical synthesis of this sort is in itself productive of an enriched understanding of the mystery.

2. In a second sense, akin to the first, but wider — and this is the sense in favor at the present time — biblical theology, considering Scripture as a totality, as, so to speak, the intelligible expression with the one word of God, takes as its point of departure the many words, and figures and themes, but tries beyond this diversity to grasp the unity of the mystery and of the design of God. Biblical theology, in this wider connotation, assumes as its basic principles the unity of Scripture and the recognition of Christ as the key to the understanding of the two Testaments. The Old Testament is Christ announced, prefigured, prepared for; the New Testament is the Old Testament realized and fulfilled — it is Christ who is and is to come. The one *Logos* resounds through both Testaments. The mystery of God is one; his design is one, but it unfolds and is progressively realized in the history of salvation, and is expressed in the succession and diversity of the inspired books. Biblical theology is wedded to the profound movement of this divine economy in which prefiguring images pass into their fulfillment, and it seeks to retrace the progress of revelation and the underlying unity of the divine purpose. The words and events of the economy of salvation as they are to be found recorded in Scripture [1] are its point of departure, and, with the literal sense as the initial step, must be interpreted at depth, according to the fullness of meaning intended by God and perhaps imperfectly perceived by the human author. The method consists in collating texts, not only of the same author but of different authors, through whom the one divine author has spoken, in the hope of arriving, through the dialectic of the sacred text at the mystery in its deep unity, presented by the divine teacher in different aspects during the course of its progressive revelation. [2]

---

1. Const. *Dei verbum*, n. 2.
2. P. Benoit, "De L'étude de l'Ecriture sainte et de sa place, dans une nouvelle structure des études ecclésiastiques," *Seminarium*, 18 (1966), p. 845.

Several examples spring to mind. The messianic theme, in the Old Testament is expressed through different figures, the king, the suffering prophet, the Son of man, the priest. Through these figures, whose development it follows, biblical theology envisages the whole organic unity of God's purpose, preparing for the coming of his Son, the mysterious Son of man, invested with the threefold title of prophet, priest and king. The mystery of the covenant is expressed in the themes of the people of God, of the Bride and Bridegroom, of the Kingdom and of the Church; it is bound up with the mission of Abraham, of Moses, of David, and of Jesus, with the institution of prophets and priests and with all the rites of the Old Testament (circumcision, different kinds of sacrifice and so on). Setting out from these themes, these persons, these institutions, biblical theology is able to discern the ways by which God pursued his purpose of union with man in order that in Jesus Christ he might share with him the divine life. In the same way the themes of sacrifice, of the Pasch and of the return to the Father express one and the same mystery, that of man's union with God, in the Spirit of love.

This kind of theology is biblical; for its point of departure is Scripture; the words, the themes, the perspectives which are to be found there. It is theology for several reasons, first of all because it sees scriptural themes not as isolated but as harmoniously bound together in a higher synthesis, the design of God. It is theology since, rising above the multiplicity and diversity of words and themes, it attains to an understanding of the divine purpose and seeks to reveal its unity. It is theology again, in the sense that the principle of unification for the biblical data may differ from one "theology" to another — it may be the covenant, the exodus, the Word of God, the action of God. Finally it is theology in the sense that it interposes principles which are not drawn directly from the text of Scripture — the unity of the Bible, and the continuity and organic connection of the different theologies of the human authors.

Understood in this second sense biblical theology still remains enclosed within quite precise limits. It does not derive its data from the Fathers of the Church or from the liturgy, but from

Scripture alone. It is a science, but a biblical science; for it deliberately confines itself within the limits of the mode of expression, the images, the categories of which God has made use in revelation. It is true that Scripture manifests the influence of diverse cultures (Mesopotamian, Egyptian, Canaanite, Persian, Greek), and that biblical theology makes use of these instruments of thought offered by God himself. But it does not make use of instruments of thought (Augustinianism, Scotism, or Thomism for instance) or of cultures (the Chinese, Indian or African cultures for instance) other than those in which revelation is expressed. Nor does it ask what answer Scripture can make to the problems of men today. To this type of biblical theology belong, with many nuances, the work of Procksch, Jacob, Eichrodt, Vriezen, Stauffer, Von Rad, the *thèmes bibliques* of J. Guillet and the monographs of the *Vocabulaire de theologie biblique*.[3]

2. *Principal biblical theologies in the twentieth century*

The principal biblical theologies of the Old Testament are those of E. Sellin (1930), W. Eichrodt (1933-9), L. Köhler (1936), P. Heinisch (1940), O. Procksch (1950), T. C. Vriezen (1950), O. Baab (1949), E. Jacob (1955), P. Van Imschoot (1954-6), J. L. McKenzie (1956), G. Von Rad (1958) and D. Barthélemy (1963). These authors underline in their work the originality of Old Testament revelation, and the unity of the divine purpose throughout the centuries of preparation for the coming of Christ. Yet each has his own way of conceiving the Old Testament's structural principle. For Eichrodt, this is the idea of the covenant between Yahweh and his people. For Jacob, it is the presence of action of God in history. For Procksch, it is the progress of history rushing towards its culmination in Christ. For Von Rad the object of biblical theology is the revelation of God in history through his words and actions, and the only unity

---

3. J. Bligh understands biblical theology in an even wider sense. See on this subject: J. Bligh, review of the work of D. M. Stanley in "Christ's Resurrection in Pauline Soteriology," *The Heythrop Journal*, 4 (1963), pp. 68-74.

acceptable is a concrete unity, that is the continuity of Israel's experience. According to Vriezen, there is no really central and dominant theme in the Old Testament, but rather a train of themes which it is simply a question of describing.

The principal biblical theologies of the New Testament are those of A. Lemonnyer (1928), re-edited and completed by L. Cerfaux in 1963, F. Büchsel (1937), F. Ceuppens (1938-48), E. Stauffer (1948), P. Feine (1949), R. Bultmann (1948-9), M. Meinertz (1950), J. Bonsirven (1951), A. M. Hunter (1957), A. Richardson (1958) and R. Schnackenburg (1961). To these one might add the four chapters written by A. Feuillet and S. Lyonnet on the major themes of the New Testament in the *Introduction à la Bible* (edited by A. Robert and A. Feuillet, Vol. II, 1959).

II. PATRISTIC THEOLOGY AND PATROLOGY

1. *Patristic theology*

The purpose of patristic theology is to give an accurate explanation of the Fathers' thought, so that we may share in their understanding of the mysteries of faith. It takes for granted, as its point of departure, a careful study of the Fathers' language, the literary forms which they used and the historical context in which they lived. The great danger which it has to avoid, is doctrinal anachronism, which consists here in reading into their work our own points of view, our own categories of thought and even our own systematizations.

It is easy to understand how important for theology is this first discursive understanding of the faith; for the work of the Fathers witnesses to the living and life-giving tradition whose fullness was transfused throughout the life and practice of the praying and believing Church.[4] One finds among the Fathers too, a pastoral sensitiveness which is not so clearly instanced among the medieval Doctors. The initiators of patristic theology were Denys Petaus and Louis Thomassin in the seventeenth century.

Patristic theology is not simply a systematization of patristic thought, but true theology; for it sets out to understand the revealed mystery, taking, as the source and guide of its procedure, the Fathers of the Church. It is an understanding of their understanding of the faith. Its definitive aim is to see, through their modes of expression, the one mystery of God. And it is to the magisterium of the Church that it has recourse to decide which among her teachers are the authentic witnesses to the word of God.

2. *Patrology*

Patrology is the science that studies the Fathers of the Church and the ecclesiastical writers of the early Church, especially their lives and their works, from a threefold point of view, philological, philosophical, and theological. It is chiefly a historical discipline. Its tasks are: (a) to give us information about the lives of the Fathers and ecclesiastical writers, about what influences operated in their formation and what occasions gave rise to their writings; (b) to establish the canon of their work, distinguishing true from false ascriptions; (c) to appreciate the character and importance of their work; (d) to expound the chief points of their doctrine; (e) to see where and in what ways they stood in relation to one another, whether in a relation of spiritual sonship or of inspiration.

Patrology has the same title to be called a theological discipline as ecclesiastical history has. It is to be distinguished from patristic theology in that it is interested above all in the lives and writings of the Fathers as sources of information, while patristic theology is interested above all in the doctrinal teaching of the Fathers, that is in their presentation and their understanding of the faith.

III. LITURGICAL THEOLOGY

From the seventeenth to the twentieth century, the liturgy was conceived by theologians to be above all a theological locus or

source, that is as a means of knowing what the ordinary magisterium of the Church taught and what the Christian community
believed, for the liturgy is a privileged expression of the faith
of the Church. In its various treatises, theology used to call it
as a witness to tradition, in order to demonstrate to adversaries
(Protestant, rationalist, and modernist) that such and such a
doctrine proposed by the Church today for our belief is authentically apostolic in origin, or else, in order to trace the stages of
dogmatic progress — a Trinitarian doxology, for instance, could
bear witness in that progress to a particular moment. In this
openly apologetic context the special function of the liturgy was
to show the organic unity of the Catholic faith, from the apostolic
age to our own. One invoked it, as one did Scripture and the
Fathers, to establish or confirm. But the legitimate use of the
liturgy as a theological locus does not reveal its full content or
what liturgical theology in its most profound sense means.

1. *The Liturgy*

It is impossible to have an accurate idea of liturgical theology
without an accurate notion of the liturgy itself, and such a notion
has been elaborated by the second Vatican Council in its Constitution on the Liturgy. Christ accomplished the work of our
salvation, says the Constitution, "principally through the paschal
mystery of his blessed Passion, Resurrection from the dead and
glorious Ascension." [5] As he was himself sent by the Father so
Christ sent his apostles, and communicated to them his Spirit,
not merely to announce the mystery of salvation, "but also to
perform this work of salvation which they announced, through
the Sacrifice and the other sacraments around which the whole
of liturgical life revolves." [6] To continue this work of salvation
through the centuries, "Christ is always present in his Church
especially in her liturgical action. He is present in the sacrifice

---

4. Const. *Dei verbum,* n. 8.
5. Const. *Sacrosanctum Concilium* on the liturgy, n. 5.
6. *Ibid.,* n. 6.

of the Mass . . . he is present by his power in the other sacraments . . . he is present in his word . . . he is present when the Church prays or sings the psalms." [7] That is why "the liturgy is considered to be an exercise of the priestly function of Jesus Christ, an exercise in which man's sanctification is manifested by signs perceptible to the senses and is effected in a way proper to each of these signs." [8] In that it is the action of Christ the priest and of his Body which is the Church, liturgical action is sacred action *par excellence,* so that no other action of the Church can have equal claim to efficacy or attain it to the same degree." [9] Doubtless the liturgy is not the whole of the Church's activity, but it is the "peak towards which her activity is directed, and at the same time the source from which she draws all her power." [10] It is from the liturgy, therefore, "and above all from the Eucharist, as from a source, that grace flows into us, and that there come, most effectively, the sanctification of men in Christ and the glory given to God to which all the other activities of the Church are directed as to their end." [11]

So the Church is the sacred community of the faithful receiving the word and sacraments of Christ. And the liturgy is the privileged meeting-place of God and his Church in a perpetual *now.* Her function is not only to offer to God due worship but also to make present and active among men, beneath the veil of signs, the mystery of salvation which sanctifies them. In this connection, the Constitution rightly stresses that the liturgy is, at the same time and indissolubly, the giving of glory to God and the sanctification of man.[12] It is the concrete means by which, under the veil of signs which are perceptible to the senses and which effect what they signify, there is pursued and accomplished from Pente-

7. *Ibid.,* n. 7
8. *Ibid.,* n. 7.
9. *Ibid.,* n. 7.
10. *Ibid.,* n. 10.
11. *Ibid.,* n. 10.
12. H. Schmidt, *Constitution sur la Sainte Liturgie, Genèse et Commentaire* (Bruges, 1966), pp. 138-144; Idem, *Introductio in Liturgiam occidentalem* (Freiburg & Rome, 1962), p. 64.

cost to the *parousia,* that history of salvation which is the mystery of Christ and the mystery of his Church, in a dynamism which is at once temporal and supernatural. Thus understood, the liturgy manifests the faith of the Church, both in antiquity and today, as a *praxis.* The liturgy is a *praxilogy.* This ritual action of the worshipping Church seen in this way as the history of salvation fulfilling itself to the end of time, is the proper contribution of the liturgy to the understanding of revelation.

2. *Liturgical theology*

Liturgical theology is a theological discipline which has as its object the mystery of Christ living in the Church and the mystery of the Church living in Christ. It considers this mystery in so far as it is present in the ritual action and worship of the Church through the centuries, and tries to have a more living understanding of it. It is a methodical reflection on the saving action of God in the world through Christ and his Church, and on the return of man to God beneath the veil of the signs which sanctify him. As true theology, it has a positive moment, when it takes scientific possession of the liturgical data, by means of philology, history and archeology, and a moment of systematic reflection upon this data. Liturgical theology is not simply the history of rites and rubrics. It is authentic understanding of the object of faith, in that the liturgy is the very mystery of salvation itself in the act of fulfillment through the centuries. The theology of the sacraments, therefore, is the chosen ground of liturgical theology. The Council has stressed the importance of this theological reflection in elevating liturgy to the status of a principal discipline in faculties of theology. It has recommended that liturgy should be taught under its theological and historical aspects as well as under those which are spiritual, pastoral and juridical.[13]

---

13. Decree *Optatam totius* on priestly formation, n. 16, which refers to nn. 16 & 17 of the Constitution *Sacrosanctum Concilium* on the liturgy.

BIBLIOGRAPHY III

Biblical Theology

ALONSO, J., « La Teología Bíblica a través de la historia : consideración de algunas tendencias », *Miscelánea Comillas*, 29 (1958) : 9-27.

BRAUN, F.-M., « La théologie biblique », *Revue thomiste*, 53 (1953) : 221-253.

DULLES, A., « Method in the Study of Biblical Theology », in : *The Bible in Modern Scholarships*, ed. by J. P. Hyatt, New York, 1965, pp. 210-216.

DURWELL, F. X., *La résurrection de Jésus, Mystère de salut*, Le Puy et Paris, 1954, introduction.

FESTORAZZI, F., « Il problema del metodo nella Teologia biblica », *La Scuola Cattolica*, 91 (1963) : 253-277 ; 93 (1965) : 215-221.

GERVAIS, J., « Thèmes bibliques et théologie spéculative », *Revue de l'Université d'Ottawa*, 32 (1962) : 5-24 (pages étoilées).

JACOB, E., « Possibilités et limites d'une théologie biblique », *Revue d'histoire et de philosophie religieuses*, 46 (1966) : 116-130.

LÉON-DUFOUR, X., *Études d'Évangile*, Paris, 1965, pp. 19-46.

LÉON-DUFOUR, X., éd., *Vocabulaire de théologie biblique*, Paris, 1962, introduction.

LYONNET, S., « De theologia biblica », in : *De peccato et redemptione*, I : *De notione peccati*, Romae, 1957, pp. 7-25.

MACKENZIE, R., « The Concept of Biblical Theology », in : The Catholic theological Society of America, *Proceedings of the tenth annual Convention*, New York, 1955, pp. 47-74.

MARROW, S. B., « Biblical Theology », *New Catholic Encyclopedia*, 2 : 545-550.

SCHLIER, H. et RAHNER, K., art. « Biblische Theologie », *Lexikon für Theologie und Kirche*, 2 : 441-451.

SCHLIER, H., « Sinn und Aufgabe einer Theologie des Neuen Testaments », in : *Biblische Zeitschrift*, N. F., 1 (1957) : 6-23.

SPICQ, C., « L'avènement de la théologie biblique », *Revue des sciences philosophiques et théologiques*, 34 (1951) : 561-574.

SPICQ, C., « Nouvelles réflexions sur la théologie biblique », *Revue des sciences philosophiques et théologiques*, 42 (1958) : 209-220.

SPICQ, C., « Biblische Theologie », *Anima*, 20 (1965) : 100-107.

WATSON, P. S., « The Nature and Function of Biblical Theology », *Expository Times*, 73 (1961-1962) : 195-200.

WRIGHT, G. E., « Reflections concerning Old Testament Theology, » in : *Vriezen Festschrift*, 1967, pp. 376-388.

Liturgical Theology

BARTSCH, E., « Liturgiewissenschaft », in : E. NEUHÄUSLER und E. GÖSSMANN, *Was ist Theologie*, pp. 310-348.

IN COLLABORATION, « Exigences du renouveau liturgique », *Lumière et Vie*, n. 81 (janvier-avril 1967).

LENGELING, E. J., art. « Liturgie », *Encyclopédie de la foi*, 2 : 480-505.

MEYER, H. B., « Liturgie als Hauptfach. Erwägungen zur Stellung und Aufgabe der Liturgiewissenschaft im Ganzen des theologischen Studiums », *Zeitschrift für katholische Theologie*, 88 (1966) : 315-335. On trouvera dans cet article une abondante bibliographie sur l'enseignement de la liturgie dans l'esprit de Vatican II.

SCHMIDT, H., *Constitution sur la sainte Liturgie. Genèse et Commentaire*, Bruxelles, 1966.

SCHMIDT, H., « Le renouveau liturgique », *Nouvelle Revue théologique*, 88 (1966) : 807-829.

VAGAGGINI, C., *Il senso teologico della Liturgia*, Roma, 1957.

CHAPTER IV MORAL THEOLOGY AND SPIRITUAL THEOLOGY

I. MORAL THEOLOGY

1. *Moral theology and dogmatic theology*

The object of moral theology is man's vocation in Christ and the moral obligations which follow from this.[1] Its primary light, therefore, is not reason, but the never-ending light of the word of God, and the faith through which we adhere to the mystery of Christ and our salvation. Moral theology is a methodical reflection upon the mystery of our calling in Christ, and upon the resonance of this mystery in our daily life.

It is immediately apparent, then, that moral theology, far from being opposed to dogmatic theology, is one and the same science. Like dogmatics it is a true theological discipline, which derives its doctrine from revelation and elaborates it in the light of faith and under the direction of the magisterium. It must, no less than dogmatics, nourish its students' spiritual life. And it should show, even more than dogmatics, how the word of God

---

1. J. Fuchs, "Theologia moralis perficienda, votum Concilii Vaticani II," *Periodica*, 55 (1966), p. 532.

can illuminate the concrete problems of men today. The division between dogmatics and moral theology which can be justified today by the demands of specialization or the convenience of teaching arrangements, is first of all a historical affair.

In the great medieval *summae* ethics is not distinguished from dogmatics. One and the same discipline treats both the Christian mysteries and Christian behavior. In St. Thomas for instance, theological morals are inseparable from the source which gives them life. From the fourteenth century onwards, however, there appeared, in more and more developed form, certain works of an essentially practical nature, called *summae confessorum,* designed as aids to confessors in their priestly ministry. In the sixteenth century, in response to the directives of the Council of Trent a new theological course was created, the *Institutiones theologiae moralis,* which lay mid-way between the learned theological *summae* and the *summae* of practical experience for the use of confessors, which were henceforth regarded as insufficient. The appearance of the *Institutiones theologiae moralis* consecrated the separation between dogma and ethics, and people even acquired the habit of talking about moral theology *tout court.* In time, the new course was considerably amplified and took on so great a degree of importance that it came to monopolize the whole moral teaching of theology, with the consequence, regrettably, that there was less and less attention paid to its scriptural and doctrinal sources and more and more inflation of casuistry. Manuals of moral theology grew more and more like *summae* of cases of conscience, concentrating exclusively on laws and special precepts, on the licit and the illicit, and talking less and less about the source and inspiration of Christian behavior, our new status as sons of God and brothers of Christ, redeemed by his blood.[2]

The history of moral theology makes it clear that there were, from the seventeenth to the twentieth century, periodic returns, of varying stability and duration, to the sources of moral theology in Scripture and dogma, but one has to wait for the twentieth

---

2. E. Hamel, "L'usage de l'Ecriture sainte en théologie morale," *Gregorianum,* 47 (1966), pp. 56-58.

century to find work which witnesses to a real re-establishment of moral theology in its source.[3]

2. *The point of view of the Second Vatican Council*

The Council's chief document on moral theology is the decree *Optatam totius,* on the formation of priests, but the full sense of this can be understood only in the light of the great constitutions which give it direction and substance. The Constitution *Dei verbum* emphasizes the primacy of the Word of God, the source of light and life. "The depths of the truth about God and about man's salvation are manifest to us in Christ, who is at once the Mediator and the Plenitude of all revelation." [4] The study of Scripture, it says, must be "as it were the soul" of all theology, and therefore of moral theology as of all the other theological disciplines.[5] The Constitution on the Liturgy declares that "the liturgy . . . is the supreme means by which the faithful can express in their lives and manifest to others the mystery of Christ and the real nature of the true Church." [6] So it is the specific note of the Christian that he expresses in his life the mystery of Christ. To be in Christ, and to act in conformity with his being in Christ; such is the supreme standard of his life. This filial way of living is a witness also to the real nature of the Church, which is a community of sons of the Father, given life by the Spirit of Christ, "growing up in Christ" through the Spirit of love. In reminding us that liturgical life revolves about the sacraments and particularly about the Eucharist, the Constitution reminds us that our moral life is essentially a participation in the paschal mystery of the death and resurrection of Christ.[7]

The moral life of the Christian must mirror the Church and its real nature. But the Constitution *Lumen Gentium* shows that the Church, as conceived by the Council, is the community of

---

3. *Ibid.,* pp. 58-63.
4. Const. *Dei verbum* on revelation, n. 2.
5. *Ibid.,* n. 24.
6. Const. *Sacrosanctum Concilium,* on the liturgy, n. 2.
7. *Ibid.,* n. 6.

the people of God, brought into being by the Spirit of love, who is always at work in it through his charisms and his gifts. Moral theology must then show the primacy of charity and of docility to the Spirit. The Constitution stresses no less the eschatological character of the Church. The Church is on pilgrimage towards the new Jerusalem; she is called to ceaseless purification in expectation of the glorious coming of her Bridegroom. The Christian life itself, therefore, must be conceived as a perpetual conversion and an unceasing vigilance, in expectation of the Bridegroom's coming.

The Constitution *Gaudium et Spes* elaborates a true Christian anthropology, where man is envisaged in his totality, in his personal and in his social dimension, in the context of history sacred and profane. This more complete vision of man is not without its effect on moral theology, which will have to be grounded in a greater knowledge of him than in the past. The theology of the family for instance will gain from being clarified by socio-psychological studies. The consideration of men's social relationships, particularly stressed today, asks of the moralist a greater sensitiveness to social problems; and correlatively, it invites the Christian to develop a greater sense of social responsibility in his personal behavior.[8]

Apart from these general indications in the great constitutions, the Council speaks explicitly in the decree *Optatam totius* about the teaching of moral theology. It recommends that "special attention should be given to the development of moral theology."[9] The reason for this recommendation is not simply the intimate relationship in which moral theology stands to dogmatics, not merely its particular importance in the conspectus of theological disciplines; it refers to the past and present state of this discipline, which calls for development and profound renovation. After expressing its hope of a renewal, the Council indicates more precisely in what spirit such a renewal must be undertaken: "more

---

8. B. Häring, "Theologia moralis speciali cura perficienda," *Seminarium,* 6 (1966), pp. 358-363.

9. Decree *Optatam totius* on the formation of priests, n. 16.

thoroughly nourished by scriptural teaching" moral theology "will show the greatness of the vocation of the faithful in Christ, and their obligation to bear fruit in charity for the life of the world." [10]

3. *Moral Theology according to "Optatam totius"*

The text cited is, as it were, a new charter for moral theology. The first objective of moral theology, says the decree, is to "show the greatness of the vocation of the faithful in Christ." Before talking about laws and special precepts, it is the task of moral theology to investigate the good news of our vocation in Christ. In expressing itself in this way the Council does not forget that our relationship to God as our Creator is, ultimately, the foundation of moral obligation. But, following Scripture, it wishes to stress that the fullness of our relationship to God is realized in Christ. St. Paul is not aware merely of man, but of the sinner reconciled by Christ (2 Cor 5, 18). Our condition as a creature ordered to God is expressed henceforth by our *being-in-Christ* (1 Cor 1, 30). This expression is repeated more than a hundred and sixty four times in St. Paul's letters.[11] We must live not just as men but as men baptized, dead and risen in Christ to a new life (Rom 6, 1-11). If this is our *esse,* so too will be our *agere.* The Christian adopts a way of life in conformity with his new condition, that is a filial way of life, following from, and on the model of, Christ's life, doing in all things the will of his Father, in the Spirit of love (Phil 2, 6-11).

In Christian morals this theme of vocation is primary, more fundamental even than that of law. The Christian is, essentially someone called by God in Christ. His vocation, which is a calling to salvation, that is to the sharing of the divine life, is a gift. For St. Paul this vocation in Christ has as its necessary corollary a life of holiness, manifesting itself in everyday behavior (1 Thess 4, 7). Just as, before, Yahweh's covenant with Israel involved

---

10. *Ibid.,* n. 16.
11. B. Häring, "Theologia moralis speciali cura perficienda," *Seminarium,* 6 (1966), p. 366.

for Israel the moral obligation of holiness of life, so now in the same way our vocation in Christ must be accompanied by fidelity to the precepts which particularize the will of God in the life of each individual. It is obvious then that moral theology must talk about laws and special precepts, under pain of failing to fulfill its task, but it must first of all teach our vocation in Christ. It must show the greatness of this vocation so that it is seen to be good news *par excellence,* and arouses a more and more lively desire to be faithful. If morals, on the contrary, is only a soulless code, it will run the risk of leading to a legalist morality of a pharisaic sort.

To show the "obligation upon the faithful to bear fruit in charity for the life of the world": these are the precise terms in which the decree *Optatam totius* assigns to moral theology its second objective. After showing the greatness of the Christian vocation, moral theology must show the obligation upon Christians to bear fruit corresponding to the sublimity of their vocation. For the Christian is called not only to labor at his own perfection, but also to bear fruit for the salvation of others. "Each of the laity," says *Lumen Gentium,* "must be a witness in the world of the resurrection and life of the Lord Jesus, and a sign of the living God. Both as a body and each individually the laity must do its part to nourish the world with the fruits of the Spirit (Gal 5, 22), and to spread abroad in it the Spirit of the poor, the unaggressive, the peace-makers, whom the Lord in the Gospel calls blessed." [12] If anyone lives the life of Christ and of his Spirit, he will bear the fruits of the Spirit.

The first of these is charity. For no-one has really in him the Spirit of Christ if he does not manifest this Spirit in love of God and love of men, following the example of Christ who gave himself for the salvation of all. "He who loves not his brother whom he has seen, how can he love God whom he has not seen?" (1 Jn 4, 20; Jn 15, 12-13) This charity like that of Christ, turns towards the world so that the world may have life and have it abundantly (Jn 3, 16; 6, 34). Moral theology must show moral

---

12. Const. *Lumen Gentium* on the Church, n. 38.

conduct in its social and apostolic dimension. Holiness of life has the value of witness. If the laity "are consecrated as a royal priesthood and a holy people (1 Pet 2, 4-10) it is to offer spiritual sacrifices through all that they do, and to bear witness to Christ throughout all the world." [13] They are called to be "in all circumstances, and in the midst even of the Christian community, witnesses to Christ." [14] Through their life, infused with faith, hope and charity, they work "from within like a leaven, for the sanctification of the world." [15]

This conception of Christian morality in terms of vocation and response gives to the Christian's moral life a personal and personalizing character. Man in Christ is called personally to a life of holiness, in an encounter of me and Thee. Moral behavior then takes on the character of a personal commitment, of a response, through one's life, to the calling of Christ. In law and special precept, the Christian sees the expression of the will of the living God, and, in full and free possession of his conscience, he takes his place as an individual within the movement of loving response which man as a whole makes to God's calling to salvation. In relating the personal response of each individual to the salvation of the world, and asking him to bear living fruit in the world and for the world, moral theology emphasizes the social character of Christian behavior and also the necessary part which personal initiative and responsibility have to play in moral conduct.

4. *The characteristics of post-Conciliar moral theology*

The decree *Optatam totius* gives an indication also of some of the characteristics which a renewed moral theology should present. First of all, it will be teaching "nourished by Scripture." Taken negatively, this expression means that moral theology should not conceive Scripture simply as an arsenal of texts, which it

---

13. Decree *Apostolicam Actuositatem* on the apostolate of the laity, n. 3.
14. Const. *Gaudium et Spes,* n. 43.
15. Const. *Lumen Gentium* on the Church, n. 31.

can draw on as a basis for its propositions. Scripture must be, first and foremost, the inspiration of moral theology, giving it its very conception of what moral life is, that is its vision of God and man and the relationship which unites them. A moral theology nourished by Scripture will have an essentially Christian character. It will be constructed in living contact with the mystery of Christ and the history of salvation. Consequently it will be something quite different from a *summa* of cases of conscience, and answers framed entirely for the use of confessors. It goes without saying that moral theology must prepare the priest for his task in the confessional, but it cannot confine itself to this as its sole objective. It must above all look into the conception of Christian morality which emerges from Scripture, and which connects the moral behavior of the Christian with the sublimity of his vocation. In his letters St. Paul begins by expounding the good news of salvation in Jesus Christ, dead and risen again for us; only afterwards does he mention the moral demands which the gift of salvation makes upon those who accept it. The direction of penitents, moreover, asks from the confessor a deep knowledge of what the Christian vocation means, and of the laws which govern its development. This granted, it remains true that a sound casuistry has its place in moral theology, as it has in Canon law, or civil law, or psychology. Properly understood, casuistry, is simply the application of general principles to particular cases.[16] In practice it should always be inspired by the virtue of prudence, and never lose sight of the deep orientations of the Gospel.

Secondly, the presentation of moral theology must preserve its scientific character. In recommending a more biblical moral theology, a moral theology more centered in the mystery of Christ and the history of salvation, the Council does not intend to transform its teaching into pure kerygmatics or pious exhortation. Moral theology must present the good news of our vocation in Christ and the obligations which follow from it, but according

16. E. Hamel, "Valuers et limites de la casuistique," *Sciences Ecclésiastiques,* 11 (1959), pp. 147-173; Idem, *Loi naturelle et loi du Christ* (Bruges & Paris, 1964), pp. 45-77.

to all the exigencies of science, notably in the matter of method and systematization. In particular it must be built upon a solid exegesis, in order to know the literal sense which the texts bear, and upon biblical theology, in order to know the full sense which follows from Scripture as a whole. More than this, it must lead to a properly theological explanation, an elaboration all the more necessary in that Scripture does not constitute a systematic exposition of Christian morality. It insists on the formation of conscience and on moral attitudes, but it does not pretend to inform the Christian about the detail of his own particular duties, or offer him an exhaustive list of his moral obligations. Nor does it tackle the new problems which human conscience poses in each generation. Rather than a sum of precepts and solutions, it is a frame of mind.

Finally, moral theology must be supported by sound anthropology. For understanding the Christian vocation presupposes understanding the man who is called. In the same way that moral theology needs the collaboration of the exegete, in order to guarantee its point of departure, that is its exact knowledge of the data of revelation, so it needs the collaboration of the human sciences, especially of psychology and sociology in order to work out a theology made to the measure of man.

II. SPIRITUAL THEOLOGY

1. *Christian life and spiritual life*

Before talking about the spiritual life and about spiritual theology it is useful to talk about Christian life. Christian life is the life begun by faith and baptism.

God, the living and thrice holy, in an initiative wholly of love, has broken his silence. In Jesus Christ the consubstantial Word of the Father, God speaks to man, summons him, tells him of his plan of salvation, and invites him to the obedience of faith as a first step towards a communion of life. If God reveals himself, it is in order to share with man his own inner life; it is in order to bring him into the communion of love which is the Trinity. Faith is man's first step, a free step, towards God.

Through faith man responds to God's calling, turns towards him and gives himself to God in friendship. When man, through faith opens himself in this way to God who has called him, and allows God's word to enter and direct him, then God and man meet, and this meeting develops into a dialogue and a communion of life. Finally, in baptism, man is admitted into Christ's community, and receives the gift of the Spirit which makes him a son of the Father, to grow to maturity under the direction of this Spirit of Christ.

This dialogue which faith begins needs ceaselessly to be deepened. The divine life whose seed is sown in us by baptism needs to grow and develop. And it is here that the spiritual life enters upon the scene. In itself the spiritual life means more than the supernatural life, which is a gift of God, an infusion of grace and the theological virtues into the soul. It means more than Christian life, which is the response of faith and admission into the Church by baptism. The spiritual life is defined by the following characteristics: by the awareness which we have of it, by the experience which we can gain of it, and by the will to make progress in it.[17] It is man's dialogue with God, but a dialogue which knows and wishes itself to be so, a dialogue which grows deeper and deeper and more and more alive.

It is "our dynamic relationship with the Father who saves us in Jesus Christ and our voluntary intention that our whole life should be actuated by this relationship." [18]

2. *Spiritual theology*

Spiritual theology is the theological discipline (founded upon the principles of revelation and the experience of the saints) which studies the organic structure of the spiritual life and the awareness we have of it, explains the laws of its progress and development, and describes the process of growth which leads the soul

---

17. F. Roustang, *Une initiation à la vie spirituelle* (Paris, 1963), p. 13.
18. C.-A. Bernard, "La conscience spirituelle," *Revue d'ascétique et de mystique*, 41 (1965), p. 447.

from the beginning of its Christian life to the summit of perfection.[19]

1. Spiritual theology, is a theological discipline, for it treats of the living God, Father, Son and Spirit as the source, example and end of the spiritual life, and of man who shares in this divine life. Since the chief material object of this discipline is man, every contribution that the human sciences can make to a better understanding of him can be of service to it in its intention to be faithful to the whole reality of man. Spiritual theology envisages man in his historical situation as a being who is sinful and saved from sin, as a creature called to a supernatural destiny, having his own personal history and yet incorporated into the human and ecclesial community.

2. Spiritual theology is a science based on the principles of revelation and the experience of the saints; these are its two standards of judgment. From revelation spiritual theology knows that God is Father, Son and Spirit; the Father who has made us and loves us as his children, the Son and Word who calls us and invites us to a communion of life with the Trinity, the Spirit who sanctifies us and gives us life; and it knows that man is called and chosen by God from before the creation of the world to be the Father's son, to be redeemed by Christ, to be given life by the Spirit, that he is destined to share in the life of the divine Persons. The experience of the saints illustrates this filial life of man in the multiplicity and richness of its concrete manifestations, and also in its progress and perfection.

3. Spiritual theology studies the organic structure of spiritual life. It is a part of what one might call supernatural anthropology, of which the organic elements are grace, the theological virtues

---

19. A. Royo Marin, *Teologia della perfezione cristiana* (Edizioni Paoline, Rome, 1959), p. 23. For the explanation of this definition we follow C.-A. Bernard, *De Principiis vitae spiritualis* (ad usum privatum, PUG, Rome, 1966-7), pp. 17-18.

and the gifts of the Holy Spirit. In this respect it is subordinate
to dogmatic theology. It studies also our awareness of spiritual
life. For if it is true that the life of grace which is the ontological
foundation of the spiritual life, is God's gift, the development of
the spiritual life and its progress depend on man's free co-operation. Spiritual theology can therefore describe the conscious activity of the spiritual man. Spiritual activity, moreover, is accompanied by a more and more lively sense of the reality and
consistency of the mystery of God, and of, as it were, the depths
of the life of faith. Our consciousness of this in the spiritual life,
is analogous to the consciousness we have of the presence of
the world perceptible to our senses.[20]

4. Spiritual theology explains the evolution of the spiritual
life and the laws of its progress. Spiritual life is, in fact, the life
of a being *en route;* plunged in temporality, it is subject to growth
and progress, in the image of the Church in her growth towards
the plenitude of the Body of Christ. Spiritual theology tries to
find out the laws which govern this progress and this growth
towards spiritual maturity in a deeper and deeper union with
God. The word "law" here is to be understood in the psychological
sense of the usual pattern of behavior, with the margin of exception which has necessarily to be allowed when it is a question
of beings who are free. So, in his rules for the discernment of
spirits, St. Ignatius describes the ordinary play of spiritual movements and their meaning, without claiming to cover all the cases.

5. Spiritual theology describes the whole process by which
the soul is led from the beginning of Christian life to the summit
of perfection. For spiritual life is not a simple succession of
experiences, but a continuous deepening, a more and more living
awareness of our communion with each of the divine Persons.
This continuous progress is indeed the characteristic note of an
authentic spiritual life.

---

20. C.-A. Bernard, "La conscience spirituelle," *Revue d'ascétique et de
      mystique,* 41 (1965), p. 459.

3. *Ascetical and mystical theology or spiritual theology*

Since the seventeenth century, there has been a habit of distinguishing ascetical theology from mystical theology, although spiritual theology includes both. Ascetical theology studies the motives and means of the ordinary, active purification of the soul which is freeing itself from sin and beginning to practice the virtues. Mystical theology teaches the ways of union with God through passive purifications and through the action in the soul of the gifts of the Holy Spirit. It treats also of the extraordinary graces which often accompany the life of union of souls more advanced in the way of perfection. This distinction between ascetical theology and mystical theology is particularly valuable to the spiritual director, who has to treat in a different way the simple beginner and the true mystic. But, with most authors today, we prefer the term spiritual theology to ascetical and mystical theology. Spiritual theology studies all levels and all modalities of the spiritual life. Active purification and the active pursuit of perfection, moreover, are not solely the lot of the beginner: they normally accompany the whole course of the spiritual life.

4. *Spiritual theology and moral theology*

1. After what we have said about moral theology we cannot maintain that its business is with precepts and sins, while the business of spiritual theology is all that concerns the pursuit of perfection. The distinction between the two disciplines lies elsewhere.

Moral theology and spiritual theology are both interested in our behavior as Christians and in the realization of our vocation to holiness through a life submitted in all things to the Spirit of love. But while moral theology is interested above all in the rightness of our orientation to God through our fidelity to the law of Christ, that is, in the *ordo caritatis*, spiritual theology studies Christian behavior from the personal and experiential point of view. It is interested in the *commercium caritatis,* and in the canons of this *commercium.* So moral theology sets before us the perfection of the Sermon on the Mount but it does not study the concrete ways of realizing this ideal of perfection within a particular vocation, or in a particular historical context. The study of styles of Christian life or of particular ways of living the Sermon on the Mount through the ages and in the personal life of the individual Christian belongs to spiritual theology.

Spiritual theology and moral theology are, therefore, two complementary ways of looking at the same object, that is our behavior as Christians: the first primarily attentive to the soundness of this behavior in its universal structure which is valid for every Christian, the second attentive rather to its personal, historical and experiential dimensions. Hence the importance in spiritual theology of phenomenology, of the experience of the saints through the centuries, of the experience today of all those who are actually living the Christian life. Moral theology, on the other hand, will attach more importance to studying the permanent structures of the human situation.[21]

2. Spiritual theology presupposes moral theology; for the soaring of the Christian life towards its perfection would not really be so if it were not founded upon the conformity of the human will to God's will. From this point of view spiritual theology is subordinate to moral theology. On the other hand, moral theology normally leads to the full flowering of the Christian life, to the restoration of that *commercium* with God whose forms and moments are described by spiritual theology. In other words the spiritual life, being a personal and historical phenomenon always presupposes, as the foundation of personal development, the objective substructure of the human condition.

---

21. *Ibid.*, pp. 451-453; R. Egenter, "Über das Verhältnis von moraltheologie und Aszetic," in *Festschrift Michäel Schmaus* (München, 1957), pp. 21-42.

BIBLIOGRAPHY IV

Moral Theology

CROTTY, N., « Biblical Perspectives in Moral Theology », *Theological Studies*, 26 (1965) : 576-595.
FUCHS, J., « Theologia moralis perficienda, votum Concilii Vaticani II », *Periodica*, 55 (1966) : 499-548.
FUCHS, J., *Moral und Moraltheologie nach dem Konzil* Freiburg, 1967.
HÄRING, B., « Theologia moralis speciali cura perficienda », *Seminarium*, 6 (1966) : 357-368.
HÄRING, B., *La Predicazione della morale dopo il Concilio*, Roma, 1967.
HAMEL, E., « L'usage de l'Écriture sainte en théologie morale », *Gregorianum*, 47 (1966) : 53-85.
MCDONAGH, E., ed., *Moral Theology Renewed*, Dublin, 1965.

Spiritual Theology

BERNARD, C.-A., « La conscience spirituelle », *Revue d'ascétique et de mystique*, 41 (1965) : 441-466.
EGENTER, R., « Über das Verhältnis von Moraltheologie und Aszetik », in : *Festschrift Michäel Schmaus*, München, 1957, pp. 21-42.

CHAPTER V PASTORAL THEOLOGY, MISSIONARY THEOLOGY AND ECUMENICAL THEOLOGY

I. PASTORAL THEOLOGY

The history of this discipline throws light on its present status. Before it became a genuine theological discipline, pastoral theology was aimed at filling a gap in priestly formation. Right up to the twentieth century in fact it was regarded simply as a finishing touch given to the formation of the future pastor, under the form of practical advice, with the intention of ensuring the success of his ministry among the faithful. As an essentially practical course, it provided a series of recipes rather than any genuine science. It was analogous in the sphere of pastoral activity, to our manuals of cases of conscience. Little by little, efforts were made to burst the bonds of this commonplace conception, and transform this mere initiation into pastoral problems, into a genuine practical theology, with the accent this time on the word theology. A throng of disciplines then sprang up, juxtaposed rather than related organically: pastoral liturgy, catechetics, homiletics, pastoral sociology, pastoral psychology, missionary-pastoral studies and the rest. At bottom all these disciplines pursued the same end, the preparation of the priest for his pastoral apostolate, but since each operated on its own account, with its own method and its own presentation, it was difficult to discern what connection they had with one another.

1. *The inspiring principles of pastoral theology*

Two basic considerations led theology to take cognizance, little by little, of the proper part which pastoral theology had to play. First of all it came to be understood that the pastoral or salvific activity of the Church was not the concern solely of priests, with the faithful having nothing to do but follow passively the directions of their pastors, but the concern of the whole Church, both priests and faithful. It is the whole Church which is responsible for the pastoral ministry, just as it is the whole Church which is the object of pastoral theology.

Again the consequences for the Church's apostolate of the economy of the Incarnation and of its historical character, also came to be better understood. These were the means chosen by God to accomplish men's salvation, and since the sanctifying action of the Church, whose presence in the world prolongs the sanctifying action of the Incarnate Word, enters into the time sequence and is addressed to men in their actual historical situation, it follows that the pastoral activity of the Church must take account of social and cultural conditions, which change with centuries and generations, with places and peoples. The Church cannot be content to be present in the world as if before a mere change of scene. The actual concrete situation of men conditions her apostolate. If the Church wishes the gospel to find an echo in the hearts of the men of our times she must take account of the conjunction of historical circumstances in which the men of our time live.

There is then a place in theology for a methodical and scientific study of the Church as a contemporary phenomenon, in this moment of her presence in the world. This study of the Church *en-situation-historique* belongs to an understanding of the Church. Consider for instance some of the problems which confront theological reflection in these terms: (a) the influence on the Church's apostolic activity of a unified world, conceived as a whole and living as a whole; (b) the relationship of the Church to secularized society, and the changes in attitudes and in forms of apostolate which this new type of society implies; (c) the relationship of the Church to other religious societies: Christian communities separated from her, and great religions of salvation; (d) the role of baptized Christians in poor countries (especially in the presence of "the third world" how is the Church to be the Church of the poor, and what forms ought her service and witness to take?); (e) the relationship of the Church to civil society(here are all the problems of toleration and religious liberty).

So while dogmatic theology treats of the Church in her essential being, that is as a mystery and an institution at once human and divine, visible and invisible, pastoral theology is a methodical reflection upon her being in motion, that is upon the mystery of the building up of the Body of Christ which is the Church, in her present, concretely realized form, and upon the conditions of this realization, on the way in which the contemporary state of the world affects the actual accomplishment of the Church's salvific mission. By "the contemporary state of the world" we mean the cultural and social changes which belong to each epoch. In every new historical situation there is an indication of God's purpose, an invitation to new tasks or at least to a continual *aggiornamento*.

2. *Pastoral theology and pastoral activity*

(a) *Fundamental pastoral theology* — This establishes the basic principles of a pastoral theology. It studies the mystery of the Church as present in the world and to the world, as operating in the world, subject to the vicissitudes of history. Its reflection is grounded in the past experience of the Church and in her permanent essence, in order the better to understand her present condition. For pastoral theology's first task is to formulate principles upon which to base the action of the Church in the world today. It is a question of a sort of existential ecclesiology. The Constitution *Gaudium et Spes* has stated some of these principles. For instance (a) the Church "realizes that she is truly and deeply linked with mankind and its history at every point";[1] she recognizes her duty to enter into dialogue with "the entire human family," to which the people of God belongs,[2] and consequently she recognizes also the necessity of understanding the world in which she lives;[3] (c) the Church is at the service of all men, but she is not unaware of the help which she herself received from their history and their development. The Church and human society serve each other;[4] (d) while she shares the earthly lot of humanity the Church must act as a leaven, playing her part in the transformation of the human family;[5] (e) it is the Church's "duty to scrutinize at every moment the signs of the times, and to interpret them in the light of the Gospel," so that she may answer the questions asked by each generation.[6]

(b) *The theology of the pastoral ministry or pastoral theology in the proper sense* — This is a methodical reflection upon the action being taken by the Church throughout the world today to establish the kingdom of God. It bears upon (a) the forms of ministry or mediation which the Church sets up to bring about men's salvation, whether these concern the written or spoken word, worship or any sort of charitable work; (b) those who exercise these ministries — the hierarchy, the clergy and the faithful, religious or lay; (c) those to whom this pastoral activity of the Church is directed — children, adolescents, adults, families, parishes, dioceses, nations, etc; (d) the relationship between the Church and the other forms of society which surround her.

Pastoral theology calls upon several of the human sciences to serve her as her auxiliaries, in particular upon anthropology, sociography, sociology, psychology and history. All pastoral action, in fact, and all reflection on pastoral action should be based on a precise knowledge of contemporary human beings. But these human beings are infinitely varied. The rural *milieu* and the *milieu* of the

---

1. Const. *Gaudium et Spes*, n. 1.
2. *Ibid.*, n. 3.
3. *Ibid.*, n. 4.
4. *Ibid.*, n. 11 & n. 44.
5. *Ibid.*, n. 40.
6. *Ibid.*, n. 4.

city present us with very different faces, and over and above this, every *milieu* contains within it an enormous variety of national and racial types. It is for the human sciences to assemble the necessary facts for a pastoral reflection which is adjusted to reality. They are to pastoral theology what philosophy, history and philology are to dogmatics.

(c) *Pastoral activity or the exercise of the pastoral ministry* — This is the putting into practice of the principles of pastoral theology. For pastoral theology, as such, is a theoretical science: it does not tell us how to respond to the precise needs of this or that particular parish. Pastoral activity makes use of the human sciences in order to identify collective realities (human groups of all sorts — social classes and so on), in order to identify social phenomena — customs and prejudices and so forth, and in order to be better able to respond to the diverse religious needs of human beings. Pastoral theology provides it with its principles and norms of action.

Because of the close connection which exists among pastoral theology, pastoral activity and the human sciences, there should be a like connection of reciprocal aid among the pastor, the theologian, the sociologist and the psychologist. The human sciences provide an intelligible description of concrete human reality from the sociological and psychological points of view. They *place* the problems which confront pastoral action and theological reflection, and offer what are already the elements of a solution. Pastoral activity stands in a direct relationship both to the human sciences and to the principles provided by pastoral theology. Psychological and sociological observation and the problems of pastoral life in their turn give rise to theological reflection. The problem of conversion, for example, cannot properly be examined without calling into play the united contributions of the pastor, the theologian, the sociologist and the psychologist.

II. MISSIONARY THEOLOGY

Missionary theology, like pastoral theology, sees the mystery of the Church in a dynamic existential perspective. But while pastoral theology is concerned above all with the faithful, those already within the institutional Church, missionary theology is concerned with the multitude of non-Christians. The missionary dynamism of the Church impels her to overflow her frontiers to extend to all men the blessing of the Gospel. The object of missionary theology is the Church's movement of expansion beyond her present limits.

The Church is missionary by nature: she is sent by Christ as Christ was sent by the Father (Jn 20, 21; 13, 20). But one can distinguish between the Church's general mission, or her apostolic activity in the wide sense, and the missions, or her missionary activity strictly speaking, which consists in bringing salvation to those who have no knowledge of the Gospel, and in gathering together all the children of God in one people and in one Body. The aim of missionary activity is to set up and consolidate the Church in the places where she does not now, as an institution, exist.

The Council's decree on missions indicates the two essential parts of missionary theology: the theology of mission, or the doctrinal principles which underlie missionary activity and which manifest its necessity, and, in the second place, the theology of missionary work itself, in its phase of realization through the preaching of the Gospel, the planting of the Church, and the constitution of young Christian communities.

1. *The theology of mission*

The decree *Ad Gentes* relates the idea of mission to God's whole design for men and to its origin in the Trinity: in doing this it gives to the missions an unparalleled theological depth. At the very outset the Trinitarian structure of the word "mission" is stated in a sentence of which the first chapter is simply a development: "The Church, during her earthly pilgrimage, is, of her nature, missionary; for it is from the mission of the Son and the mission of the Spirit that she takes her origin, according to the design of the Father." [7] The mission given by Christ to his Church (Mk 16, 15; Mt 28, 18) draws its life from God, and from the life of the Trinity: "As my Father has sent me, I send you" (Jn 20, 21). It is to the Father, to God who is love, that we must return to understand the primordial movement which explains mission. It is from the divine charity in its overflowing that creation proceeds and the design of salvation is born, and in its most complete expression this is mission. "The design of God," says the Council "flows from that fountain of love or charity within the Father, from him who is Origin without origin, of whom the Son is begotten and from whom, through the Son, the Spirit proceeds. It is in his great and merciful goodness that he has freely created us, and that he has called us, through grace, beyond our created being, to communicate in his own glory and in his own life." [8]

So charity is the primordial energy which moves the design of salvation. It is in an action *ad extra* of the Trinity, from the Father, through the historical missions of the Son and the Spirit, that this charity reaches human history. Christ, in the name of the Father, founds the Church, and sends the Spirit. From this time onwards, from Pentecost to the *parousia,* the Church and the Spirit act indissolubly to build up the Body of Christ, and to finish the work of salvation which he began.[9] The mission of the Church prolongs in time the movement of the Trinity's love, begun in the missions of the Son and the Spirit: "the mission of the Church," says the Council, "is fulfilled in that activity by which, in obedience to Christ's command and in response to the grace and love of the Holy Spirit, she is made present to all men and all nations as the sacrament of salvation." [10] The Church is the sacrament of the love of God, and her missionary activity is an overflowing of everlasting charity, which we see in the graciousness of our Savior Christ. The Church is the love of God

---

7. Decree *Ad Gentes* on the missionary activity of the Church, n. 2.
8. *Ibid.,* n. 2.
9. *Ibid.,* nn. 3-4.
10. *Ibid.,* n. 5.

invading the world to save it. The love of the Holy Spirit gives life to the mystical Body of Christ, and urges it, as a whole and in each of its members, to the extension of that love to all men in which missionary activity consists. The primordial power that informs all mission, in the Trinity, in the Church, in the heart of the missionary and in the life of each Christian, is love.

The movement of love through which God makes himself present in the world to save it takes a sacramental form: it is through the flesh of Christ, through the visible Church, through her institutions and her sacraments, and through the presence of the missionary, that the Gospel reaches men and invisible grace transforms their hearts. And this movement in which love is extended to all men to gather them into a unity in the triune image must pass through the pivotal point of the cross. That is why missionary activity, and the coming of Christ to men and to societies of men, are always accompanied by suffering, by persecution, and even by the shedding of blood.

The immediate purpose of missionary activity is to lead man to the obedience of faith and make of them one people of God, one Body of Christ, one temple of the Holy Spirit, so that all men together recognize the God of our Lord Jesus Christ and can say, "Our Father." [11] In this same end lies the completion of God's glory: his design of love offered to all men, known to all men, and recognized by all men. "Men give full glory to God when they accept consciously and fully the salvation which he has accomplished in Christ. The giving of glory, that is the recognition of God's love, is the ultimate purpose of missionary activity. To the movement of love from God to man there corresponds the return of man to God, the response of man's love to the pressing invitation of God's love.

2. *Missionary work and its implications*

Chapters II and III of the decree *Ad Gentes* describe the three steps, or the three-fold rhythm of missionary work: preaching

---

11. *Ibid.,* nn. 7 & 9.

the Gospel, planting the Church, and forming the young Christian community. This rhythm, illustrated by Christ himself in his life on earth, is preceded by a preliminary phase, the phase of what is called pre-evangelization. Pre-evangelization is a preparation. Before explicitly preaching the Gospel, one must show it to be present and active in human lives which it has transformed, so that the sight of this abundance of life will arouse the desire to share it. It is a question of preparing the way for the Gospel by showing the salvation which it brings in actual operation in our world. Pre-evangelization includes the following.

(a) *The presence and witness among non-Christians of a really Christian life* — Wherever they live, but especially in mission countries, Christians "are bound to show by the example of their lives and by the witness of their speech, the new man which they put on at baptism, and the power of the Holy Spirit by whom they were strengthened in confirmation." [12]

(b) *Charitable work* — Following the example of Christ, who went about through towns and villages curing every kind of disease and infirmity as a sign that the kingdom of God had come, the Church must translate her love into works of charity, especially for the poor and those who suffer, in the form of schools, social work of every kind, and the struggle against hunger and disease and ignorance.[13]

(c) *Preliminary dialogue* — As Christ led men to the light through patient and loving conversation, so it is necessary to come very gradually to the point of explaining to non-Christians what inspires the charity of his disciples. Deeply imbued with the spirit of Christ himself, his disciples should know the people among whom they live, and talk to them, so that they themselves may learn through sincere and patient dialogue what spiritual riches God, in his deep generosity, has distributed among the nations of the earth. At the same time, however, let them try to illumine these riches with the light of the Gospel, to free them

---

12. *Ibid.*, n. 11.
13. *Ibid.*, n. 12.

and bring them under the sway of the God who is their salvation.[14]

The first step of missionary activity begins with preaching in the proper sense of the word. "The chief means" of implanting the Church, says the decree "is the preaching of the Gospel of Jesus Christ." [15] Before being a baptismal and eucharistic community the Church must be an evangelical community, that is, one brought together by the word of God. This preaching, like that of the apostles, has as its object the mystery of Christ, salvation through faith in Christ and through baptism, which effects the remission of sins. The fruit of preaching is faith and conversion, through the action of the Holy Spirit. This conversion, the decree points out, is a beginning by which a man turns away from sin and turns towards Christ in complete adherence. It obviously needs to develop and grow to maturity.[16]

The second step of missionary activity is the planting of the Church. To plant the Church is, first of all, to create living communities of faithful Christians who exercise the three-fold function which God has entrusted to them, prophetic, priestly and royal. The first step in planting the Church is the catechumenate. This, says the decree, "is not a mere expounding of dogmas and precepts, but a formation for the whole Christian life, an apprenticeship" by means of which the catechumens are initiated into a new kind of life, "the life of faith and liturgy and love which God's people lives." [17] They are then ready to receive the sacraments of Christian initiation, baptism, confirmation, and the Eucharist. And in this way the Christian community, the "sign for the world of God's presence" [18] comes into being.

The full planting of the Church is the setting up of the institutional Church with its own essential organs, in this particular *milieu*: with its own catechists, its own deacons, its own priests

---

14. *Ibid.*, n. 11.
15. *Ibid.*, n. 6.
16. *Ibid.*, n. 13.
17. *Ibid.*, n. 14.
18. *Ibid.*, n. 15.

and above all its own bishop. "When the congregation of the faithful has become sufficiently rooted in social life and adapted to local culture to have a certain firmness and stability the work of the Church in a given community reaches a kind of milestone." [19] The rhythm of the third step of missionary activity, which is the crown of the whole, can be distinguished by the following characteristics: (a) the congregations of the faithful become more and more consciously communities living a common life of faith, liturgical celebration, and love; (b) their families become seminaries for the apostolate and nurseries of vocations; (c) the laity are a leaven of justice and charity in civil society and the lay apostolate becomes organized; (d) the young Christian communities themselves become missionary; (e) they assume into the Christian faith to its benefit the values of their own local traditions. "The individual traditions of all the national families, with their characteristic qualities illumined by the light of the Gospel, are taken up into Catholic unity." [20]

3. *Present problems in missionary theology*

In recent years theological reflection upon revelation, faith, the history of salvation and ecumenism, has raised a whole conspectus of new problems about the missionary activity of the Church. Let us simply mention some of them.

(a) Since substitute routes to salvation appear at every turn people ask what can be the *raison d'être* of the visible Church and the preaching of the Gospel. Are we not running the risk of depriving the missions of their urgent character, and of sacrificing

---

19. *Ibid.*, n. 19.
20. *Ibid.*, n. 22. The study of the theological principles of mission and of missionary activity obviously does not exhaust the whole of missionary science. This has a historical department (notably the history of missions) and a practical department (the concrete knowledge of the different *milieu* to be evangelized, missionary canon law, missionary pastoral theology, etc.).

the transcendence of revelation to individual good faith? There is here an obvious danger of subjectiveness and relativism.

(b) What is the position of non-Christian religions in relation to the history of salvation? And, in a general way, what is the theological sense of the word "paganism"?

(c) The idea of an apostolate through "witness" or holiness of life is everywhere underlined by the Council and by the decree *Ad Gentes*: it belongs to missionary theology to work out what this means in detail, and to show the special dynamism of witness in relation to other forms of the apostolate. From another point of view, if holiness is to be found in all religions, how can the holiness of the Church still have value as a sign?

(d) Since there is a theology of the laity, what light can it throw on what action the Church should take to serve and help developing nations?

(e) How is the Church's missionary responsibility, to begin with that of the bishops, to be translated into fact, and structured according to the conciliar directives?

(f) What is the role of the Holy Spirit in the mission of the Church? The problem of personal charisms is connected with this action of the Spirit.

(g) In what does the planting of the Church consist? What are the essential elements of Christianity, and what are those which arise solely from the culture and thought-forms of the evangelizing peoples? How far can the philosophy and culture of the converted peoples contribute to the understanding of the Christian faith?

III. ECUMENICAL THEOLOGY

The ecumenical movement, in the sense the expression has for us in the twentieth century, arose from the problem of missions in a Protestant context. In this respect the international missionary conference held at Edinburgh in 1910 is an important point of reference. Some of the subjects discussed at this conference (the preaching of the Gospel in an non-Christian world, the missionary planting of the Church, the promotion of Christian unity) were obviously ecumenical subjects. There was an experience at Edinburgh of real dialogue among Christians of different tendencies about the general problems which concern Christianity as a whole, and it was discovered how much divergencies of faith injure missionary work. It was also at Edinburgh that the idea of universal doctrinal conferences germinated what came to be known as conferences on *Faith and Order*.[21]

The deep suffering felt by the Protestant Churches faced with the disunity of Christian confessions had the effect of making Catholics themselves more conscious of the scandal of divisions among Christians. Catholic ecclesiology in the twentieth century, renewed by the return to Scripture, and bent upon considering the mystery of the Church, in order the better to grasp its aspects and tensions, was led in its turn to ponder upon the mystery of broken unity.

1. *Catholic ecumenical principles*

The ecumenical movement from the Catholic point of view as from that of our separated brethren was born of the desire to eliminate the scandal created by division among Christians, who are all members of the religion of love. The aim of the ecumenical movement, then, is to restore among Christians the unity so deeply desired by Christ for his disciples: 'that they all may be one; as thou, Father art in me, and I in thee, that they also may be one in us: that the world may believe that thou hast sent me" (Jn 17, 21). To promote unity among Christians was also "one of the chief ends" of the second Vatican Council.[22]

"The 'ecumenical movement' means those activities and enterprises which, according to the various needs of the Church, and

---

21. G. Thils, *Histoire doctrinale du mouvement oecuménique* (seconde édition, Louvain & Paris, 1962), pp. 13-16.
22. Decree *Unitatis redintegratio*, on ecumenism, n. 1.

as occasion offers, are begun and organized for the fostering of unity among Christians. These are: first, every effort to eliminate words, judgments and actions which do not correspond in truth and fairness with the condition of our separated brethren, and which make our relations with them more difficult; then, 'dialogue' among competent experts from different Churches and communities. In meetings organized in a religious spirit, each explains the teaching of his communion in greater depth, and brings out clearly its distinctive characteristics." [23] In short, the ecumenical movement tries to eliminate all that offends against truth (its negative aspect), and to foster a fruitful dialogue among experts from different Christian communities (its positive aspect).

Ecumenism, in the Catholic Church, is founded upon a more biblical vision of the Church as the people of God and as the sacrament of unity for the world as a whole. It implies then as its basis, dogmatic teaching and dogmatic principles, but it is, as such, a movement of *rapprochement* through a renewal of ecclesiology and by various other means, among which the most striking is dialogue between Christian communities: the Catholic Church on the one hand, and on the other the Orthodox Churches and those inspired by the Reformation.

The fruits of this dialogue should normally be: (a) a more exact knowledge of each communion's doctrine, and a deeper appreciation of the riches of its past and present life; (b) a wider collaboration; (c) union in prayer; (d) an examination of conscience on the part of each communion upon its faithfulness to the will of Christ and upon the necessity of a sustained effort in renewal and reform.

The ultimate end of the ecumenical movement — which at the moment is only a hope — is that "little by little, as the obstacles to perfect ecclesial union are overcome, all Christians will be gathered together in eucharistic celebration in the unity of the one and only Church." That is, the Catholic Church believes that the unity which Christ has given to his Church "dwells inalienably

---

23. *Ibid.*, n. 4.

in the Catholic Church." [24] Other communities are in a communion more or less perfect with her, according to how many of the elements of salvation they have preserved or abandoned. The decree mentions among these elements "the written word of God, the life of grace, faith, hope and charity, other inner gifts of the Holy Spirit, and other visible elements." [25]

Since the restoration of unity among Christians is a work of grace, it is in the renewal of the Church and in a greater faithfulness to her vocation that the ecumenical movement seeks support. It is the whole of the Catholic community which is called upon to give a clearer and more faithful witness to the teaching and institutions which Christ has transmitted through the apostles.[26] For there can be no true ecumenism without inner change. "Change of heart and holiness of life, united to public and private prayer for Christian unity should be regarded as the soul of the ecumenical movement, and can rightly be called spiritual ecumenism." [27] The mystery of unity is a mystery of love and of supplication. To the spirit and soul of ecumenism therefore it belongs: (a) to care deeply and effectively about the promotion of Christian unity, each doing so according to his circumstances; (b) to make an objective and sympathetic study of "the teaching, the history, the ritual and spiritual life, the religious mentality and the characteristic culture of our separated brethren";[28] (c) to recognize and appreciate in the concrete the Christian values, the virtues and the acts of heroism which are to be found in different Christian communities;[29] (d) to eliminate every feeling and every appearance of scorn, hatred, or antipathy towards others and to have a positive attitude towards them of humility, gentleness, generosity and welcome;[30] (e) finally, to live the Christian life deeply

24. *Ibid.,* n. 4.
25. *Ibid.,* n. 3.
26. *Ibid.,* n. 4.
27. *Ibid.,* n. 8.
28. *Ibid.,* n. 9.
29. *Ibid.,* n. 4.
30. *Ibid.,* n. 7.

so that the light of Christ may shine in its full splendor without diminution or adulteration.

2. *Aspects of the ecumenical movement among our separated brethren*

The ecumenical movement arose as we have seen, among our separated brethren, from the missionary movement, and the desire to give full effect to this. Confronted by the scandal created, in the countries evangelized, by the multiplicity of witness which presented itself in the name of Jesus Christ, the Protestant confessions understood the urgency of mending their broken unity. The history of the ecumenical movement is therefore the history of the overtures towards one another, and groping attempts at *rapprochement,* made by the separated Christian communities. In outline one can distinguish the following stages: (a) the establishing of the first contacts and of a true form of dialogue among the different bodies; (b) the first forms of collaboration with the official approval of the Churches concerned; (c) the federation of communities. In this respect an important stage was reached with the forming of the Ecumenical Council of Churches at Amsterdam in 1948, for the common study and solution of the problems of evangelization, for promoting Christian education in the pagan world, for helping to meet the needs of under-nourished populations, and for studying in common the means of promoting Christian unity. The World Council of Churches held important sessions in 1954 at Evanston and in 1961 at New Delhi. Although the Council is not a Church, it opens up wide vistas upon the possibility of a gathering together of all Christian communities in the one Church of Christ. An increasing preoccupation with unity emerges particularly in the desire to preach one unique Gospel, to share one eucharistic table, and to possess one universally recognized ministry. Today, the ecumenical movement among our separated brethren exhibits two distinct tendencies, towards establishing closer and closer links between different communities on the level of dialogue and collaboration, and towards defining the essential elements of that unity which Christ desired for his Church.

3. *Ecumenism and theology*

The second Vatican Council stressed the necessity of giving students in theology a sound knowledge of the separated Christian communities. The decree on the formation of priests, says: "Taking into consideration particular conditions in different places, students should be introduced to a deeper knowledge of churches and ecclesial communities separated from the apostolic Roman See, so that they can contribute to the restoration of unity among all Christians according to the directives of the Council." [31]

In the theological sphere most of the problems which touch on ecumenical activity are problems of ecclesiology. They can be grouped about two subjects:

(a) All Christians today agree in saying that the Church as instituted is realized in history. But there arises immediately the problem of the conjunction of the human element, exposed to the relativism of history, and the divine element, definitive and unchanging. Hence the problem of the institution and the event: in particular the problem of definitive unity and unity in the form in which it has been realized, the problem of necessary unity and legitimate diversity within this unity, the problem of the holiness of the Church and the sin of the Church, and so on — all problems which have a bearing on ecumenism.

(b) All Christians agree equally in saying that the Church as instituted must proclaim the message of Christ to the whole world. But how is this proclamation to be conceived? As proclamation by words, or as proclamation by the tradition of the sacramental life, or as proclamation by both at once? How are we to conceive of the relationship between Scripture and tradition, between the magisterium and the personal witness of the Holy Spirit in each of the faithful? What is the nature of the

---

31. Decree *Optatam totius* on the formation of priests, n. 16.

sacraments? All these problems have to be considered from the
Catholic, Orthodox and Protestant points of view.

But in theology, ecumenism is not only a problem of ecclesiology: it is also a problem of mentality and of methodology.
"Theology and other disciplines, especially those of an historical
sort, must be taught from an ecumenical point of view, so that
they may correspond more accurately with the facts." [32] A
theology ecumenically disposed must certainly be careful to
give a faithful presentation of the doctrine of the Church, but
it must be a faithful presentation which fosters dialogue with
separated Christians.[33] The decree gives valuable indications on
this subject. It states, as a general principle, that "the method and
manner of expressing Catholic belief should not place any ob-
stacle in the way of dialogue with our separated brethren.[34]

This means in practice a number of things: (a) The exposition
of Catholic doctrine must avoid being in any way polemic: it must
be serene.[35] (b) It must be clear and entire, avoiding all false
irenicism, which would tend to soften or be silent about dogmas
which might offend our separated brethren. "Nothing is more
foreign to ecumenism than this false irenicism, which damages
the purity of Catholic doctrine and obscures its real and undoubted

---

32. Decree *Unitatis redintegratio* on ecumenism, n. 10.
33. L. Volken enumerates in this connection, seven principles which can
    ensure that theology is ecumenically designed. It should: (1) distin-
    guish what concerns the Christian faith or the Christian life from what
    is purely human, constituting non-theological factors; (2) distinguish
    in a Christian doctrine between its substance and its expression; (3)
    remember that in Christian doctrine, everything is not of the same im-
    portance; (4) remember that even the substance of the faith is not to
    be taken in a static sense; (5) remember that there is theological pro-
    gress if the content of a doctrine unfolds progressively, but that there is
    not always organic development; (6) remember that every truth or part
    of a truth must be seen in its true perspective; (7) remember that one
    must try and bring to light the truth which is the latent cause of error,
    that one must go in search of the perhaps sound intention which lies
    at error's base. See L. Volken, *L'Action oecuménique* (Paris & Friburg,
    1967), pp. 137-146.
34. Decree *Unitatis redintegratio* on ecumenism, n. 11.
35. *Ibid.*, n. 10.

sense." [36] Truth and charity must be together, after the example given us by John XXIII. (c) Doctrine must be explained in a way that is at the same time profound and precise, and in language intelligible to our separated brethren. (d) It should be remembered when expounding doctrine that "there is in Catholic teaching a hierarchy of truths, since they vary in their relationship to the foundation of Christian faith." [37] There is, in effect, a distinction in the importance of different revealed truths, which should be respected when doctrine is being explained. One will not put the same emphasis on the Assumption of Mary as on the dogma of the Trinity. It is no less necessary to distinguish a truth of faith, a truth theologically certain, a theological hypothesis etc. The criterion of a truth's place in the hierarchy of Catholic doctrine is its relationship to the foundation of Christian faith, that is the mystery of God the Savior in Jesus Christ and through Jesus Christ. (e) It should be remembered that among our separated brethren, especially among Protestants, the word of God as contained in Scripture is in the foreground of religious life and theological reflection (to give to Scripture all the importance which has been restored to it in the sphere of Christian reality, and to show how the doctrine of the Church is based on the facts of Scripture can be singularly effective in fostering ecumenical dialogue).[38] (f) It should be remembered in the same way, that a greater attention to the liturgical basis of faith can contribute to a *rapprochement* with the Eastern Churches.[39] In short in all its disciplines, and in all the subjects which it treats, theology must show itself more attentive to the ecumenical dimension and the ecumenical implications of its work.

---

36. *Ibid.*, n. 11.
37. *Ibid.*, n. 11. According to O. Cullmann, this is the most important statement in the decree from the point of view of fostering dialogue among Christians. Cf. O. Cullmann, "Comments on the Decree on Ecumenism," *The Ecumenical Review,* 17 (1965), p. 94.
38. Decree *Unitatis redintegratio* on ecumenism, n. 21.
39. *Ibid.*, nn. 14-15.

BIBLIOGRAPHY V

Pastoral Theology

ARNOLD, F. X., *Pour une théologie de l'apostolat*, Tournai, 1961.

ARNOLD, F. X., RAHNER, K., SCHURR, V., WEBER, L. M., *Handbuch der Pastoraltheologie*, I, Freiburg-Basel-Wien, 1964.

BRENNAN, J. H., « Pastoral Theology », *New Catholic Encyclopedia*, 10 : 1080-1084.

DE CONINCK, L., « Les orientations actuelles de la théologie pastorale », *Nouvelle Revue théologique*, 76 (1954) : 134-141.

DE LAVALETTE, H., « Réflexions sur la théologie pastorale », *Nouvelle Revue théologique*, 83 (1961) : 593-604.

FEIFEL, E., « Pastorale », dans : *Encyclopédie de la foi*, 3 : 320-328.

KNAUBER, A., « Pastoraltheologie », *Lexikon für Theologie und Kirche*, 8 : 164-165.

LIÉGÉ, P.-A., « Pour une théologie pastorale catéchétique », *Revue des sciences philosophiques et théologiques*, 39 (1955) : 3-17.

RAHNER, K., « Pastoraltheologie », in : *Was ist Theologie*, pp. 285-304.

SCHUSTER, H., « Wesen und Aufgabe der Pastoraltheologie », *Concilium*, 1 (März 1965) : 165-169.

SPIAZZI, R., *Teologia pastorale Didattica, Kerigmatica e Omiletica*, Roma, 1965.

ZALBA, M., « Theologia pastoralis in Concilio Vaticano II applicata », *Periodica*, 56 (1967) : 149-198.

Missionary Theology

GLAZIK, J., « Missionswissenschaft », dans : *Was ist Theologie*, pp. 369-384.

HENRY, A. M., *Esquisse d'une théologie de la mission*, Paris, 1959.

KAMPHAUS, F. et OHM, T., art. « Mission », *Encyclopédie de la foi*, 3 : 85-94.

LOFFELD, E., *Le problème cardinal de la missiologie et des missions catholiques*, Rhenen, 1956.

MASSON, J., « Fonction missionnaire de l'Église. Réflexions sur le Décret *Ad Gentes* de Vatican II », *Nouvelle Revue théologique*, 88 (1966) : 249-272.

OHM, T., *Faites des disciples de toutes les nations*, 2 vol., Paris, 1964-1965.
RÉTIF, A., *Introduction à la doctrine pontificale des missions*, Paris, 1953.
SANTOS, A., *Introducción a la Missiología*, Santander, 1961.
Protestant Point of View: ANDERSON, G. H., ed., *The Theology of the Christian Mission*, New York, 1961 ; AAGAARD, J., « Some main Trends in modern protestant Missiology », *Studia theologica*, 19 (1965) : 238-259.
Orthodox Point of View : YANNOULATOS, A., « The Purpose and Motive of Mission », *International Review of Missions*, 54 (1965) : 281-297.
Commentaries on the Decree *Ad Gentes*: A. SANTOS, Madrid, 1966; J. MASSON, Torino, 1966; *Misiones Extranjeras*, 50 (1966); *Euntes Docete*, 19 (1966).

Ecumenical Theology

BELL, G. K. A., *The Kingship of Christ*, St. Albans, 1954 ; *Christianity and World Order*, New York, 1940.
BLÄSER, P., « Oekumenische Theologie », in : *Was ist Theologie*, pp. 385-411.
LAMBERT, B., *Le Problème œcuménique*, 2 vol., Paris, 1962.
LAMIRANDE, E., « La formation à l'œcuménisme », *Revue de l'Université d'Ottawa*, 37 (1967) : 593-610.
QUINN, J., « Ecumenism and Theology », *The Heythrop Journal*, oct. 1967, pp. 373-380.
ROUSE, R. and NEIL, S., ed., *A History of the Ecumenical Movement*, 1517-1948, London, 1954.
SCHEPERS, M. B., « Ecumenism in the wake of the Council », *Angelicum*, 44 (1967) : 174-186.
THILS, G., *Histoire doctrinale du mouvement œcuménique*, deuxième édition, Louvain et Paris, 1962.
VOLKEN, L., *L'action œcuménique*, Paris et Fribourg, 1967.
Commentaries on the Decree on Ecumenism: DUMONT, C. J. et BEAUPÈRE, R., « Le Décret conciliaire sur l'œcuménisme », *Istina*, octobre-décembre 1964, pp. 353-544 ; ABBOTT, W. M., New York, 1965 ; BARTZ, W., Trier, 1965 ; BEA, A., Brescia, 1966 ; CONGAR, Y., Paris, 1965 ; JAEGER, L., Paderborn, 1965 ; JAVIERRE, A. M.,

Torino, 1965 ; Leeming, B., London, 1966 ; Nicolau, M., Madrid, 1965 ; Thils, G., Tournai, 1965 ; Franquesna, A., Barcelona, 1965 ; Jiménez Urresti, T. I., Madrid, 1965 ; Nicodemo, E., Roma, 1966.

CHAPTER VI   CANON LAW

1. General conception and theological basis

Canon law is the law of the Church, as the divine-human society founded by Christ, the Incarnate Word; it is made to govern the lives of baptized Christians and to lead men to salvation. The existence of canon law is based on the very nature of the Church as a society at once visible and invisible, at once the mystical Body of Christ and a hierarchical society organized juridically. "Just as the assumed nature indissolubly united to the divine Word serves him as a living medium of salvation, so the whole social structure of the Church serves the Spirit of Christ which gives it life so that his mystical Body may grow." [1] Like every visible society the Church needs a social and juridical organization. For her as for every such society the principle "*ubi societas ibi ius*" is valid, and this necessity follows also from the explicit mission with which Christ entrusted her, the mission to govern the people of God with the help of the Holy Spirit, as a community of salvation (Mt 16, 19; 18, 18; 28, 20; Jn 20, 21-23). It is Christ's will on which this society of baptized Christians

---

1. Const. *Lumen Gentium* on the Church, n. 8.

is founded and which gives to it its purpose, its authority and its means of sanctification. The law of the Church derives its specific nature from the fact that it is the law of a supernatural community, divinely founded and built up by divine word and divine sacrament. The proclamtion of the word derives its juridical character from the fact that it is done in the name and by the command of the Lord, and from the fact also that it is addressed to the people of God to be lived by it. The salvation announced by the word is accomplished by the sacrament. But in so far as it is a visible sign and has a social character, the sacrament is susceptible of juridical control (that is of the conditions of its administration and of its valid reception). Word and sacrament are the two essentials in the visible building up of the Church. And canon law contains the norms of life and action for the organization of preaching and for the fostering of the full development of the sacramental life, and thus of growth in the union between Christ and his members.[2]

In virtue of this supernatural end, the juridical organization of the Church has a supernatural character, so that it differs essentially from secular law. Canon law is strictly speaking a theological discipline, which makes use of legal expression and juridical method.

In the wide sense canon law embraces all that the Church universal has decreed as a rule of the Church's life, that is the codes which govern its life in the East and in the West, particular diocesan legislation, and the special rules of orders or communities inspired by special charisms of the Holy Spirit and approved by the Church.

From the point of view of origin, the Church's laws can be divided into: (a) divine laws inscribed by God in human nature or revealed by God and contained in Scripture and tradition (this is divine natural law and divine positive law, and the Church in this case simply promulgates the law in a precise form, and interprets it); (b) laws made by the Church herself, human laws and therefore subject to change and adaptation (for instance ritual

---

2. K. Mörsdorf, art. "Droit canon," *Encyclopédie de la foi*, 1, pp. 381-391.

modes and clerical obligations; it is in this that the greatest part
of canon law consists); (c) finally civil laws which the Church,
living in the midst of the world and in contact with political society
makes her own and makes "canon." It must remembered that the
Church, in the course of the centuries, has had to undertake duties
which do not follow directly from the divine mission given her
by Christ, but from social necessity at various points of her
history, for instance the duty of determining the age required to
contract a valid marriage, or the degrees of consanguinity and
affinity which make a marriage invalid.

In the matter of divine law, it is important to distinguish the
permanent and immutable doctrinal element from the concrete
and historical forms in which the law is expressed. Thus the hierarchy of orders, and of jurisdiction (the pope, bishops, priests, deacons, subdeacons) rests in the last analysis on the mission of the
Twelve and on the special mission of Peter. But the concrete juridical forms in which, historically, the Church has lived this mission
will always remain under the influence of a certain coefficient of
variability. Consider for instance the new forms of collegiality
among bishops and priests. The same distinction has to be made
in the case of the sacramental life, the preaching of the word and
all ecclesiastical institutions. One must never confound the underlying doctrinal element with its concrete and variable expression.
There will always be found at the level of a law a process analogous
to what happens in the development of dogma.

2. *Canon law and other theological disciplines*

Canon law is intimately connected with other theological
disciplines, specially with dogmatic theology and with moral theology.

First of all it is bound up with dogmatics. The decree on the
formation of priests says explicitly: "In the explanation of canon
law . . . the mystery of the Church, as set forth in the Dogmatic
Constitution on the Church should be kept in mind." [3] The law

---

3. Decree *Optatam totius* on the formation of priests, n. 16.

of the Church is indeed rooted in a conception of the Church, an ecclesiology. One might even say, "as the ecclesiology is, so will the law be." Just as the code of 1917 records the theological reflection aroused by the first Vatican Council, particularly in the matter of the primacy and infallibility of the Roman pontiff, so the new code should develop in the light of the second Vatican Council and the Constitution *Lumen Gentium*. The present code already contains a rich conspectus of doctrine on the Church, on its structure, its powers, and its ministers, upon preaching and upon the sacraments, and upon the relationship between Church and state, etc. It also contains directives which have, little by little, created a mentality which has prepared the way for the work of the second Vatican Council, in for example its insistence on the pastoral duties of bishops, and in a more spiritual conception of the power of the Church which has helped her to disentangle herself from temporal power.

Moral theology and canon law are also complementary disciplines. Often indeed they treat the same subject from different points of view. While moral theology is concerned with the order which governs the life of the Christian community, it is concerned with this only in so far as it is the object of moral obligation, at the level of the individual conscience in confrontation with the law of God, proclaimed and determined by the Church. Canon law on the other hand is specially concerned with the norms which govern the social organization of Christian life. So canon law defines the common good of the Church, the right of the Church as an institution, and the individual rights of the faithful. It maintains the order to which their communion in the social life of the Church must conform, judges offences against this order and prescribes penalties. At this level it judges the conformity or non-conformity of specific actions with the established law. While canon law is concerned with the exterior observance of the precepts of the Church (for its end is to ensure an ordered social life in the Church), moral theology is primarily concerned with the intention which inspires human actions and their conformity to the moral order. Moral theology, therefore, is essentially concerned with what is interior. But it should be remembered that the Church's juridical order, like that of civil society, touches conscience, in that the faithful are "bound in conscience" to observe this order. Law without moral inspiration would be nothing but legalism, but on the other hand a morality which completely ignored law would run the risk of being dissipated in a vague "spiritualism," and of paying little attention to the social character of the Church's Christian life.[4]

3. *The new code*

The present code of canon law, promulgated half a century ago, inevitably calls for a certain degree of transformation. It is not a matter of calling in question the Church's juridical organization, but rather, in a Church which is in process of *aggiornamento,* of making her law a perfect instrument of the renewal to which the Council has called her. It is in faithfulness to the very mission of the Church that canon law needs periodically to be rejuvenated. The Church's law is designed to lead baptized Christians of all times and all places to their eternal home. Consequently there is in it both a permanent element and a variable moving element, the inevitable consequence of a pilgrim Church. Canon law, like the Church herself must keep step with the rhythm of the generations and answer the new questions which each generation asks. The history of canon law and the diversity of rites, witnesses to this necessity, a necessity created by the living faith of a Church incarnate in time.

The present code, and canon law in general, are at the moment the object of a good deal of criticism, some of it well-founded, some of it hardly so. Canon law is accused of maintaining the Church in a formalistic and legalistic state. Would it not be more accurate to say that the temptation to juridicism threatens not only canon law but all sacred sciences, all ecclesiastical institutions, and even all human life? It is important surely

---

4. K. Mörsdorf, "Kirchenrecht," *Lexikon für theologie und Kirche,* 6, pp. 246-250; W. Bertrams, "Die Eigennatur des Kirchenrechts," *Gregorianum,* 27 (1946), pp. 526-566.

to distinguish between canon law and a legalistic mentality. In the same way, the present code is accused of having constructed a pyramidal Church, where everything depends on the pope, without giving enough consideration to the traditional collegial institutions. Yet it should be remembered that it is this same code which affirms the supreme power of the council, and which prescribed provincial councils and diocesan synods. History will perhaps reveal that the bishops themselves have rather stressed their personal power than created or put into practice a true collegiality as authorized by the code. Again canon law is accused of being the expression of a clerical mentality which leaves no place in the Church for the laity. It is true that the code remains centered on pastoral responsibility, but it would be excessive to say that it forgot the laity, since all that concerns the fundamental rights of baptized Christians and all that concerns the sacramental life is addressed to the laity as much as to the clergy. We should remember, too that the code is not the only record of the Church's legislation. In both the universal and the diocesan charters granted to Catholic Action the laity were given a law which prepared the way for the decree on its apostolate. Nevertheless we should recognize that the present code does not sufficiently reflect the importance assigned to the laity by the second Vatican Council.

Other grievances would appear to be better founded. Some think that civil law and philosophy have at times exercised an exaggerated influence on canonical science, for example in the interpretation of what jurisdiction means and in the conception of the role of the bishop, which has been understood rather in terms of civil law than in pastoral terms. One hopes therefore, that the new law will draw more inspiration from the data of revelation and from what can be learned from theology. Again it is said that the present code, if it ensures the unity of the Church, does not take sufficient account of its necessary diversity on a local plane. This diversity, recognized by the Council in the institution of episcopal conferences, should be reflected in the new code, especially in the matter of administration. One notices, moreover, that a good many of the canons no longer correspond to actual fact, in the realm of censures for instance. All in all, it is to be hoped that there will be more suppleness in the formulation of law, more distinction between universal laws and local customs, and more place given to custom and to jurisprudence.

Canonists recognize, with an ever increasing degree of unanimity, the necessity of basing the new law on a sound theology, and especially on an ecclesiology.[5] It would need to be shown how, in a true ecclesiology, law has a necessary place. This theology of the Church must be the soul of her law. The second Vatican Council has, in *Lumen Gentium* and in its manifold decrees, presented a theology of the people of God and of the different orders in the Church, the episcopate, the priesthood, the diaconate, the laity. In the synthesis of this vision of the Church as a whole, clergy and faithful are better placed in relation to each other; power itself is conceived in terms of service rather than in terms of rights and prerogatives: the bishop is the pastor, the shepherd, and the priest is the minister, the servant, of God. If the new law succeeds in assimilating all this theological richness which is to be found in the Council and in registering the orientations which it implies, it can be the instrument of a great renewal in the Church. If, on the contrary, it allowed itself to remain at a distance from the renewal of life called for by the Council, serious damage could follow, for the whole Church.

A dialogue therefore is necessary between canonical science and other theological disciplines, dogmatics, moral theology, liturgy, patristics, missiology. Canonical science and the life of the faithful should bear fruit in each other. Theology provides law with its guiding principles and its inspiration. But the living practice of the Church, which the law expresses, asks in its turn, for reflection by the canonist. In this way, the Church's laws on the formation of the clergy, on the religious life, and on the administration of the sacraments exercise their influence on the life of the faithful, which, in its turn, through the attitudes which

---

5. D. Composta, "Prospettive per una theologia del diritto," *Salesianum,* 29 (1967), pp. 28-69; L. Orsy, "Towards a theological conception of the canon law," *The Jurist,* 24 (1964), pp. 383-392.

it reflects, provokes theological reflection. Without a theological basis and without an awareness of concrete reality, canonical science would be impoverished and become mere legalism. The new law should be in the image of the life of the Church as it is lived today and of the present renewal in the theological sciences.

4. *New orientations*

In conclusion let us give some indication of the present preoccupations of canonical science.

(a) Speaking in a general way, there is a characteristic return to the primary sources of canon law (in Scripture and tradition), and a more vigilant attention to present signs of the times. Since it has to regulate the present life of the Church, canon law is seeking to reflect the face of the Church as it is today and the preoccupations of the Church as they are today.[6]

(b) There is a consideration of the law of the Church not only from an exegetical point of view, but also from an evolutionary point of view. For canon law is a witness to the living tradition of the Church: it is a witness, for instance, to the different forms of the religious life throughout the centuries.

(c) There is a tendency to place more emphasis upon the sacramental value of the Church's law. Since the Church is the sacrament of salvation instituted by Jesus Christ, her canonical power has also the character of a mediating sign of salvation.

(d) A more just balance is being sought among the legislative powers (the pope, bishops, councils, episcopal conferences, synods, chapters of religious orders), the executive powers (the Roman congregations and diocesan officials) and the judiciary of the Church (the Rota and local tribunals). On a just balance among these depends the law's respect for the rights of individual persons. It is specially to be hoped that the administrative exercise

---

6. As an example see: E. Pin, "Les Instituts religieux apostoliques et le changement socio-culturel," *Nouvelle Revue théologique,* 87 (1965), pp. 395-411.

of judiciary power will be better regulated and less secret, giving more attention to the right of those on trial to make their defense.

(e) There is a tendency to take more account of custom. Since 1917 the conditions demanded for the juridical recognition of custom have been so rigorous that it was practically excluded. If the new code wishes to reflect tendencies which are already manifesting themselves in the post-conciliar period (for example in legislation on the liturgy) it will need to be more receptive to the idea of custom.

(f) There is a tendency to distinguish more sharply between universal law and particular law. Up to now universal law has been plainly predominant. In the future, perhaps, there will be a distinction between a briefer, universal code addressed to the whole Church and particular codes in which the precise applications of the universal code will be worked out for different regions.

(g) There is a greater respect for the charismatic element in the life of the Church, especially with regard to new forms of the consecrated life among clergy and laity. Up to now the laity have been directed from above, for example in Catholic Action. In the future life of the Church it will certainly be necessary to take more account of lay charisms and of the new forms of apostolate which can arise within the laity.

(h) Since the Council has rightly insisted on the character of service which must distinguish the pastorate, canon law should express this character in the regulations which determine obligations and responsibilities. A pastorate conceived in terms of service must know how to listen, how to engage in dialogue, how to foster initiative and co-operation. Hence the importance of the synod of bishops (the pope and the bishops), of senates of priests (the bishop and the priests of a particular diocese, or those working in the same area). Hence the necessity of pastoral councils and commissions, with a real and operative representation of the laity.

(i) In her relationships with the state, the Church is tending to a new sort of harmony. It is not yet possible to assess the influence upon the search for this new sort of harmony which a document as important as the declaration on religious freedom will have. In the past the Church used to ask official recognition by the state (the regime of the *concordat*). From now on it would seem that the two societies are tending to develop each in its own sphere (temporal and spiritual) with mutual respect each for the other's different end.

(j) In her action in the midst of the earthly and political city the Church must take account of its reality while at the same time conforming to her own true mission of sanctification. The Church must be incarnate in the life of the city, not in dominating it, but in an apostolate of presence and the giving of life. She must act more and more from within, as a leaven, sanctifying the laity who in their turn sanctify institutional life. Hence the importance of secular institutes.[7]

BIBLIOGRAPHY VI

COMPOSTA, D., « Prospettive per una teologia del diritto », *Salesianum*, 29 (1967) : 28-69.

CORECCO, E., « Il rinnovo metodologico del diritto canonico, *Civitas*, janvier et avril 1966, pp. 1-31.

DE ECHEVERRÍA, L., « Théologie du droit canonique », *Concilium*, n. 28 (oct. 1967) : 13-20.

HANLON, G. P., *De Codicis juris canonici recognitione*, Romae, 1964.

HEIMERL, H., « Aspecto cristologico del derecho canonico », *Jus canonicum*, 6 (1966) : 25-51.

HEIMERL, H., « Esquisse d'un droit constitutionnel dans l'Église », *Concilium*, n. 28 (oct. 1967) : 59-67.

HUIZING, P., « La Réforme du droit canon », *Concilium*, n. 8 (1965) : 91-117.

HUIZING, P., « Nature et limites de la future codification de l'ordre ecclésial », *Concilium*, n. 28 (oct. 1967) : 31-39.

MAY, G., « Kirchenrecht und Kirchenrechtswissenschaft », *Was ist Theologie*, pp. 266-283.

---

7. J. Beyer, "L'avenir des Instituts séculiers," *Gregorianum*, 46 (1965), pp. 545-594; Id., "Les instituts séculiers, ferment du laïcat," *Choisir*, mars, 1964, pp. 24-27.

ÖRSY, L., « Vie de l'Église et renouveau du droit canon », *Nouvelle Revue théologique*, 85 (1963) : 952-965 ; ID., « Towards a theological Conception of the Canon Law », *The Jurist*, 24 (1964) : 383-392.

SCHMITZ, D. H., *Die Gesetzessystematik des Codex Juris Canonici Liber I-III*, Coll. Münchener Theologische Studien, München, 1963.

SHANNON, P., « Le Code de droit canonique 1918-1967 », *Concilium*, n. 28 (oct. 1967) : 51-58.

STICKLER, A. M., « Das Mysterium der Kirche im Kirchenrecht », in : F. HOLBÖCK und T. SARTORY, *Mysterium Kirche in der Sicht der theologischen Disziplin*, Salzburg, 1962.

URRESTI, T. I. JIMÉNEZ, « L'Église comme institution », dans : *La nouvelle image de l'Église*, ouvrage collectif sous la direction de B. LAMBERT, Paris, 1967, pp. 83-98.

URRESTI, T. I. JIMÉNEZ, « Droit canon et théologie : deux sciences différentes », *Concilium*, n. 28 (oct. 1967) : 21-29.

CHAPTER VII ECCLESIASTICAL HISTORY AND THE HISTORY OF DOGMA

I. ECCLESIASTICAL HISTORY

1. *Christianity, the religion of history*

The Church's historical interest is derived from the very nature of Christianity, which is the religion of God's intervention in history. The God of Israel is essentially a living and personal God, who comes into history and changes its course with a sovereign liberty. The God of revelation is a God who is mixed up with history, and who reveals himself there in accomplishing the salvation of his people.[1] The whole Bible is the history of what God did to save Israel, and what it encloses is the history of salvation. For God's design is revealed and realized in successive stages, according to a disposition or economy of great wisdom. His interventions constitute in universal history a kind of out-crop, as it were, of the divine in time. The choosing of Abraham, the calling of Moses, the exodus, the covenant on Mount Sinai, kingship, prophecy, exile, these events scan the history of salvation, and there is a peak in this history, the coming of God among us in the Person of Christ. The whole of the Old Testament

---

1. Const. *Dei verbum* on revelation, n. 2.

is oriented to this. Jesus Christ is the consubstantial Word of God, incarnate and manifest in history. He is the epiphany of God in the flesh and in time, the Event *par excellence*. In him the history of salvation is accomplished, and between his coming in the flesh and his coming in glory, there intervenes the time of the Church, that is the time when the mystery revealed and accomplished in Jesus Christ reaches all men and all times. This is the time when the Gospel is preached to every creature (Mk 16, 15), the "favorable time," the day of salvation (2 Cor 6, 2), the "today" of God, during which each is called to conversion (Acts 3, 20; Heb 3, 7-10; 4, 7). The time of the Church is the time of mission and apostolate, the time of the growing up of the Body of Christ to the stature of the perfect Man. The history of salvation is always being continued.[1a]

Christianity is so much the religion of history that it is Christianity, may we say, that has given to the world the very conception of history. For cyclic time, which is only repetition and perpetual beginning again, it has substituted linear time, in three dimensions. Outside Israel and Christianity, which is the prolongation of Israel, one scarcely finds in fact any firmly established idea of a continuous succession of temporal events which embrace past, present and future, and which are connected by a direction and end. Christianity is the religion of the *Epaphax*. The pasch and the covenant are not repeated; they are recounted and celebrated. Redemption is not repeated but it is actualized.[2]

1a. R. Latourelle, *Theology of Revelation*, pp. 416-434.

2. M. Bloch writes with justice, "Christianity is an historian's religion. Other religious systems could find their beliefs and their rites on a mythology more or less exterior to human time. The sacred books of Christians are books of history, and their liturgies commemorate, with the episodes in the earthly life of a God, the annals of the Church and the saints." M. Bloch, *Apologie pour l'histoire ou métier d'historien* (3rd. edition, Paris, 1959), p. 9. On Christianity as the religion of history, see O. Cullman, *Christ et le temps* (Neuchâtel, 1957); M. Eliade, *Le mythe de l'éternel retour* (Paris, 1949); J. Mouroux, *Le mystère du temps* (Paris, 1962); R. Latourelle, *Theology of Revelation*, (Alba House, New York), pp. 348-351.

2. *History of the Church and theology of the Church*

"In expounding ecclesiastical history," says the decree on the formation of priests, "the mystery of the Church should be kept in mind, as it was set forth in the Dogmatic Constitution on the Church, promulgated by this Council." [3] The Church as described in *Lumen Gentium* is at once institution and mystery, at once a religious society and the mystical Body of Christ. As an institution she is subject to historical observation, and history can describe the concrete vicissitudes of the Church within the general framework of secular events. History can recount the Church's outer life, discuss the men who influenced her inner life, describe her relations with the world and with secular powers. But on the other hand, because she shares in the divine-human mystery of Christ, the Church is a mystery of faith. Her real nature and the secret of her deep dynamic power are known to us only through a revelation which is an object of faith. In consequence, any conception of the Church's history implies a particular way of understanding her, that is it implies a theology of the Church. According to whether we accept the options of Bultmann's theology or those of Catholic theology, all our ways of looking at the history of the Church will be modified. A history of the Church is then, whether we like it or not, founded on a theology of the Church. What are the essential lines of this theology and what are its repercussions on our understanding of the Church's history?

1. The Church is the people of God. The society founded by Christ is not a collection of individuals, but a solidly structured community governed by responsible leaders. Yet if it is true that the hierarchy has its importance in the Church, since its members, the pope and the bishops, are God's representatives and have power, by his mandate, to teach, to govern and to sanctify, the history of the Church cannot be reduced to the history of the

---

3. Decree *Optatam totius* on the formation of priests, n. 16.

pope and bishops, for then it would no longer be the history of the people of God. Ecclesiastical history must be equally interested in all the faithful, clerical or lay. The hierarchy itself, moreover, exists in order to serve the people of God, and its role cannot be understood except in terms of its function in relation to the people of God, to whom it must transmit faithfully the words of life and the means of salvation.

2. The Church is a visible society, involved in the temporal city, but she is also the temple of the Holy Spirit, the Body of Christ, a *milieu* of supernatural life. Ecclesiastical history therefore cannot be reduced to the mere politico-religious aspects of the Church's life, the relations of Church and state, the interventions of the Church in the public life of nations, the interventions of civil power in the organization of the Church. These aspects cannot be neglected, since the Church is an incarnate Church, and lives upon the frontiers of the temporal and the spiritual, but what is to be seen there is only the "phenomenal" aspect of the Church. The essential aspect, which lies within the deep core of her life, is her life of faith and love and the special character of the new life which this life of the theological virtues inspires. So the history of the Church has to recount not only her struggles against heresy, and her theological controversies, but also, in so far as the documents allow, her progress in the deepening and exercising of her faith, as manifested for instance in apostolic and charitable work, in forms of prayer and ritual, in the flowering of her life in the saints, in the foundation of orders and communities. All this belongs to the face of the Church.

3. Like Christ, at once Man and God, the Church is at once human and divine. The law of incarnation governs every act by which man is divinized. Because Christ's Church is truly human, made up of men who retain their temperaments, their personalities, their qualities and their defects, it follows that there is room in the Church, in the hierarchy and in the life of the faithful, for error and sin. The second Vatican Council declared over and

over again that the Church "embraced sinners within her"; that is why "she is always in need of being purified" and of "pursuing unceasingly the path of penitence and renewal." [4] Catholics must strive "to conquer sin" [5] and "to purify and renew themselves." [6] Since this is so, why should we be surprised that the actions of members of the Church, taken in the constant play of freedom and grace, exhibit like all human actions, ingredients that are only too human, motives and limitations which it is possible to recognize, analyze, and assess? We shall find them shabby, lacking in information, slow in reading the signs of the times and in adaptation to new situations — in short exhibiting the whole theoretical catalogue of historical errors. Add to all this the real infidelities, the scandals (favoritism, abuse of power, attachment to wealth, reputation and status, dissimulation), the immoralities, the whole gamut of sin. And these are the sins of those who govern as well as of those governed. A sound theology of the Church helps us to understand these shores where light and shadow meet and intermingle in the life of the Church. And ecclesiastical history must not fear in its turn to point out the qualities and defects of Churchmen. All these things exist equally it must be added in communities separated from the Church.

4. The object of ecclesiastical history is the Roman Catholic Church. There could be no question for her of regarding this Church as one among many Christian confessions. The Church is unique: there is only one mystical Body, only one Church which is the Body of Christ, the Church founded by Christ, that is the Church whose head on earth is the Bishop of Rome. But it does not follow that the other Christian communities are without interest or without life, like so many dead branches. Such an attitude would contradict the statements of the decree on ecumenism.[7] Each of the separated communities has its own value

---

4. Const. *Lumen Gentium* on the Church, nn. 8 & 9.
5. *Ibid.*, n. 65.
6. *Ibid.*, n. 15; see also Const., *Gaudium et Spes*, n. 43 & Decree *Unitatis Redintegratio*, n. 6.
7. Decree *Unitatis Redintegratio* on Ecumenism, n. 3.

and has something to give to others. Ecclesiastical history must pay attention particularly to the following considerations: (a) the responsibility for these divisions which have rent the Church is a shared responsibility; (b) if in the storm the Church has not been overthrown, she has been weakened and impoverished and she has sometimes lost her balance; (c) the separated communities have often made better use than we have done of the spiritual blessings which they have preserved. In consequence, the Catholic Church can be enriched through treasure exploited in the separated Churches, the value set upon the word of God, the sense of God's transcendence and of the gratuity of grace among Protestants, and the sense of mystery and of liturgical prayer in the East. Ecclesiastical history should explain how the misunderstandings and enmities which led to separation arose, and show also how the separated communities have profoundly influenced the life and development of the Catholic Church, in theology, in spirituality, in liturgy, in the realm of art.

5. Finally the Church is a dynamic and catholic unity. She is the Church of mission and evangelization, and she is in the phase of her expansion to the ends of the earth. A history of the Church could not then confine itself to being a history of the West at the expense of the East, of Europe at the expense of other continents, or even of Southern Europe at the expense of Northern Europe. Since the Church extends throughout the world ecclesiastical history is not confinable to a privileged geographical terrain.

Without sacrificing in any way the exigencies of historical method, ecclesiastical history must take account of this multiplicity of aspects, all of which belong to the mystery of the Church.

3. *The object, method and nature of ecclesiastical history*

"The object of ecclesiastical history," writes H. Jedin, "is the growth in time and space of the Church founded by Christ. In so far as it receives its subject matter from the science of faith and is based on faith, it is a theological discipline, and distinct from a history of Christianity." [8] The mystery of the growth of the Church can be likened to the mystery of the grain of wheat which germinates and develops without losing its identity.

In the dimension in which the Church has a past and a history, she is subject to the demands of historical method. The history of the Church is bound up with its sources, and the laws of historical criticism apply both to the documents and to the facts disclosed, just as in any other historical discipline. The way in which the facts disclosed are connected, the perception of the motives which inspired and governed the actions of Churchmen as they emerge in the documents of the past, the genesis and development of ecclesiastical institutions, all these things are a matter of historical observation and historical method.

Nevertheless ecclesiastical history is distinct from secular sciences and from a simple history of Christitianity. Because of its object (the Church as institution and mystery) and the originating principles which illuminate it (revelation and faith), it is a true theological discipline. The history of the Church, taken as a whole, cannot in fact be otherwise conceived than as the history of salvation in application and actualization, from Pentecost to the *parousia,* and its meaning can be perceived only by faith. The history of the Church is the continuous presence of the Word of God in the world through the preaching of the Gospel and the constitution of the Body of Christ. It is the growth of this Body, of the holy people redeemed by his blood. Ecclesiastical history, in so far as it is understanding of the mystery of salvation in its phase of realization (through the Church's ministries, through the sacramental life, and through the charisms) and in its fruits, which anticipate the new Jerusalem (the manifold sanctity of doctors, martyrs, confessors and so on) is a part of theological understanding. It is through the life of the Church developing through the centuries that we develop in our understanding of

---

8. H. Jedin, ed., *Handbuch der Kirchengeschichte* (Freiburg, 1962), introduction; Id., "La position de l'histoire de L'Eglise dans l'enseignement théologique," *Seminarium,* 19 (1967), pp. 133-135.

the mystery of the Church, of the wealth of content in Christianity and of the ways of God with men.

There is, therefore, scarcely need to insist on the necessity of ecclesiastical history for every Christian, and above all for every minister of God. It is through the *historia salutis* that we come to understand more of the *mysterium salutis*. To this general reason we may add three others suggested by the major problems which confront the Church in the twentieth century. The first is the problem of our knowledge even of Christ, of his message and of the signs of his mission. Is it possible for the Christian today, and to what degree is it possible, to know the Christ of Nazareth and to hear his true message? To what extent is the primitive Church a distorting screen between the Christ she preaches and the Christ who existed? This problem, one of the most disturbing at the present time, is, no doubt, a problem of hermeneutics, but it is also a problem of historical research, which can be resolved only by a more complete knowledge of the primitive Church, of her activities, of her different *milieu* and of the influence which they exerted upon her. The second problem which confronts the Church in the twentieth century is that of atheism, and an atheism which, in its dangerous and aggressive form, is an historical materialism, based upon the past. Thirdly, the need of the post-conciliar Church to pursue her own *aggiornamento*, demands a very lively sense of tradition and renewal, which is equally remote from blind conservatism and a naive belief in progress. A sound historical sense and an intimate familiarity with the past can help to dissipate a certain cloudy mythology of progress and also certain dreams about the purity of its origins.

4. *The history of ecclesiastical history*

It can be said that ecclesiastical history began with the *Acts of the Apostles,* which is at the same time a history of events and a theological interpretation of the sources of the Church's life. Throughout the early centuries three preoccupations, especially, dominate work of a historical nature, the desire to preserve the memory of the martyrs (*The Acts of the Martyrs*), the desire to preserve the traditions of local Churches (Hegesippus) and an apologetic preoccupation. But we owe the first Christian works of history in its sense of an objective knowledge of the past which sets out from documents, to Eusebius of Caesarea, the father of ecclesiastical history, and to those who followed in his footsteps, Socrates, Sozomen, Theodoretus of Cyrrhus, Rufinus, St. Jerome, Sulpicius Severus, Prosper of Aquitaine, St. Isidore, and St. Bede.

In the Middle Ages hagiography was prevalent, with a very obvious intention to improve the moral and spiritual life of the faithful. This is also the age of chronicles (of dynasties and pontificates) and of annals (of local Churches or of monasteries). These works, even when they have a real objectivity, are written for the "edification" of the Christian community. One can say in a general way that history was not one of the dimensions of medieval thought. Among the scholastics logical and systematic exposition outweighed historical exposition. It is not until the sixteenth century that ecclesiastical history begins to discover its scientific status, as a methodical and objective form of knowledge. The Renaissance was interested in antiquity for its own sake, and in what the face of antiquity was really like. The Protestant reformers for their part, making use of what the humanists could give them, called upon history to support their doctrinal positions. The most imposing war-machine set in motion by the learned Protestants of the sixteenth century was the *Centuries of Magdebourg,* published between 1560 and 1574, which gave occasion to Caesar Baronius to write his *Annals,* from 1588 and 1607.

In the seventeenth and eighteenth centuries the controversy between Protestants and Catholics, and also the Gallican and Jansenist disputes, were the source of an admirable efflorescence of historical work. The need was felt to establish dogma, ritual, and institutions on a sound basis. This is the time when Bollandus, Petaus, Du Cange, Mabillon, Baluze, and Muratori appear, as well as syntheses like Claude Fleury's *Histoire ecclésiastique* (1690-1720), and Sebastian Le Nain de Tillemonts' *Mémoires pour servir à l'histoire ecclésiastique des six premiers siècles* (1693-1712).

This is also the time when history became more scholarly with the appearance of the great collections (the collections of conciliar texts, the work of the Benedictines of St. Maur and of the Bollandists) and the development of the auxiliary sciences (diplomatics in Mabillon, paleography in de Montfaucon). It is the time too when history became more specialized, for instance in the doctrinal history of D. Petau, and L. Thomassin, in history of contemporary divisions, like Bossuet's *L'Histoire des variations des Églises Protestantes* in 1688, and in history of the missions like de Charlevoix's ethnographic studies in *Relations des Jésuites de la Nouvelle-France.*

The first half of the nineteenth century is poor in output. Nevertheless between 1842 and 1849 there appeared in twenty-nine volumes Rohrbacher's *Histoire universelle de l'Eglise,* which is mainly a catalogue of events. Towards the end of the century, with the help of philological and critical science there was a definite renewal of ecclesiastical history, of which the most illustrious example is surely Louis Duchesne's *Histoire ancienne de l'Eglise.* From now on research was shared with the laity, whose contribution, beginning with pioneers like Pastor's *Histoire des papes* (1884-1925), opened out in all directions at once. Leo XIII's decision to open part of the Vatican archives to scholars gave a powerful impetus to historical research.

Ecclesiastical history as we know it in the twentieth century is the result of all this activity. It takes extremely varied forms: collections and critical editions of texts, great dictionaries like the *Dictionnaire d'archéologie et d'histoire ecclésiastique,* general history, like *Histoire de l'Eglise* of Fliche and Martin, conciliar history, like the work of Hefele and Leclercq, monographs of all sorts, a proliferation of reviews. Ecclesiastical history tends to cover every aspect of the life of the Church.

II. THE HISTORY OF DOGMA

The history of dogma is connected with ecclesiastical history. It did not become a scientific discipline until history itself became so in the nineteenth century. Its chief representatives are Harnack, Schwane, Tixeront, De Groot, Loofs, Seeberg and Landgraf.

The history of dogma is bound up with the recognition of dogmatic developments in the Church. Dogma is the statement, in human terms, of revealed mystery. What develops through the centuries is not revelation itself, not the mystery but our understanding of the mystery, in the successive explanations which we give of it in order to manifest its inexhaustible content. We multiply these formulations in order to translate into human terms our whole effort at assimilation. So dogma can always develop towards a formulation which is more exact, more detailed and at the same time richer in meaning, more adequate to the reality which is being stated and to new aspects of it which have been discovered. Strictly speaking, a dogma is the statement of a religious truth, contained in the deposit of revelation and proposed as such by the universal magisterium of the Church, in normative forms, the acceptance of which is a *sine qua non* because of the Christian's adherence to the faith.

In practice, however, the history of dogma as it is conceived today, extends beyond this notion of dogma. It is the history of Catholic doctrines whether these doctrines have or have not been the subject of a solemn conciliar or pontifical definition by the Church. It is concerned with the way in which doctrinal themes have, from the time of revelation onwards, developed, become deeper, more precise and better formulated through the long labor of reflective thought. It retraces the sources, the stages, the pauses, the hesitations, the progress of this development. If, for instance, one consults the installments of the *Handbuch der Dogmengeshichte,* one finds that the study of doctrinal themes begins in a wide biblical exposition (of words, of categories, of biblical perspectives) and continues through the writings of the Fathers, the first theological systematizations, the medieval *summae,* and the interventions of the magisterium, right up to the elaborations of contemporary theology. The history of dogma, understood in this way, tends to absorb several disciplines (particularly patrology and the history of theology), and to be indistinguishable in practice from a factual *dossier* of the great doctrinal themes of the Catholic faith. It gathers its materials from Scripture and tradition, from the documents of the magisterium, and from theological tradition right up to our own day.

BIBLIOGRAPHY VII

Ecclesiastical History

AUBERT, R., ROGIER, L.-J. et KNOWLES, M. D., *Nouvelle histoire de l'Église*, Paris, 1963, Introduction, vol. I, pp. 7-26.
CONGAR, Y., « Histoire », *Catholicisme*, 5 : 767-783.
DENZIER, G., « Kirchengeschichte », in : *Was ist Theologie*, pp. 138-168.
JARRY, E., « Histoire ecclésiastique », *Catholicisme*, 5 : 785-799.
JEDIN, H., ed., *Handbuch der Kirchengeschichte*, Freiburg, 1962, introduction, pp. 2-11 ; ID., « Kirchengeschichte als Theologie », *Stimmen der Zeit*, 178 (1966) : 148ss. ; ID., «La position de l'histoire de l'Église dans l'enseignement théologique», *Seminarium*, 7 (1967) : 130-147.
LORTZ, J., *Storia della Chiesa nello sviluppo delle sue idee*, Alba, 1966, introduzione, pp. 1-8.
WODKA, J., « Das Mysterium der Kirche in Kirchengeschichtlicher Sicht », in : F. HOLBÖCK und T. SARTORY, *Mysterium Kirche*, Salzburg, 1962, vol. I, pp. 347-385.

History of Dogma

ALSZEGHY, Z., FLICK, M., *Lo sviluppo del dogma cattolico*, Brescia, 1967.
GEISELMANN, J. R., « Dogme », *Encyclopédie de la foi*, 1 : 364-380.
HEINZMANN, R., « Dogmengeschichte », in : *Was ist Theologie*, pp. 169-189.
POZO, C., « Dogmenentwicklung », *Sacramentum mundi*, 1 : 926-935.
RATZINGER, J., *Das Problem der Dogmengeschichte in der Sicht der Katholischen Theologie*, Köln, 1966.
SCHMAUS, M., « Vorwort », in : *Handbuch der Dogmengeschichte*, Band IV, Faszikel 3, Freiburg, 1951, pp. V-XI.

PART IV
THEOLOGY AND CHRISTIAN LIFE

CHAPTER I THEOLOGY AND PREACHING

The end, after all, of theological studies is the formation of
the apostle and the priest. But the first mission of the priest is to
announce the word of salvation from God the Savior: "Priests
have as their first duty," says the decree *Presbyterorum Ordinis,*
"to proclaim the gospel of God to all men. In this way they fulfill
the Lord's command, 'Go into the whole world and preach the
gospel to every creature' (Mk 16, 15), and the people of God
is born and grows." [1]

The priest, like the prophet of the Old Testament is God's
herald. In a perpetual *hodie* he announces that salvation has come,
and asks men to make the choice of faith. "Woe to me," said St.
Paul, "if I do not preach the gospel" (1 Cor 9, 16). "Christ did
not send me to baptize but to preach the gospel" (1 Cor 1, 17) —
not because the sacraments are needless, but because the sacramental life itself depends on the news of the Word. In order
that Christ may be known and men may give glory to the Father,
there must be lips to speak the good news. For "how can men call
upon God unless they believe in him, and how can they believe
in him unless they have heard of him, and how can they hear

---

1. Decree *Presbyterorum Ordinis* on the ministry and life of priests, n. 4.

of him without a preacher?" (Rom 10, 14-17). Preaching the
word of God is part of the prophetic mission of the Church,[2] a
mission which is necessary and irreplaceable in the present economy of salvation.

If he is to be the lips of Christ and the instrument of the
Holy Spirit in the proclamation of the word of God, the apostle
must himself be entered and possessed by the word. This being
possessed by the word is the work of assiduous reading, of prayer
and of study, and it is here that the contribution of theology
to the ministry of preaching lies. Certainly theology and preaching will always remain two different levels of presentation, each
with its own laws and its own methods. But let us not go on
exaggerating the differences. The object to be understood and
presented is in both cases the word of God. And we may believe
that a theology which fulfills exactly its own function will be
an excellent preparation for fulfilling the essential demands of
preaching.

1. *The Mystery of Christ and the unity of the Christian mysteries*

The object of Christian preaching is the Christian mystery,
that is the design of salvation hidden in God from all eternity
and now revealed, through which God establishes Christ as the
center of the new economy and constitutes him, through his
death and resurrection the one source of salvation, for Gentile
and Jew alike; it is the divine plan as a whole (Incarnation, redemption, grace, election, glory), which in the end brings us
back to Christ and the unfathomable depths of his Mystery. For
in him all was made and all was remade. This one Mystery of
Christ, as it were, is pluralized in particular mysteries, all bound
together in a harmonious and powerful synthesis. How many
Christians have let the life of faith become an insipid affair in
them because they have never suspected the unfathomable depths
of this mystery? They have the feeling of living in a poor, shabby
legalist religion. They have never experienced like St. Paul the

---

2. *Ibid.*, n. 4.

stammering of a man dazzled by the magnificence of the design of salvation, the work of infinite wisdom, the unheard of expression of love. And how will they ever be able to experience this if the preacher never speaks to them of the splendor of the Christian Mystery, if he never presents Christ as the living focus of the whole history of salvation and as the center of unity for all the mysteries? And how will the preacher himself be able to do this, if he has not first perceived through long and careful study the manifold links wihch bind the mysteries together, and if he has not been seized, as it were, with a sort of vertigo before the scope and splendor of the divine poetics? It is through theology that he will see the one Mystery in the many mysteries, will see it ordered there in an organic synthesis, through certain central mysteries (the Trinity, the Incarnation, grace) which so to speak, articulate the whole. The theologian goes from the mysteries to the Mystery, trying to reconstitute in them the harmonious synthesis which is the human reflection of the divine design. This vision of the Mystery and the mysteries as a totality will also protect preaching from a certain sort of one-sidedness which consists in giving a privileged place to certain mysteries of Christianity to the detriment of certain others, which are more fundamental and richer in meaning but which one is afraid of presenting to the faithful because they are more difficult to explain — the mystery of the Trinity for instance.

2. *The salvific value of the Mystery*

Theology enlightens us not only about the object of revelation, that is to say the Mystery, but also about its salvific value. In fact it is in the truth of dogma that theology discovers its salvific bearing; for if God reveals himself, it is in order to save us from sin and bring us to everlasting life. It is part of theology's function to show how each mystery has been revealed to us in order to tell us in what our salvation consists and how we should orientate ourselves to it; for, it must be said again, it is the truth of the Mystery that is ordered to salvation. In this sense theology, in its essential function, serves Christian life.

It is therefore, a mistake to see, as certain advocates of kerygmatics believe they do, a dichotomy between the scientific explanation of the object of faith on the one hand and its salvific value on the other. We cannot arrive at the objective value of dogma and of the Christian mystery except in and through the truth of the objective reality of revelation. The better the real meaning or truth of the content of faith is understood and formulated, the clearer also will be its salvific value. It is the deeper and more exact understanding of dogma itself which will make clear to us its salvific dimension.

It is no doubt true that this knowledge in the scientific order does not — at least immediately — move the heart and will as much as knowledge in terms of concrete images, but it enriches the mind and spirit, and provides the preacher with the possibility of presenting the object of faith and its value for salvation in an authentic way. It is also a protection against a false and one-sided emotionalism. If a man has succeeded in grasping the content of his faith scientifically, he will have advanced so far in understanding the Mystery that, even outside theology, in preaching for instance, he will find himself able to master the most varied situations, provided, obviously, that he has the natural gifts necessary for communication and an experience in his own life of the concrete reality of men. His scientific penetration into the object of faith makes him free to present dogma at various levels and to various groups with a rigorous regard for orthodoxy. A theology, on the other hand, which is deprived of this scientific exactness is incapable of ensuring a preaching which is at once sound and adaptable.

3. *The liturgy of the word and the Sunday sermon*

The Constituion on the Liturgy [3] and the decree on the ministry of priests [4] have given back to preaching all its importance and

---

3. Const. *Sacrosanctum Concilium* on the liturgy, n. 52.
4. Decree *Presbyterorum Ordinis* on the ministry and life of priests, n. 4.

all its scope in the liturgical life of the Church. The homily especially has become the privileged place for proclaiming the word
of salvation. But preaching, says the Constitution, "should draw
its content primarily from scriptural and liturgical sources, since
it is the proclamation of the wonderful things God has done for
us in the history of salvation, that is, of the Mystery of Christ." [5]
The homily "should explain from the sacred text, the mysteries
of faith and guiding principles of the Christian life.[6] The Constitution on Revelation says in its turn, "The ministry of the
word, which includes pastoral preaching, catechesis, and all other
Christian instruction (in which the liturgical homily should have
a special place) should also go to Scripture for sound nourish-
ment and supernatural strength." [7]

To put this programme into practice the preacher needs
experience of exegesis and theology. For preaching should adapt,
but not distort, aim at simplicitly but not at poverty, and if one
is to present accurately the message which is to be found in
Scripture without distorting it or impoverishing it, that message
needs first to have been raised to a scientific level. To comment
upon Scripture is not easy. The preacher must study and understand the sacred text; that is he must decide exactly what its literal
sense is, grasp its historical and social context and be able to
appreciate the literary form in which it has come to us. Every text
moreover, carries meaning at a deeper level, which is its full
meaning, and though this meaning is to be found in the text
itself, it is in the text as it is organically related to all the other
parts of Scripture, in the context of the whole of revelation. And
to assess the relative importance of a text, to distinguish in Scripture what is peripheral and what is central, it is necessary to know
and possess the Christian synthesis, the key to the understanding
of which is Christ. All this presupposes that the preacher never
ceases to be an exegete and a theologian.

---

5. Const. *Sacrosanctum Concilium* on the liturgy, n. 35.
6. *Ibid.*, n. 52.
7. Const. *Dei verbum* on revelation, n. 24.

It is not enough then, for the preacher to use scriptural texts and images and think that in this way he is fulfilling his task as the servant of the word, as if the text of Scripture should act *ex opere operato*. If he is going to talk about the mystery of the Church, for instance, and set out from the great scriptural images, the people of God, the Bride, the Vine, the Body and so on, he must make a careful inventory of all the places where these figures are used, examine the content of their meaning in each context, and decide the exact contribution which each has to make. In short he must go from the symbolic language of Scripture to the more technical language of exegesis and theological explanation, in order to return to the biblical sources and find there a message of which, without losing any of the evocative power of scriptural language, he can grasp, thanks to rigorous hermeneutic work, the real and inexhaustible meaning.

4. The "actualization" of the word

Preaching needs not only to offer the word of salvation, but also to "actualize" it, so that the man of the twentieth century, with his twentieth century culture and mentality and problems, feels that it impinges upon him as concretely as it did upon the man of the first century. But how is one to fill the obvious gap which exists between Scripture and the man of today? How is the word addressed to the Jews of the Old Testament or the Christians of the primitive Church to find a like echo in the minds and hearts of our contemporaries?

There is no doubt that as the Christian community becomes more and more familiar with the scriptural themes and symbols which have fashioned the soul of Christianity the gap between Scripture and the man of today (which has unfortunately been widened by the centuries of almost total abandonment of Scripture) will be gradually lessened. Even so it still remains for the preacher, if he is to express the message of Scripture in terms intelligible to the man of today, to train himself first to understand his faith in terms of the scriptural categories, and to feel before the sacred text, as one feels before a familiar landscape. This familiarity should be one of the results of theological teaching.

But more still is required. This work of "actualizing" the word of God is part of a process which began in the very beginnings of the Church and has never been interrupted. The Church has never ceased to meditate upon the word of God and to offer it afresh to each new generation. So the text of the parables in the synoptic gospels is already a re-reading and actualization of our Lord's parables, in the slightly different context of the early Church. How, then, can present-day preaching ignore this long tradition of the Church, with all its rich harmonies set up by the one unique word of God? How can preaching become part of this tradition and prolong it if it does not take account of the uniform development of what it prolongs?

Without a knowledge of the word in its source, and without a knowledge of the interpretation given to it through the centuries, present-day preaching, even if it were to set out from a sound knowledge of our contemporaries and their problems, would run the risk of becoming impoverished and going astray. Those whose *métier* is preaching know this well enough: the real problem of preaching is not so much a problem of adapting oneself to the country as a problem of being sure of supplies. And what is used up soonest is the supply of doctrine. A serious theological formation, apart from giving a priest something to say, gives him the confidence which he needs to say it, a confidence as remote from self-sufficiency as it is from an inferiority complex.

Theology does not, for all that, solve all the problems posed by the presentation of the message of salvation in terms intelligible to the man of today, just as a theoretical knowledge of psychology does not necessarily make a good psychologist. Besides, the adaptation necessary is not to be made simply in terms of language but much more, above all indeed, in terms of persons. The preaching of the same point of doctrine calls for almost infinite adaptation, according to the age, the culture, the social group of the persons to whom it is preached. The only permanent element which one can be sure of mastering is knowledge of the

message itself. The rest depends less on faculty or seminary courses
than on the intensity of the preacher's personal religious life and
his natural gifts of expression and communication.

5. *The theology of preaching*

Finally — and it is not its least important function — it is the
task of theology to study, in the light of revelation, the place of
preaching in the economy of salvation: its nature, its object, its
subject, its end, its necessity, its effectiveness, its forms and so on.
This dogmatic reflection upon preaching, begun about 1936 under
the inspiration of J. A. Jungmann, is in the course of developing
to its full dimensions. It has been stimulated by Protestant theology which is particularly active in this field, and it has benefited
also, both from the liturgical renewal, with its stress on the ritual
value of preaching, and from the rapid progress of the biblical,
patristic and liturgical sciences. The Constitution of the Liturgy
recognized and consecrated all this activity. In liturgical celebration the table of the word is inseparable from the eucharistic
table.[8] From now on theology is in a position to construct a
theology of preaching in close connection with a theology of the
sacraments.[9]

Such a theology of preaching will recognize that preaching
today, following the example of apostolic preaching, should have
the following characteristics. (a) It should be historical and
biblical, that is to say it should have as its axes the history of
salvation, and Scripture which contains this history; for the primitive *kerygma* was not presented as a "higher metaphysic,"
which would answer the questions asked by the human intellect,
but as a sacred history. (b) Since preaching announces the sal-

---

8. Const. *Sacrosanctum Concilium* on the liturgy, nn. 51 & 56; Const. *Dei
verbum* on revelation, n. 21.
9. See, for example, D. Grasso, *L'annuncio della salvezza* (Naples, 1965);
T. Soiron, *Die Verkündigung des Wortes Gottes* (Freiburg, 1943); O.
Semmelroth, *Wirkendes Wort* (Frankfurt, 1962); A. Gunthoer, *Die
Predigt* (Freiburg, 1963); S. Maggiolini, *La Predicazione nella vita
della Chiesa* (Brescia, 1961); R. Spiazzi, *Scientia Salutis* (Rome, 1963).

vation historically accomplished by Christ, it must respect the organic structure of this history. It must be Christocentric like the plan of salvation itself, following a concentric rather than linear arrangement, so that each mystery will lead back to Christ from whom it comes. (c) It must be Paschal, since among all the mysteries of Christ, the most important is the resurrection. Properly speaking it is the Resurrection which makes the Gospel good news. (d) It must be ecclesial, not only because the ministry of preaching has been entrusted to the Church, but also because the history of salvation is continued in the Church, whose work is to build up the Body of Christ. (e) It must be liturgical, for the salvation which the kerygma announces, and which catechetical instruction elaborates, is realized in the liturgy, in the sacraments, especially in baptism and the Eucharist. It is above all in the Mass that preaching reaches its complete fulfillment as a sacred, living and present word: the whole of the first part of the Mass is a liturgy of the word, the proclamation in the Church of the message of salvation. (f) It must be eschatological, that is it must present the word as the word of the living God, who asks man to make a decisive choice, involving his last end. (g) Finally, it must be a witness, that is it must show in the life of the preacher the power of the Gospel to transform human existence.[10]

BIBLIOGRAPHY VIII

BOUYER, L., *Le sens de la vie sacerdotale*, Tournai, 1959.
IN collaboration, « La Prédication », *Lumière et Vie*, n. 46, janvier-mars, 1960.
IN collaboration, *Parole de Dieu et Liturgie*, coll. « Lex Orandi », n. 25, Paris, 1958.
GRASSO, D., *L'annuncio della salvezza*, Napoli, 1965.
GRELOT, P., «La Parole de Dieu s'adresse-t-elle à l'homme d'aujour-d'hui », *Maison-Dieu*, n. 80 (1964) : 151-200 ; ID., « Exégèse, théologie et pastorale», *Nouvelle Revue théologique*, 88 (1966) : 3-13, 132-148.

---

10. R. Latourelle, *Theology of Revelation*, pp. 224-227.

HAENSLI, E., « La prédication d'aujourd'hui, fruit d'une théologie vivante », dans : *Questions théologiques aujourd'hui*, III, Bruges et Paris, 1966, pp. 63-89.

HENRY, A.-M., éd., *L'annonce de l'Évangile aujourd'hui*, Paris, 1962.

O'CONNOR, J. M., *La prédication selon saint Paul*, Paris, 1966.

1. *Possible tension*

Pastoral action and theology are closely bound together, as theory and practice, life and reflection on life. Nevertheless in the concrete the co-ordination of the two activities remains difficult. If it is true that exact theological reflection can give to pastoral action the security it needs, it is nonetheless true that the two abilities are rarely met within the same person. Theologians and pastors constitute two groups sociologically distinct and differentiated. It even happens that tensions arise between pastors engaged in apostolic action and theologians consecrated to university teaching or research.

From the nature of the case, the theologian himself is incapable of mastering the whole field of theological science. He must specialize in a particular discipline, more often than not occupying a restricted territory in this discipline. Within the modest sector he explores the bibliography is immense. From his post there he hears well enough the voices of the world and the pastor's appeals, but it is not always possible for him to answer them. If he listens only to his own apostolic zeal, he risks failing to follow the rhythm of scientific production; he even runs the risk of abandoning the austere labors of research for the more immediate and consoling results of the priestly ministry to the great loss of pastors themselves, since things will be even worse if no-one is faithful to his own duties. However, that may be, the isolation of many theologians devoted to research can give the impression that theology is, as a branch of knowledge, a luxury reserved for an intellectual aristocracy, and that it treats of problems other than those of our time in an unintelligible language which cuts it off from real life.

On their side priests engaged in apostolic life know well enough in theory that they need to be enlightened by theology, but how, in the midst of a feverish round of duties leaving no intervals for reflection, are they to find the time and means to confront the problems of the apostolate as theology suggests they should? A good many glance hastily through the reviews which deal in theological popularization, and thus take cognizance in a vague way of the results of research. Others attend conferences and study days, but realize that they are unable to make the transfer from scientific knowledge to practical adaptation in terms of their pastoral work. And in some cases there exists a positive contempt for theology, an open anti-intellectualism.

The result is that there can be tension between those who believe in action and those who put their trust in the fruitfulness of disinterested study. Pastoral priests ask what can be the use of speculation which does not begin from the concrete problems posed by Christians today. And on their side theologians ask how overworked pastors in more or less continuous motion can give satisfactory answers to the often difficult questions which people ask. Is the risk not too great?

In Christian antiquity and in the hey-day of the Middle Ages these tensions did not exist or existed conspicuously less. Theology was nourished on Scripture, and pastoral and spiritual writing was scarcely distinct from theological writing. There was a continuity between Scripture and life. In the Middle Ages themselves, however, as theological knowledge became more and more considerable, theology began to be differentiated and departmentalized. With the Renaissance the study of the Bible became more and more scientific, and in this way the unity which had existed in antiquity was gradually broken up and theological disciplines began to proliferate, each one operating on its own account, more or less on the margin of life. Are pastors and theologians then condemned never to meet again?

2. *Necessary collaboration*

Before talking about the possible forms which collaboration between theologians and pastors might take, it is important to recognize that such collaboration is essential and can be fruitful for both.

The pastoral priest needs theology and the theologian. For theology is not simply a stage in priestly formation to be gone through once and for all. Like the word of God, whose servant it is in the understanding it gives of this word, it should never cease to nourish priestly life. If it does not, faith itself grows anemic and dies. For theology is the cultivation of faith. If certain pastoral gestures seem poor, especially in the matter of the liturgy, is it not because the pastor does not see the wealth of doctrine which they express? And how is the pastor to confront the problems which are placed before him without appealing to the theologian: problems of education and religious denomination, problems of religious liberty, problems of married and family life, of the relationships of Catholics with civil society and with non-Christian religions? Ecumenical dialogue with the separated Christian communities growing everywhere more eager and intense is possible only on the basis of a sound theology. Again the pastor has constant need of the theologian to make sure that there will be a real encounter between the word of God and the man of a technological culture.

On the other hand, the theologian needs the pastor. For the laboratory where the theologian works is not confined to the sources of antiquity but embraces also the whole life of the people of God as it is today. And it is the pastor who, by the very nature of his office, listens like a physician to the life of the Church. His pastoral duties place him at the cross-roads where all its agonies and problems and appeals for help meet. He sees the signs of the times in their concrete manifestations. And so it is in keeping in constant contact with the pastor that the theologian will remain aware of what the Church asks of him, that he will experience the need to investigate more deeply the content of the faith. If it can be said that there is no real pastoral progress without theological progress, it can also be said that there is no real theological progress without attention to what pastors say, and to the problems which they propose. The great conciliar constitutions are after all only the theologians' answer to the questions which pastors have long been asking in the exercise of their ministry, in their confrontation wtih a new world and new structures of thought. Similarly, the distinguished works of present day theology are written in response to the demands of apostolic life.

If they are really conscious in this way of how theology and pastoral activity stand in mutual need of each other, theologians and pastors will not seek isolation but seek to meet.

3. *Forms of collaboration*

Collaboration between pastors and theologians presupposes as its point of departure that both are aware of the common bond which unites them, that is the service of the word of God. Their audiences and the degree of technicality with which they speak to them may be different, but their objective remains the same, to serve the Church and to serve men. In this connection one should stress that theology today is more anxious to serve than it was formerly. Not to take cognizance of this new orientation would be to ignore the real state of affairs. If it has for a long time been possible to accuse theology of operating on the periphery of life that reproach is today only a half-truth. Certainly, by the very demands of theological science, theology will always be obliged to deploy its forces on several fronts, some rather remote from life, like research and textual criticism, editions of texts, the analysis of sources, others half-way between pure research and pastoral activity, like its teaching functions. This is, in any case, the fate of all the sciences. But what distinguishes the activity of contemporary theology taken as a whole is its consciousness of being at the service of the Church, and of the Church as she is today.

After acquiring some understanding of the word of God, the theologian tries to make it accessible to the men of his own time, and the men of every age have their own problems and their own language. Challenged by the new situations and new questions of men today the theologian makes it his business to respond to them by ceaselessly returning to the one word of God. He is the liaison officer between the word of God and the word of men and "his function makes him an interpreter of the word of God for his contemporaries." [1] What distinguishes the theology of men like Chenu, Guardini, Congar, Rahner, Semmelroth and Schillebeeckx, Mouroux and Von Balthasar and Häring, is their effort to disclose the riches of the word of God to the men of our own time, and to make its message accessible to them. Theology today is attentive to the movements of contemporary thought and to the repercussions of these movements as they affect the Church. It serves the Church's mission in the world and is the locus of her dialogue with the world. It never ceases to show that Christ is at all times the Light of men, yesterday, today and tomorrow. In this respect theology is eminently pastoral. At a more highly technical level, therefore, the preoccupations of the present day theologian coincides with those of the pastor. It should be realized too that theology's task today is particularly difficult because the rhythm of life has been accelerated. Life is outstripping reflection.

Apart from this form of collaboration constituted by their mutual consciousness of a common mission, there are many practical forms which collaboration between pastors and theologians can take.

It was evident at the time of the Council how fruitful dialogue between specialists (*periti*) and pastors could be, whether in the form of occasional consultation or in the form of working together

---

1. P. Grelot, "Exégèse, théologie et pastorale," *Nouvelle Revue théologique*, 88 (1966), p. 140.

on commissions. In a great many dioceses throughout the world changes of structure are being made in order to encourage a habitual exchange of views between pastors and theologians. The following are a few examples.

(a) Study sessions or refresher courses allow priests engaged in the ministry to become *au courant* of contemporary theological work and aware of results of research which can be assimilated into pastoral practice. These meetings give them also an opportunity for renewing and reunifying themselves, for laying the foundations of pastoral action and saving their thought, in its struggles at close quarters with manifold and diverse circumstances, from being disintegrated or exhausted. And there is no less profit for theologians, who, thanks to their colleagues, leave the security of sources and syntheses to make contact with the problems of life.

Refresher courses and study sessions are, however, exceptional means. What is needed is really permanent formation. The common life among the priests of a diocese encouraged by the Council,[2] would perhaps if it were to become general, be a way of ensuring this permanent formation, which ought to come about not through the withdrawal or isolation of individuals but through some structure which would include every priest. In an age when everything is organized and provided for in advance, would it not be possible to arrange the pastoral life of priests in a way which would give a special place to theological information and theological reflection?

(b) At a diocesan level there is the formation of pastoral teams, which count among their members one or more theologians who take part in the work of the team and who live together. These relay-theologians can exercise a role between that of the pastor and the theologian exclusively consecrated to research. One could not indeed ask specialists to be always in the public eye at the mercy of the questions asked by the faithful without depriving them of time indispensable to research. The role of these

---

2. Decree *Presbyterorum Ordinis* on the ministry and life of priests, n. 8.

relay-theologians would be, for example, to ensure a certain quality of preaching in the diocese, to work of the revision of catechisms, to resolve complicated cases of morals, to throw light on doctrinal problems. In a pastoral theology which takes in the whole field of action these mixed teams of pastors and theologians seem to be a necessity even, for apostolic work.

(c) Lastly, at the level of priestly formation in seminaries and faculties of theology, the organic connection between the study of the word of God and its impact on the problems of men today is being better and better made. The decree on the formation of priests says explicitly: "Let them learn to look for solutions to human problems in the light of revelation, to apply eternal truths to the changing conditions of human affairs and to communicate them in a manner adapted to the men of our time." [3] Normally these indications from the Council would involve changes in the very structure of ecclesiastical studies, in order to give the future priest at the same time a sound understanding of the Mystery and a more intense pastoral formation. When the living synthesis of what preoccupies the theologian and the pastor has been made at the very level of priestly consciousness at the time of its formation, a divorce between pastors and theologians, without being impossible will surely be more rare.

BIBLIOGRAPHY IX

DENIS, H., *Pour une perspective théologique*, Paris, 1967.
DUQUOC, C., « Théologie et mission de l'Église », *Lumière et Vie*, n. 71, janvier-février 1965, pp. 55-80.
GRELOT, P., « Exégèse, théologie et pastorale », *Nouvelle Revue théologique*, 88 (1966) : 3-13, 132-148.
KLOSTERMANN, F., « La formazione pastorale del Clero alla luce del Vaticano II », *Seminarium*, 18 (1966) : 626-674.
LAMBERT, B., « Les deux démarches de la théologie », *Nouvelle Revue théologique*, 89 (1967) : 257-280.

---

3. Decree *Optatam totius* on priestly formation, n. 16.

MAZIERS, M., « Le pasteur et les théologiens », *Lumière et Vie*, n. 71, janvier-février 1965, pp. 3-14.

SEMMELROTH, O., *Le ministère spirituel*, Paris-Fribourg, 1965.

CHAPTER III   LAY THEOLOGIANS

Formerly even the idea of a layman followng a theological course leading to a doctorate, and still more the idea of a layman teaching theology in a university, was a matter of exception. The Church was represented as a society divided into two classes with quite distinct functions; on the one hand there were the hierarchy, the religious and the clergy, the depositories of authority, the custodians of the word and the sole persons qualified to propound or investigate it, and on the other hand there was the laity, on its knees before the altar, seated in front of the pulpit, sometimes called upon to undertake teaching duties but at an inferior level. The second Vatican Council has fortunately abolished this image.[1]

1. *Historical summary*

It is, besides, a relatively recent image. They were laymen, not clerics who were the first theologians of the Church: Justin,

---

1. E. Hamel, "Aequalitas fundamentalis omnium Christifidelium in Ecelesia secundum Concilium Vaticanum II," *Periodica* 56 (1967), pp. 247-266.

Tertullian, Pantaenus, Clement, Origen (afterwards ordained a priest), Victorinus, Pamphylius, Sextus the African, Lactantius, Prosper of Aquitaine, Evagrius and so on. Many of the Fathers of the Church began their theological work as laymen, men like St. Cyprian, St. Basil, St. Gregory Nazianzus, St. Jerome, St. Paulinus of Nola, St. Augustine. "It is a very modern idea and foreign to the patristic era," says Marrou, "this distinction between a religious culture reserved solely for the clergy and a secular culture legitimate for the laity." [2]

During the early centuries of the Church the laity took an active interest in theological problems, and theological thought owed much of its progress to them. It was an accident of history which handed over to the clergy the upper reaches of religious culture, namely the overthrow of the Roman Empire by the barbarians and the salvage of western culture by Churchmen — by bishops and monks. In the east, which was spared this ordeal, both theological culture and culture as such have been less monopolized by the clergy.

The humanist movement, by enlarging the laity's cultural world and their share in the sacred sciences, fostered their reintegration into the compass of religious thought, so that men like S. Piccolomini, Contarini, and Reginald Pole wrote, as laymen, theological treatises. The line of lay theologians was continued in the seventeenth and eighteenth centuries with the help of Jansenism and Gallicanism, and then in the nineteenth century in the anti-Gallicanism debate, with Veuillot and de Maistre.[3] Several apologists of modern times have been laymen, Auguste Nicolas, Pascal, Chateaubriand, Brunetière, Chesterton, Blondel, Jacques Maritain and Jean Guitton for instance. Finally it should be stressed that many of the themes of modern theology have been presented and even expounded by laymen in literary form, both

---

2. H. I. Marrou, *Saint Augustin et la fin de la culture antique* (Paris, 1938), p. 383.
3. Y. Congar, *Jalons pour une théologie du läicat* (Paris, 1953), pp. 428-432.

in the novel and in poetry. The works of Péguy, Claudel, Mauriac and Bernanos spring to mind.

To tell the truth however it is in the twentieth century, with the birth of organized Catholic Action, that the Church has taken a more lively cognizance of the laity's role in the Church, of their prophetic function and consequently of the need for a sound religious formation to prepare them for their teaching tasks. This cognizance, which has been growing for more than half a century, reached its climax during the recent Council. The second Vatican Council was characterized by a deepened understanding of the mystery of the Church. It is in her effort to define herself better that the Church has given the laity its proper place and it is in becoming an ecclesiology of the whole Church that theology has made explicit the laity's function there.

2. *The laity's position and mission according to the second Vatican Council*

By the term "laity" the Council means "all the faithful except those in holy orders or in a religious state sanctioned by the Church; that is, the faithful who after being incorporated into Christ by baptism are defined by their membership of the people of God, and so made in their own way sharers in the priestly, prophetic and kingly functions of Christ, playing their own part in the Church's mission both in the Church and in the world." [4] Just as Christ is the supreme prophet, since he is the Father's Son in Person, revealing to men through his words and his manner of life their vocation as sons and daughters of God, so he makes of all those whom he incorporates into his Body his prophets and his witnesses.[5] In virtue of their baptism and their confirmation, the laity are sent as apostles.[6] "Upon all Christians is laid the splendid burden of making God's message of salvation known

---

4. Const. *Lumen Gentium* on the Church, n. 31.
5. *Ibid.*, n. 35.
6. *Ibid.*, nn. 10, 11, 12, 31, 42.

and accepted by all men throughout all the world." [7] The laity work for the evangelization of the world, but in their own way, that of men living in the world.[8]

The laity share in the prophetic office of Christ through the united witness of their lives and their words. Their life of faith, hope and charity, in accordance with the Gospel, is already a living teaching, an existential language. In showing what the Gospel is in practice, they reveal to those about them a new way of living, a way which is completely filial, surrendered to the Father's will as expressed through Christ.[9]

The laity are asked also to witness explicitly to the word of God and to teach. The decree on the apostolate of the laity declares that the laity should take an active part "in the investigation and defense of Christian principles and in applying them in a way adapted to the problems of our time." [10] "They are asked to collaborate fully in spreading the word of God, especially through catechetical instruction." [11] In missionary territories they should be ready to collaborate in a more immediate way with the hierarchy, to fulfill a special mission in preaching the Gospel and communicating Christian doctrine, in order to strengthen the nascent Church.[12] The Council praises the laity who "in universities and scientific institutes advance by their historical or scientific- religious research, the knowledge of peoples and religions." [13] It encourages the laity moreover, to devote themselves to theological teaching and research. "It is to be hoped," says *Gaudium et Spes,* "that many of the laity will receive an adequate formation in the

---

7. Decree *Apostolicam Actuositatem* on the apostolate of the laity, n. 3.
8. Const. *Lumen Gentium* on the Church, n. 35.
9. R. Latourelle, "La sainteté, signe de la Révélation," *Gregorianum,* 46 (1965), pp. 50-52; Id., "Les laïcs, ferment de la société," *Relations,* January 1967, pp. 3-5 and February 1967, p. 34; Id., "La testimonianza della vita segno di salvezza" in *Laici sulle vie del Concilio* (Assisi, 1966), pp. 377-395.
10. Decree *Apostolicam Actuositatem* on the apostolate of the laity, n. 6.
11. *Ibid.,* n. 10: Declaration on Christian education, n. 7.
12. Decree *Ad Gentes* on the missionary activity of the Church, n. 41.
13. *Ibid.,* n. 41.

sacred sciences, and that some of them will take up these studies professionally and engage in theological research." [14]

The apostolate of teaching at all levels can reach its full effectiveness only through a more complete and more varied formation. If the mission of the laity is defined by its function in the Church, it follows that it cannot exercise its mission without a formation appropriate to that function. So the Council, after insisting on the apostolate of the laity, stresses with the same insistency the necessity of an adequate formation.

This formation for the apostolate presupposes an education in the humanities, a spiritual formation, and "a solid doctrinal knowledge in matters theological, moral and philosophical." [15] To be prepared to engage in dialogue with believers and unbelievers the laity should attend the study centers and institutes of higher learning founded for this purpose.[16] In the declaration on Christian education the Council recommends that those who teach in Catholic schools should be "trained with particular care" and have a sound religious knowledge "certified by an appropriate diploma." [17] Later on it adds, "In Catholic universities lacking a theological faculty, an institute or chair of theology should be established to provide lectures for both lay and clerical students." [18] Future theologians, in both teaching and research, should be educated at the great centers of university life.

There is no doubt that the laity are asked to accept a serious theological formation to prepare them to be dispensers of Christian truth not only at the level of catechetical instruction but also at the strictly university level, with both the teaching and research duties proper to this.

These indications from the Council correspond moreover, to the necessities of the present time. Up to now, religious teaching has in effect in many countries been in the hands of the clergy

---

14. Const. *Gaudium et Spes,* n. 62.
15. Decree *Apostolicam Actuositatem* on the apostolate of the laity, n. 29.
16. *Ibid.,* n. 32.
17. Declaration on Christian education, n. 8.
18. *Ibid.,* n. 10.

and of religious. From now on, with the growth of population and the consequent explosion of the educational bulge, it is the laity themselves who should take over to a greater and greater extent this duty of the Church. It will be necessary gradually therefore to form and educate lay teachers for every level of theological work. The laity should not only teach, moreover, but write, collaborate in the revision of catechetical work, edit reviews, write books for the laity. Another vast and important department, that of the means of social communication (the press, radio, the cinema and television) is making an equal demand on those with special qualifications, for their work gives them daily opportunities of making value judgments on religious problems and problems with religious implications. So the decree on the means of communication recommends "a considerable increase in the number of schools, university faculties and separate institutes in which journalists, film, radio and television writers . . . can be given an integrated education permeated by a Christian spirit." It adds that "literary critics and critics of films, radio and television should be thoroughly trained so that each may have the best possible understanding of the criteria involved in his own special sphere of value judgments, and at the same time be educated and encouraged to make judgments in which moral issues are presented in their own intrinsic light." [19]

It remains now to consider the sort of teaching the laity need and the position of the laity as teachers and research workers in theology.

3. *The teaching of theology to the laity*

There already exist in the Church different forms of religious teaching designed for the laity. Sometimes it is a matter of mere lectures for adults who want to complete their religious formation. Apart from this there are real centers of religious education with regular courses extending over a period of two or three years, leading to a diploma which allows its holder to teach in Catholic

---

19. Decree *Inter mirifica* on the means of social communications, n. 15.

schools. These centers are either of a university type or attached to universities. The theology taught in them is often of an excellent quality and given by teachers of remark. But it may also happen that it is nothing more than a sort of popularization of the teaching given to the clergy, a theology liberated from its scientific rigors and long demonstrations, a theology without tears. In many places the laity find themselves restricted to separate courses, leading, it is true, to diplomas but not to diplomas equivalent to the degrees conferred on the clergy. It has still not been resolutely decided to open faculties of theology to the laity and to give them a theological teaching not less rigorous than that given to the clergy.

In 1944 John Courtney Murray rightly insisted, in two remarakable articles, on the necessity of giving to the laity, not a mere abridged version of the teaching in seminaries, but a really scientific theology; on the other hand he exaggerated, it would seem, the difference between a theology for the laity and a theology for the clergy.[20]

Theology, as taught to the clergy, he said, is essentially aimed at preparing them for the priestly ministry. It makes of the cleric a member of the teaching Church, at the service of the magisterium in its function as the guardian and interpreter of the word. It prepares him to be the dispenser of the sacraments. The layman on the other hand, is involved in the world, and in a world more and more secularized. It is in this world that he has to act, as a mediator between the Church and civil society; it is in this world that he has to prolong the action of the Church where the hierarchy cannot penetrate. The laity do not have to administer the sacraments but to act as a leaven in the life of the world. So, John Courtney Murray concluded, they need a theology that really is so, but a theology with its own distinct character, in accord with their function and their mission in the Church. This theology will attach great importance to the actions and personality of the pro-

---

20. J. C. Murray, "Towards a Theology for the Layman: the Problem and its Finality," *Theological Studies* 5 (1944), pp. 43-75; "The Pedagogical Problem," *Ibid.*, 5 (1944), pp. 340-376.

fessor and to his knowledge of the contemporary world. In the exposition of revealed truth it will adopt a historical order, that is the order of the economy of salvation itself, rather than a logical order. Consequently it will be more biblical, more Christocentric, more soteriological, after the manner of the Scriptures and the Fathers of the Church. It will stress the inner and organic harmony of the Christian mysteries and their power to give life to the whole of Christian existence. It will avoid polemics and apply itself to expounding a serene synthesis of the wealth of the Christian Mystery. In a world indifferent to it, it will act by the injection of life and the diffusion of light. It will set out to demonstrate in Christianity a new order which embraces everything, a message with a universal import, which gives consistency to the whole of reality.

When one re-reads these articles, after twenty years, in the context of the second Vatican Council, one cannot help noticing that the essential demands which John Courtney Murray makes of a theology for the laity practically coincide with the declarations of the Council on the theological formation of the clergy.[21] In faithfulness to revelation and to the tradition of the Church, says the Council, theology must be more historical and more biblical. It must be more Christocentric, since Christ is the epiphany of God in the world, the apex of the history of salvation. It must show how each of the mysteries can nourish the dialogue of the soul with God. It must be adapted to the needs of contemporary man and based on a deepened awareness of his mentality and his aspirations.[22]

In the light of the conciliar texts on the formation of priests and on the preparation of the laity for their prophetic office the difference between the theological education of the clergy and that of the laity does not seem so great. At the level of teaching degree and of the doctorate this difference does not exist. At the level of basic theological formation (a conspectus of theology) there doubtless exist problems peculiar to each of the two groups —

---

21. Decree *Optatam totius* on the formation of priests, n. 16.
22. *Ibid.*, n. 16; Const. *Gaudium et Spes*, n. 62.

the administration of the sacrament of penance, for instance, in the case of the clergy. But the points in common are from the outset more numerous, the explanation of dogma, the teaching of Scripture, moral theology and history. Even the problems formerly regarded as reserved for the laity, lay spirituality, the theology of terrestrial values and so on, cannot but gain by being discussed before clergy and laity together in the same faculty. In order to address itself specifically to the laity modern theology has only to pay attention to the laity's problems, which are also the problems of the faith and of the Church, and to become more aware of the problems of conscience which present themselves to the believer today.

To open universities and ecclesiastical faculties to clergy and laity alike seems a more and more consistent tendency in the Church. This orientation will be wholly beneficial, to the clergy, who will thus come out of their isolation, and to the laity, who will feel visibly incorporated into the people of God and asked to play their part according to their state of life, in the prophetic function of the Church. To meet the special demands of the laity and of the clergy, it will be only a matter of making syllabuses more flexible and providing a certain number of options, with seminars or practical work. The era of seminaries and scholasticates separated from the universities and in isolation from the laity certainly seems over. If there is no reason to exclude the clergy from the secular sciences, there is even less reason to deny the laity access to faculties of theology. Every Christian has a right to investigate and deepen his faith and to devote himself to theological research. Here too the Council has brought the clergy and the laity together: it has reduced distances which are more apparent than real.

4. *The teaching of theology by the laity*

The Council, as we have seen, hoped that many of the laity would devote themselves to theological teaching and research. The theological function, in effect, is not a prerogative of the hierarchy and the clergy, but a function common to every Christian.

At the level of theological research, there is no difference between the clergy and the laity. The latter, like all the faithful, clerical or lay, are subject to the magisterium. As experts in their own field they are subject to the judgment of their peers, to whom it belongs to assess their competence and their integrity. The experience of the Council demonstrated, in the commissions where *periti* or experts united to study a problem, that there is no difference made among experts, whether they are bishops, priests, religious or lay. The arguments of a lay expert, when they were well-founded, had no less weight than those of a bishop.

Similarly it can happen, and it will happen more and more often in the future, that the laity, as doctors in theology, teach in ecclesiastical universities or state universities. At this level of higher education in theology is there any difference between the position of the clergy and that of the laity?

We know that the Church in her entirety is a priestly and prophetic people. Through baptism, all Christians are members of Christ, and have their part to play in the mission of the whole Body. But all the members of Christ have not the same function. In order that the Church may accomplish her mission, it is necessary that Christ should be present in her and act through her. It is for this reason that Christ has chosen ministers whom he makes capable of acting in the Church in his name, and with his own authority as Head of the Body.[23] Because they share in the charge given to the apostles, "God gives to priests the grace which makes them ministers of Christ among the nations, serving in the sacred office of the Gospel, so that the nations may be an acceptable offering sanctified by the Holy Spirit." [24] It is then in virtue of his priestly ordination, and not only by delegation of the bishop, that the priest receives from God the mission to preach and to teach. The first function of the priest, and also his first responsibility, is to "announce the Gospel of God to all men" [25] including non-Christians and lapsed Christians. Every priest is consecrated in order

---

23. Decree *Presbyterorum Ordinis* on the ministry and life of priests, n. 2.
24. *Ibid.*, n. 2.
25. *Ibid.*, n. 4.

to be a *doctor,* a teacher. This teaching function at the level of the *kerygma* and of catechetical instruction obviously presupposes a sound theological formation, but it does not mean that the task of teaching theology, as *the science of the faith,* is attached to the priesthood as such. If the priest teaches theology, this task may be considered as a normal prolongation of his function as minister of the word but not as a duty of his priesthood.

At the level of the deepening of faith by theological teaching, clergy and laity are in an identical situation. The laity indeed, though they share in the prophetic mission of the Church, not in virtue of being ministers of Christ the Head, but in virtue of their baptismal incorporation into the people of God, are nevertheless, also called to witness to Christ through their lives and their words.[26] The specific character of their witness is that it is made within the texture of the world. When the laity exercise their prophetic mission at the level of science, through teaching theology, they do so in virtue of the same right as the clergy, that is in virtue of their baptism and in virtue of a charism, or special gift of the Holy Spirit for teaching the Gospel. The Council points out on this subject that priests "discerning spirits with the eye of faith, should know how to discover the charisms of the laity in all their forms, the humblest and the most exalted; they should recognize them with joy and eagerly develop them." [27]

The situation of the laity then, at the level of theology as a science, does not differ from that of the clergy. For theologians to teach, whether they be lay or clerical, it is enough that they should be qualified by a sound university education, formally attested to by one of the higher degrees (a master's degree or a doctorate).

The lay theologian, whether engaged in teaching or engaged in research will bring to theology an original, irreplaceable contribution.[28] What distinguishes him as a member of the laity, is his

---

26. Const. *Lumen Gentium* on the Church, n. 35.
27. Decree *Presbyterorum ordinis* on the ministry and life of priests, n. 9.
28. "Promuovere la cultura teologica in Italia," *La Civiltà Cattolica,* 118 (1967), p. 317; P. Foresi, "Vi possono essere teologi laici?" in *I laici e la teologia* (Roma, 1967), pp. 24-25.

life in the world and so what could distinguish lay theological teaching and research is the vision of the message of the Gospel from the point of view of its incarnation in the world. For the realities of the world have an intrinsic value, willed by God himself, and should therefore, be assumed by the Gospel (as flesh was assumed by the Word) and led towards Christ. In this task of incarnating the word in the world, it would seem normal that the laity, carrying more consciously within them the voice of the world, of its anxieties and its struggles, would light upon more exact answers to contemporary problems and needs. Since they are involved in the life of the world they see further into the implication of dogma for Christian life in the world, perceiving aspects which escape the clergy. Their role is particularly important in problems where theology abuts on other disciplines in the theology of the sciences, in the theology of terrestrial values, in questions of the relation between theology and sociology and between theology and psychology. One should add that the laity seem sometimes to be more creative than the clergy, not hesitating to blaze new trails, while the clergy, because of their special function as guardians and servants of the word (1 Tim 6, 20) sometimes exhibit more timidity in the face of new situations.

It is to be hoped then that in the post-conciliar period lay and clerical theologians will collaborate in research, just as it it is hoped that theologians will collaborate with pastors. The reflections of the cleric, roused by lay presence to a sense of the concrete and of the urgent demands of the earthly city, will be more attentive to the signs of the times and run less risk of raising their constructions in an unreal world. And on the other hand the lay theologian, awakened to an awareness of the mystery and of the heavenly city, which the priest recalls and signifies by his presence in the world, will not cease to respond to the tensions of the present world and the world which is to come, after the imperfect and provisional manner of all our responses until the day of eternal vision.

BIBLIOGRAPHY X

BRUGNOLI, P., *La Missione dei laici nel mondo d'oggi*, 2ª ed., Brescia, 1967, pp. 125-128.

CHENU, M.-D., « Laïcs en chrétienté », dans : *La Parole de Dieu*, vol. II, *L'Évangile dans le temps*, Paris, 1964, pp. 71-83.

CONGAR, Y., *Jalons pour une théologie du laïcat*, Paris, 1953.

COULSON, J., ed., *Theology and the University*, London, 1964. Spécialement : FRANSEN, P., « The Teaching Theology on the Continent and its Implications », pp. 78-104.

IN collaboration, « Laïcs et mission de l'Église », *Lumière et Vie*, nn. 63 et 65 (1963).

FORESI, P., FAILLA, C., FALLACARA, G., ZANGHI, G., *I laici e la Teologia*, Roma, 1967.

LUYTEN, N. A., éd., *Recherche et Culture. Tâche d'une Université catholique*, Fribourg, Suisse, 1965.

MARTELET, G., *Les Idées maîtresses de Vatican II*, Bruges et Paris, 1966, pp. 231-256.

MURRAY, J. C., « Towards a Theology for the Laymen : the Problem and its Finality », *Theological Studies*, 5 (1944) : 43-75 ; « The Pedagogical Problem », *ibid.*, pp. 340-376.

ÖRSY, L., « Theological Degrees for the Laymen », *The Month*, december 1964, pp. 297-304.

PATTARO, G., « L'impegno teologico del laicato », *Humanitas*, febbraio-marzo, 1966, pp. 233-244.

PORTIER, V., *Anthropologie et apostolat des laïcs*, Paris, 1965.

« Promuovere la cultura teologica in Italia », *La Civiltà Cattolica*, 118 (1967) : 313-318.

CHAPTER IV   THEOLOGY AND INTERIOR LIFE

1. *The antinomy of science and praxis*

Quite a number of students in theology find difficulty in establishing a just balance between their spiritual life and their intellectual life. Theology, the science of God, seems to put them at a distance from God, to dry them up instead of nourishing them. As a consequence they may ask themselves anxiously, and then bitterly, whether theology itself is not responsible for this spiritual anemia. At least they ask how they can escape this danger, and reconcile their desire to know with their desire to love God.

First of all let us bear in mind that theology is not, in itself the interior life. It would therefore be vain to ask it to be what it is not, to transform itself into a sermon or a spiritual exhortation. Theology is a *discursus* or discursive exercise of the mind, seeking to understand the mystery believed and possessed in faith. It is the cultivation of faith. On the other hand, the malaise experienced, or the sense of rupture between theology, as the science of God, and life in God is not a necessary effect of theology, since Doctors like Augustine, Basil, the two Gregories, Bernard, Anselm, Bonaventure, Thomas Aquinas, Peter Canisius and Robert Bellarmine drew men through the living flame of their charity. They accomplished in themselves the harmonious synthesis of science and sanctity. The science of God and life in God are not then irreconcilable. It seems even, that theology, when it succeeds, opens into the ground of sanctity.

The antinomy which can exist between theology and spiritual life is only one instance of the still more radical antinomy which affects the whole of man. As a result of sin the unity between knowledge and love is left in a fragile state. Man does not do all the good he knows and his life often accords ill with the truth which he professes. The understanding and the will have a tendency to function each on its own account. The intellect can live in, as it were a close circuit, and seek to be self-sufficient, and this is the more likely in that since the possession of truth gives the mind a certain satisfaction, there is a danger that it will simply delight in this, and ignore the practical demands which truth makes. Loss of balance of the opposite sort can also happen, that is in action which is without intellectual roots and without considered orientation. In his thirst for life a man may fall into what constitutes in practice a contempt for intelligence. It is in this way that there arise all the deviations of a spiritual life which is lacking in insight.

2. *Faith, the principle of unification*

How then are we to ensure the unity which is always in danger, the unity between knowledge and love, between the science of God and life in God? Normally the unifying factor in our being is faith. All authentic spiritual life must be based on an authentic knowledge of God and of Christ. But this knowledge is given to us through revelation and through faith, which is the free entrusting of the whole man to God who is revealing and giving himself, a full submission of both intellect and will.[1]

We can progress in our understanding of revelation of the word of God in a two-fold way, by a discursive effort of the

---

1. Const. *Dei verbum* on revelation, n. 5.

mind, seeking to understand more fully the mystery received in faith, or by way of an affective connaturality with the Mystery revealed, that is through charity and the gifts of the Holy Spirit. And these two modes of knowledge, both within the compass of faith, are intended to bear fruit in each other and to nourish the life of the soul.

The discursive knowledge of the object of faith, being the work of a believing Christian, that is of a man living in a communion of thought with the Thought of God, should normally contribute to the progress of the interior life. Theology, which is, as it were, an inventory of the unfathomable riches of the Mystery of Christ, discloses the infinite dimensions of this Mystery which sheds light in all directions. Not only does theology seek the specific intelligibility of each mystery as such, but, more than that, it seeks a perception of the manifold bonds which unite the mysteries among themselves, a synthetic vision of the wonderful economy which they constitute. Through analysis, it reaches up to a contemplation of the whole Mystery in its rich and complex unity. All this work of investigation of the Mystery is accompanied for the theologian by daily converse with the word of God. Is it possible, therefore, that this familiarity with Scripture, this contemplation of God's saving design in all its wisdom and splendor should not arouse wonder and love? Normally every insight should bear fruit in love, and end in deeper commitment. Would there not be something fearful and abnormal in the situation if this progress in the knowledge of God did not involve a progress in love? Theology does nourish the interior life, but in its own way, that is to say, in enlightening the understanding, in releasing from the Mystery the light of its intelligibility, in manifesting its value as salvation: it is in offering it as a good (and in that its truth consists) that it makes it capable of being desired.

Theology can serve the life of the soul in a valuable way also by protecting it from the multifarious deviations of the spiritual life: illuminism, quietism, emotionalism, activism, superstition, a throng of secondary devotions, and so on. Again it can rectify and purify our ways of conceiving divine reality, and so lead us to a truer knowledge of God and a better grounded spirituality.

The object of faith may be assimilated also through supernatural contemplation, grounded in a union of love with Christ and his Mystery. In this mode of knowledge, the fruit of charity and of the gifts of the Holy Spirit, the soul is more passive than active: she allows herself to be entered and possessed by the Mystery and experiences it within herself. We know that simple and unsophisticated people with little education can penetrate more deeply into the Mystery by this way of love, than powerful and cultivated minds, through all the resources and laws of reason. For the Mystery of God, being a personal Mystery and a Mystery of grace, can really be known only to him who loves: "He who has my commandments and keeps them, he it is who loves me, and he who loves me will be loved by my Father, and I will love him and manifest myself to him" (Jn 14, 21). Faith, when it is thus nourished by charity becomes the source of vision. Doing the will of God attracts the eyes of Christ, who reveals himself to his disciple. The immanence of Christ in the soul, veiled up to now, begins to be revealed, and at the same time the immanence of the Father in the Son (Jn 14, 9-10). The Holy Spirit infuses into the soul of him who loves an affective consent which is the source of understanding. He who does Christ's will grasps Christ's thought, shares in the tastes and inclinations of Christ. The spirit of Christ makes him live on the thought and the love of Christ. In some privileged souls, God can enlarge still more if he wishes, this knowledge of living faith, even to extraordinary mystical graces.

When faith is authentic, that is wholly nourished by love, discursive knowledge helps the supernatural illumination of affective knowledge, and this, in its turn, stimulates, under the pressure of love, the quest of the mind. It is in this way that harmony between the science of God and life in God is realized.

3. *The primacy of charity and of prayer*

This deeper unity of faith and charity, like that of knowledge and love in the natural order, remains always fragile, always threatened, and always to be safe-guarded. Without totally disappearing, charity can become weak and languid. Progress in the theoretical knowledge of truth does not necessarily go hand in hand with progress in love. One can know much without loving much. A disproportion then, if not a rupture, is always possible between the Gospel as known and the Gospel as lived. He who hears the word of God does not always put it into practice (Mt 7, 21-27), and does not always bear fruit in his life (Mt 13, 18-23). Striking intellectual achievement does not always coincide with striking sanctity; for the measure of sanctity is love. There can be a real threat of a dichotomy between science and life in that scientific specialization curtails the opportunities for exercising charity.

Progress in the science of God will not be accompanied by a corresponding progress in life in God unless we maintain in the very midst of our life of study, the primacy of love and of a love which expresses itself in terms of fidelity in action: fidelity to the commands of love itself, to the very duties which priestly formation imposes on us, fidelity to the Church, fidelity to the inner guidance of the Holy Spirit. We shall increase in a real knowledge of the word of God in the measure of our fidelity to it. To walk in the truth is the means to possessing it (Jn 8, 32). Christ, who is the Truth of the Father, always does the Father's will (Jn 8, 29).

The great Doctors of the Church reached this union between theoretical knowledge and life. In them submission to Christ and to his word was a total submission. So a theology which wishes to be authentic must listen to the word which it seeks to understand. For this word, being the word of God, demands a docility which is a docility of mind and of will and of life. But this docility itself is not the result of human effort, but a gift of God. To obtain it one must pray. It is in prayer that theology must approach the Mystery, in prayer that it must seek understanding, in prayer that it must accomplish its research. Study and prayer must remain in a constant union, so that study, made fruitful by

the spirit of love, may be experienced as food as well as light.[2]
True theology proceeds from a living faith, which seeks to understand in order to love better and which loves in order to understand better. When faithfulness to God, implored in prayer, goes
thus hand in hand with theology, the discursive knowledge of
God and life in God will go forward together in a harmonious
union.

BIBLIOGRAPHY XI

DUPUY, M., « Expérience spirituelle et théologie comme science »,
Nouvelle Revue théologique, 86 (1964) : 1137-1162.
SOIRON, T., *La condition du théologien*, Paris, 1952.
VOILLAUME, R., « Théologie, vie intellectuelle et perfection évan-
gélique », dans : *Au cœur des masses*, deuxième édition, Paris,
1952, pp. 339-366.
VON BALTHASAR, H. U., « Théologie et sainteté », *Dieu vivant*, n. 12
(1948), pp. 17-32.

---

2. St. Thomas says, "Ex plenitudine contemplationis derivari debet doctrina
et praedicatio" (*S. Th.*, 2-2:188:6).

PART V
THEOLOGY'S PRESENT ORIENTATIONS

CHAPTER I   PRINCIPLES OF ORIENTATION

In the sixteenth century theology bore the imprint of humanism; in the eighteenth century it fell under the influence of rationalism, in the nineteenth of scientism. It could be said that twentieth century theology has developed in terms of history and of man in his historical situation, and in terms of intersubjectivity. This orientation of theology is itself a reflection of the life of the Church, whose action "in the world in which we live" shows signs of the pheomena described as "socialization" and "personalization." [1]

1. *Theology in terms of history*

In this respect the theology of the Middle Ages and twentieth century theology look different enough. In the Middle Ages, in order to solve the problems presented by Scripture and by the writings of the Fathers of the Church, the mind turned spontaneously to explanations of a logical type; in the twentieth century, theology at once interrogates history and the historical context. The Middle Ages elaborated above all a theology of the mysteries

---

1. Const. pastorale *Gaudium et Spes*, nn. 4 & 6.

as they are in themselves. Present day theology, without despising the essence of the mysteries, is much more conscious of the economic aspect of revelation, that is of the realization of God's design in history, and in its functional aspect, that is in revelation as revelation for us, for our salvation.

Man today has discovered the historical dimension; he has taken cognizance of the necessary historicity of man and of the human situation. He conceives man, not now as a universal, after the manner of Pascal or Racine, but as a *sujet-en-situation-historique,* a consciousness operating existentially. Theology has not escaped this change in mentality: while at the beginning of the century the expression "history of salvation" was almost unknown in Catholic theology, today it is omnipresent. The Council envisages the renewal of ecclesiastical studies from the point of view of "a more living contact with the Mystery of Christ and the history of salvation." [2]

This return of theology to the historical dimension is, to tell the truth, simply faithfulness to revelation, which is essentially the intervention of God in human history. Revelation indeed took the form of a history, the history of salvation, which begins in Israel and culminates in Jesus Christ. The whole of the history of salvation is related to Christ, who is the Event *par excellence,* that is to say God entering into the history of human society. This historical dimension of revelation has been specially stressed in *Dei verbum.*[3] In its turn the time of the Church is the time of the building up of the Body of Christ until the glorious manifestation of Christ and of the children of God. In consequence we cannot reach a theology except through the economy of salvation.

It might be said without exaggeration that the present renewal of theology is due in great part to the fact that the historical dimension has been introduced consciously and methodically into every department of theology. The fruit which history can bear in theology is particularly obvious in the renewal of biblical, and patristic and liturgical studies, as also in the admirable progress

---

2. Decree *Optatam totius* on priestly formation, n. 16.
3. Const. *Dei verbum* on revelation, nn. 3 & 4.

of ecclesiastical history and the history of dogma. Under the influence of this renewal in positive theology, theological reflection itself has experienced a new impulse. A new synthesis is being worked out, or at least is being sought after, which will gather up and organize the results of this extensive inventory of historical facts.

2. *Theology in terms of man and of the human person*

Under the influence of existentialist philosophy and of phenomenology, present day theology has turned towards man. This anthropocentric point of view is evident everywhere.[4] Theology is interested in the mysteries not only in themselves but also, and perhaps more, in that they are for man and for his salvation. Theology's orientation mirrors contemporary thought, which is structurally anthropocentric. In Kierkegaard especially, man is no longer just an object among other objects: he is the center of everything, the universal point of reference. From now on, all knowledge of God passes through man, even knowledge of the God of revelation. There is no knowledge of God without a previous understanding of man. Bearing upon it the impress of anthropology, theology today wishes to be more in continuity with man and the questions of man, and therefore with philosophy.

Scholastic theology was an effort to understand the Mystery of God, the object of our faith. Contemporary theology, more existentialist and more anthropocentric, is devoted to showing the meaning of the Christian Mystery for man. It is not just an understanding of the word of God, but also an understanding of man, to whom this word is addressed, and of the circumstance in which this word was and is heard.[5] The question of man is al-

---

4. C. Dumont, "Pour un conversion anthropocentrique des clercs," *Nouvelle Revue théologique,* 87 (1965), pp. 449-466; C.-J. Geffré, "Les courants actuels de la recherche en théologie," *La Vie Spirituelle,* Supplement, February, 1967, pp. 5-21; J. B. Metz, *Christliche Anthropozentrik* (München, 1962); B. Lambert, "Les deux démarches de la théologie," Nouvelle Revue théologique, 89 (1967), pp. 257-280.

5. K. Rahner, *Hörer des Wortes* (München, 1963).

ways implied in the question of God. Theology asks questions about man as he is in the world, as he is in time, about man as the man who believes and man as the man who does not believe, about the God-Man and about man who cannot understand himself without this God-Man. Theology today wants to be present in all human problems, in problems of love and family life, in problems of profession and nationality, in the problems of humanity as a whole and its progress, in problems of culture and techniques, in problems of the cosmos. Its assimilation of sociological and psychological facts witnesses to this spirit. In a word the aim of theology today is to make a synthesis of anthropology and theology. It talks about the mysteries "in a way designed to join to a deep perception of what they are in themselves, a living explanation of what they are for us." It wants "to join an anthropology directed towards God to a theology directed towards man." [6]

Under the influence, as it always is, of the currents of contemporary philosophical thought, theology is insisting on the "personalist" and "personalizing" character of the Christian Mystery. This "personalizing" demand is to be seen especially in the theology of revelation, of faith, of grace, of the theological virtues and of the sacraments. Revelation is the personal approach of the living God and the manifestation of his personal mystery. God enters into a relationship with man which is a relationship of person with person. The I Am of God speaks to the I am of man. Before revealing anything God reveals himself in his mystery. The Trinity reveals Persons.[7] Faith, in its turn, is the opening of man's being to God, the free response of man to the calling of God, the giving of the whole of man to God in a completely filial submission and trust.[8] The theology of grace is elaborated in terms of friendship between persons, in terms of God's giving of himself to man and of man's sharing in the personal life of God.

---

6. Y. Congar, "Le Christ dans l'économie salutaire et dans nos traités dogmatiques," *Concilium*, n. 11 (1966), pp. 24-25.

7. R. Latourelle, *Theology of Revelation* (Alba House, New York, 1966).

8. J. Alfaro, "La foi, abandon personnel de l'homme à Dieu et acceptation du message chrétien," *Concilium*, n. 21 (1967), pp. 49-59.

All the theological virtues are characterized by a quality of union and of the I-thou relationship.[9] Lastly, for each one of us the sacraments are the privileged place of our saving meeting with Christ.[10]

3. *Theology in terms of "the whole"*

Throughout the nineteenth century and during the first half of the twentieth century theology never ceased to differentiate this from that, and to proliferate in every sense. It multiplied disciplines and special departments, discovered new objects and created new treatises to study them. Inside the treatises themselves different questions and distinctions flourished. Theology itself was surrounded by a constantly increasing number of auxiliary disciplines. In fact, in order to absorb this more and more massive body of knowledge, the syllabuses of seminaries and theological faculties became swollen beyond measure, so that information became more important than formation and learning than culture.

For a decade or two theology has been reacting against this atomization of theological knowledge. Without denying the legitimacy and necessity of specialization, it tries to avoid the excesses to which it leads: the isolation of those engaged in research and their incomprehension of one another's work, the shrunk and partial way of looking at problems. Theology today is preoccupied with the desire for unification and unity. It is experiencing the need to bring together what has been separated, to regroup, to build organic syntheses. It is being worked out in terms of the "totality." This preoccupation with grasping the whole of the real is expressed in many different ways.

In studying the Christian mysteries theology would not wish to lose sight of any of the aspects of reality, but rather to assume them all into a harmonious unity. It is afraid of giving importance to one aspect at the expense of another, and so being the occasion,

9. J. Alfaro, "Persona y gracia," *Gregorianum*, 41 (1960), pp. 5-29; J. H. Walgrave, *Parole de Dieu et existence* (Paris, 1967).
10. E. Schillebeeckx, *Le Christ, Sacrement de la rencontre de Dieu* (Paris, 1960).

among the Christian communions separated from the Church, of misunderstandings which are fatal to ecumenical *rapprochement*. One could give an endless list of examples of this. For instance, instead of opposing revelation as event to revelation as doctrine, revelation as "encounter" to revelation as truth, theology today tries rather to show that revelation is, according to the point of view from which one looks at it, at once divine action, historical event and history, witness and message, meeting and communion. In discussing faith it stresses not only its character as assent to revealed truth, but also its character as total self-giving (of intellect and will) to God who is revealing himself and giving himself to man. In the theology of grace it stresses what actual and habitual grace, created and uncreated grace, have in common. In the Church it sees not only the institution, but also the mystery, the sacrament, the communion. In revelation and the Resurrection it does not separate as radically as before, the fact and the mystery, the apologetic significance and the dogmatic significance. In studying the signs of revelation, it assigns equal importance to the view of the subject (man) and the view of the object (the signs). The theological treatises themselves are undergoing a process of regrouping, in the interests of a greater degree of unification. So the theme of *God* brings together the *de Deo uno* and the *de Deo trino;* sacramental theology recovers the questions distributed to moral theology, liturgy, and canon law; Christology includes the *de Christo legato,* the *de Verbo incarnato* and the *de Christo redemptore;* mariology becomes a chapter of ecclesiology; the *de Virtutibus* is added to the treatise on grace, and so on. In short, theology (like the Council with its unceasing, *"et . . . et, una cum"*) is anxious to bring together, to co-ordinate, to integrate, to unify, to make one.

It is like a preoccupation which is making theology more alive to the necessity of collaboration among the different disciplines. Theology today refuses to separate dogma from moral theology, moral theology from spirituality, theology from pastoral studies, reflection from prayer. No discipline can be self-sufficient, for the mystery itself shines in all directions at once. The different theological disciplines are in union with one another, and all must give their own contribution to the understanding of the mystery. Theologians like Karl Rahner and Yves Congar are so conscious of this that they are by turns dogmatic theologians and moral theologians, spiritual theologians and pastoral theologians, ecumenical theologians and missionary theologians according to the demands of the problem studied. When, moreover, in the decree *Optatam totius,* the Council entrusted to dogmatic theology the task of assuming into a higher synthesis the conclusions of particular disciplines, and when the Council itself, in its treatment of the themes which are the subjects of the great constitutions (revelation, the Church, the liturgy, the Church in the world), interrogated Scripture and tradition and then showed the resonance of each mystery in the moral, spiritual and pastoral life of the Christian community, it confirmed and made official what was already established practice in present-day theology.

On the other hand, it is more and more obvious that this "totalizing" vision of the object of faith and of the problems of the Church cannot be the work of one man, even if he were a great genius like St. Thomas, but must rather be achieved by teams of experts working together in brotherly collaboration. In theology, just as in the secular sciences, it is, from now on, teams of research-workers who must operate, trying in this way to arrive at a contemporary understanding of the faith. The Council has shown how fruitful such a research formula can be.

4. *Theology in terms of dialogue*

Following the example of God, who first emerged from his mystery to enter into dialogue with man, and of the Church, who engages in dialogue with the world, theology today works out its problems in a spirit of dialogue. The word means more here than a verbal exchange. It means a general attitude of openness to others, an attitude of welcome and mutual give and take. At the root of dialogue there is a deep respect for the other, and a willingness to be at his disposal, to be available, which is the beginning of love. Each enters magnanimously into the ways to truth which are offered, recognizing them as such. Each brings something and each received something. Theology today seeks to be a theology of dialogue and a theology of service.

Dialogue first began to be established among theologians themselves, trying to put the fruit of their research at the disposal of the common good, rather than wear themselves out in sterile and scandalous disputes. There was an increase in undertakings in which individual theologians collaborated as witness not only dictionaries [11] and reviews, but also the countless symposia which have appeared in recent years, where specialists share in studying a subject from different aspects. International conferences, the exchange of lectures between different universities and different faculties, the appearance of international periodicals are similarly manifestations of this dialogue-orientated theology.

Dialogue among Catholic theologians themselves is being prolonged outside the Church. Much more than in the past, theology is engaging in dialogue with other Christian communities, with the great world religions and even with modern atheistic humanism. There is an attitude of openness which rests on the recognition that other systems of thought and belief contain truth. This ecumenical orientation enables Catholic theology to recover aspects of the faith which have been, not rejected, but perhaps rather put in the shade, aspects that the separated communities have sometimes made better use of than we have done. It also means that Catholic theology is obliged to consider more carefully than before, the legitimate questions which the eastern churches and the churches which have arisen from the Reformation do not cease to put to the Catholic Church.

One of the most intensive forms of dialogue today is that which was inaugurated only a little while ago with contemporary philosophy. For a long time theology has been incapable of meeting contemporary thought frankly; it has remained on the defensive

---

11. For instance: *Sacramentum mundi, Handbuch der Dogmengeschichte, Handbuch der Pastoraltheologie, Lexikon für theologie und Kirche, Mysterium salutis, Catholicisme, Dictionnaire de spiritualité, Handbuch theologischer Grundbegriffe, New Catholic Encyclopedia*, etc.

or in a sulky frame of mind. It has taken refuge in scholasticism in which it put its trust. Now, theology has the courage to set up a dialogue with the thought of our own time, especially with phenomenology.[12] It no longer considers St. Thomas as sole master of its thought, but rather as an example of the theologian who is not afraid to confront his faith with what he has learned from reason. In the encounter between St. Thomas and Aristotelianism there was dialogue; for theology and philosophy both received something. It is in the same spirit that theology today makes contact again with contemporary philosophy. This is a necessary dialogue; for theology cannot be a contemporary understanding of the word without basing itself on a real understanding of the situation of contemporary man. And if this situation is bound up with the experience of man in the past, with that of medieval or patristic man, it is nevertheless a very different and quite specific situation.[13]

5. *Theology in terms of service*

The subject of service is connected with the subject of dialogue. Theology today presents itself as an ecclesial function and as a function of service. If, in certain periods, it has been possible to accuse theology of being a kind of indoor game for intellectuals, shut off from the world and from the problems of the Christian community, a sort of art for art's sake, that accusation no longer carries any weight. Theology wishes to serve the Church, and to serve the Church of today. If it is true that the Council has offered us a new image of pope and bishops, an image whose dominant characteristic is that of the *pastor,* it is just as true that the dominant characteristic of the new image of theology is that of service. Even when it is being rigorously scientific, as it must

---

12. A. Kolping, *Katholische Theologie gestern hund neute* (Bremen, 1964), pp. 250-251; P. Fannon, "The Changing Face of Theology," *The Clergy Review,* January, 1967, pp. 6-7.
13. E. Schillebeeckx, "Ecclesia in mundo hujus temporis," *Angelicum,* 43 (1966), pp. 347-348.

be, theology today always preserves a pastoral intention, a willingness to serve.[14] It is at the service of the word, which it tries to read in its original context (in both the literal and the plenary sense), and to re-read in the context of the questions addressed to it by the man of today; it is at the service of the magisterium (the pope, the congregations, the bishops) whose work it supports through commissions of experts or technical advisors; it is at the service of the whole people of God through teaching, writing and research.[15]

An attentiveness to history and to the historicity of the human situation, an anthropocentric pattern, a personalist orientation, a preoccupation with grasping reality as a whole, a willingness to engage in dialogue and to serve, these are the characteristics to be found in the treatment of each of the great theological themes. They are, as it were, their soul.

---

14. P. Fransen, "Three Ways of Dogmatic Thought," *The Heythrop Journal* 4 (1963), p. 20.
15. This subject is treated more at length in Part II, Chapter V under the title: *Theology, faith and the magisterium.*

CHAPTER II   THE MAIN AXES OF CONTEMPORARY THEOLOGY

Under the influence of the renewal in biblical, patristic and liturgical studies, and also under the influence of the second Vatican Council, the word of God, Christ and the Church seem, as it were, the main axes of contemporary theology, the centers of co-ordination for the intellectual aspirations of our time. It is not by accident that the constitutions of the Council are called *Dei verbum,* centered on the word of God and on Christ, and *Lumen Gentium* and *Gaudium et Spes,* centered on Christ and the Church. Other themes, like grace, the sacraments and eschatology continue to be renewed in a christological and ecclesiological context, under the influence of the principles enumerated in the last chapter.

1. *The theology of the word of God*

The attention given to the data revealed could not be given without an equal attention to the God who reveals. The return to biblical sources has had, as a corollary, a stress on the primacy of the word and the revealing action. After being long neglected, the subject of revelation has become one of the chosen subjects of contemporary theology, Catholic as well as Protestant. Mono-

graphs proliferate on all sides, on revelation itself, on its transmission through Scripture and tradition, on its actualization in
liturgical preaching, catechetical instruction and the missionary
Kerygma.

Contemporary theology is aware of how rich and manifold
the aspects of revelation are. While previous theology has a tendency to give the doctrinal aspect a specially privileged place,
theology today distinguishes and balances better the different aspects of the reality: action, event, history, economy, message and
encounter. It rightly insists on the specific quality of Christian
revelation, which is not in any way a revelation of the philosophic
or gnostic type, but the disclosure by God of a design of union
or covenant, made progressively throughout a history, into whose
sense and implications the people of God penetrate under the
direction of the prophets. Consequently theology stresses the historical character of revelation. The God of revelation is a God
who comes into history and intervenes in it through a series of
events which culminate in the central event of the Incarnation.
Theology tries to measure the consequences for a right understanding of revelation of this choice made by God of an economy
so bound up with history and with the human situation. In the
same way it is aware of the movement of revelation, and the unique
place which Christ occupies. In this respect *Dei verbum* well
reflects the present view of the problem. The whole of history
rushes on towards Christ whom it announces and typifies, for
whom it is a preparation. In Jesus Christ, the Son of the Father,
the eternal Word of God, revelation reaches its term and its
perfection. It is Christ who gives revelation its unity: he is its
author, the mediator, the summit, the plenitude, the sign.

Another characteristic of revelation which theology stresses
today is its interpersonal character: it stresses the personal over-
ture made by the living God, who addresses man, enters into
dialogue with him, discloses to him the secrets of his own inner
life so that man may enter into a communion of thought and love
with the divine Persons. It insists therefore in revealed truth on

the reality revealed, on the mystery itself, on the Person who is revealing himself, and not only as often in the past on the statements and propositions which give to the mind its grasp of the mystery or the Person. Finally, theology today underlines the essentially supernatural and salvific character of the very fact of revelation. Revelation and grace are two aspects of the same salvation. God who reveals is God who gives himself, who invites us to be his friends and who saves us.[1]

If the main lines of the theology of revelation are clearly enough defined, many problems still remain. One may indicate a few of them. If men existed for millions of years before Abraham, what are we to think of their knowledge of God, their faith, their salvation? What is the position of the "Gentiles" today, who lives under the influence of Christ's grace but without being aware of the light of the Gospel? What is the place of the great non-Christian religions in the economy of revelation and of salvation? What does it mean for Christ to be the first to benefit from revelation, and how could he express humanly, in reflective terms, his consciousness of being the Son of God?

Many problems are concerned with the language of revelation. What, in particular, is the role of the symbol in the communication and apprehension of revelation? How can our minds make contact with the mystery of persons except through symbols? Is it even possible to free revelation from symbolic expression? How can a revelation expressed in the language and categories of a particular period really be addressed to men of all times? What is the extent of the Church's action as compared with the word? How should the Church's role as interpreter of the word be understood? On man's side, what are the conditions for hearing the word of God? What is the efficacy of this word, before the response of faith, and within the response of faith? These are some of the questions which crave attention. In a certain number of cases

---

1. R. Latourelle, *Theology of Revelation* (Alba House, New York, 1966). E. Schillebeeckx, *Révélation et Théologie* (Bruges, 1965). G. Moran, *Theology of Revelation* (New York, 1966); A. Dulles, "Theology of Revelation," *New Catholic Encyclopedia,* 12, pp. 440-444.

research upon them is already at an advanced stage; in others, on the contrary, it has still to identify and describe the problems.[2]

2. Problems of Christology

All revelation has a center and an apex, which is Christ. In Jesus Christ revelation is consummated and accomplished. From the beginning the cosmos, man and his history are orientated towards Christ. The history of Israel is the prelude to and the development of the history of Christ. And the whole faith of the Church rests upon Christ who has come and comes now. Nothing of more moment can happen in history, for he is the epiphany of God among men, the consubstantial Word of the Father uttered in history to be the Light and the Life of men. Present-day theology, espousing the very movement of revelation, and rediscoveiing the spirit of the liturgy, is more and more centered in Christ and in the paschal mystery.

In fundamental theology, the primordial question is, more than ever, "Who is Jesus Christ?" Is he really God in the flesh intervening in our history? Or is he simply the privileged place of our vertical encounter with God, after the manner of a prophet, as Bultmann suggests? What signs have we of this unbelievable presence of the Son of God among us? As a consequence of the odium into which apologetics fell, these questions were for a time relegated to second place in theological reflection. Now they are coming back at full tide, ineluctable and more disturbing than ever — so disturbing that a good many Christians prefer to take refuge in a sort of fideism rather than face them bravely. Fundamental theology has come back to them, but this time with a more vigilant critical sense, better equipped in the sphere of exegetics and history, more aware too of the complexity of the prob-

---

2. A. Dulles, "The Theology of Revelation," *Theological Studies*, 25 (1964); pp. 43-58; G. Moran, *Theology of Revelation* (New York, 1966); G. Thils, *Propos et problèmes de la théologie des religions non chrétiennes* (Tournai, 1966).

lems which it is tackling and in consequence less categorical in its statements.[3]

The question of the witness of Jesus, in the actual context, seems to be above all a hermeneutical problem. Even if contemporary criticism as a whole rejects the radical skepticism of Bultmann upon the possibility of knowing the Christ of history through the Gospels, it continues to ask what type of knowledge we can arrive at, and what its limits, its quality, and its certainties are. After concentrating for a long time on the period of the formation of the evangelical tradition (*Formgeschichte*), attention is now being concentrated on the phase of redaction, that is on the work of selection, organization and interpretation of the tradition by the evangelists. When this new research was first begun, the screen constituted by the editorial work of the evangelists appeared no less opaque than that of the primitive community about which Bultmann talks. Now that it is seeing things more in perspective, present-day criticism recognizes that the work of the evangelists is certainly more important than was hitherto believed, but at the same time as it is discovering their literary processes it is discovering also their profound fidelity. The intention of the evangelists, like that of the primitive *kerygma,* is to convey to us the facts about the Christ of Nazareth, and the teaching of the Christ of Nazareth, as seen and heard. Criticism of the Gospels in the last few decades has had the effect of making our understanding of them considerably more flexible. It has taught us to read them as they were written, never separating the events from their theological significance. It has also shown clearly that the Christ of history is one and the same as the Christ of the *kerygma.* The use of the Gospels as sources of the witness of Jesus to himself seems an infinitely more complex

---

3. R. Latourelle, "Apologétique et Fondamentale. Problèmes de nature et de méthode," *Salesianum,* 28 (1965), pp. 256-273.

4. S. Neill, *The Interpretation of the New Testament,* 1861-1961 (London, 1966); J. Bourke, "Le Jésus historique et le Christ kérygmatique," *Concilium,* n. 11 (1966), pp. 27-43.

operation than it did before, but it restores confidence.[4]

The study of the signs of revelation also is affected by the study of sources. But what characterizes it is the care taken to reattach the signs to Christ and to his Person. The signs of revelation are not outside Christ or separate from him. They are Christ himself in the radiance of his presence and of his manifestation in the world. Christ is at once the Plenitude and the primordial Sign of revelation. As *Dei verbum* puts it,[5] the same realities which communicate revelation serve also to authenticate it. Christ reveals through his words and his actions, through his death and his resurrection, through "his whole presence and manifestation of himself in the world." But because Christ is among men as the Son of the Father, there is in the sublimity of his teaching, in the holiness of his life, in the power which he deploys in his miracles and in his resurrection, in the extreme of charity manifested by his death, a radiation of light which is properly speaking his glory, and which designates him as him whom he claims to be, the Father's Son. All the signs emanate from Christ and lead back to him: they are in reality nothing but the multiform radiance of his epiphany among men. It is Christ whole and entire who is the enigmatic Sign which asks to be deciphered.[6]

In dogmatics, Christology, drawing support from the data of modern anthropology, pays more attention than it did, not only to the fact of the Incarnation, but to its consequences for an understanding of the economy of salvation. It insists on the fullness and on the reality of the Incarnation.[7] The Son of God is personally man, and this man is personally God: there is a refusal to depersonalize in any way the humanity of Christ. A human act of Jesus is a personal act of God under a human form. God is Charity, but it is in man that he shows it: his human love

---

5. Const. *Dei verbum*, n. 4.

6. R. Latourelle, "Le Christ, Signe de la Révélation selon la Constitution *Dei verbum*," *Gregorianum*, 47 (1966), pp. 685-709; Id., "L'économie des signes de la Révélation," *Sciences Ecclésiastiques*, 19 (1967), pp. 7-31.

7. K. Rahner, "Réflexions théologiques sur l'Incarnation," *Sciences Ecclésiastiques*, 12 (1960), pp. 5-19.

is the human form of his redeeming divine love. The words of Christ are the human words of God; the actions of Christ are the actions of God in a humanly visible form. In Jesus Christ the Son of God, through a human word, speaks to man, as person to person.

This fresh attention to Christ's human condition, and to the human depth and abundance of his human being, has brought about the renewal of a great part of Christology, and first of all of the theology of revelation. If, through the Incarnation, there is a veritable "inhumanization" of God, it follows that all man's dimensions are assumed in order to serve as the expression of the absolute Person. It is through his actions, his gestures, his attitudes, his typical modes of behavior, his entire manner of life, as well as through his words that Christ exercised his prophetic function — a point of view which is recorded in *Dei verbum*.[8]

As a consequence of the central place which Christ takes in the theology of revelation, the theology of faith itself is more, as it were, centered on Christ. Faith is not conceived simply as a sublime act, suspended so to speak from the word of God, but scarcely passing by way of earthly reality or through Christ. It is firmly Christocentric: faith in God, but in God manifested and communicated in Jesus Christ.

Similarly, theology is in some sort rediscovering the great mysteries of Christ: the Baptism, the Transfiguration, the Passion, the Resurrection. In soteriology it is not interested merely in the moral or juridical value of Christ's death, but in the concrete action through which our salvation was accomplished, the Agony, the Passion in the flesh, the nailing to the cross, the Death of Christ. The economy of the salvation of the flesh from sin through the Passion and Crucifixion of the flesh of Christ is not without importance in understanding the mystery of Christ's satisfaction and our redemption.[9] The Incarnation is no longer a mere episode, now over, in God's activities in the world (the redemption of

---

8. R. Latourelle, *Theology of Revelation*, (Alba House, New York, 1966).
9. K. Rahner, "Problèmes actuels de Christologie," in *Ecrits théologiques* I. (Bruges & Paris, 1959), pp. 115-181.

humanity, the foundation of the Church): the Son is for ever the incarnate Word. As he reveals and gives glory to the Father here on earth beneath the veil of signs and in the darkness of faith, so the glorified Christ will manifest and communicate the fullness of his eschatological glory to those whom the Father has given him.[10]

One of the most important expressions of this theology of the Incarnation renewed through anthropology and psychology is the renewed interest in a major christological problem, that of Christ's knowledge and consciousness. This problem has been studied in recent years, especially by E. Gutwenger, K. Rahner, B. Lonergan, E. Schillebeeckx, M. Cuervo and F. de P. Sola.[11] For a long time inadequate even *simpliste* solutions were given to it, setting up in the soul of Christ logical departmentations which were hard to reconcile on a psychological plane. Christology today tries to coincide more nearly with what we learn from Scripture. It considers, with K. Rahner, that Christ made use of the words, images and concepts of his *milieu* to express little by little the primary and fundamental datum of his soul that is the consciousness of his identity as the Son of God. This immediate awareness of his divine sonship expressed itself reflectively when it was given occasion by its encounter with the surrounding *milieu*.[12]

3. *The theology of the Church*

The first centuries of the Church were especially preoccupied with the great Trinitarian and christological problems. Medieval theology studied the redemption and the sacraments. The twentieth century seems to be the century of the Church. The second Vatican Council was in a special way the Church's encounter with herself

---

10. J. Alfaro, "Cristo Glorioso, Revelador del Padre," *Gregorianum,* 39 (1958), pp. 234-239.
11. E. Gutwenger, "La science du Christ," *Concilium,* n. 11. (1966), pp. 81-94. Id., *Bewusstsein und Wissen Christi,* (Innsbruck, 1960).
12. K. Rahner, "Dogmatische Erwägung über das Wissen und Selbstbewusstsein Christi," *Trierer Theol. Zeitschrift,* 71 (1962), pp. 65-68.

(*Lumen Gentium*) and with the world (*Gaudium et Spes*). Ever since the first Vatican Council, whose work because of circumstances remained unfinished, there had been a deeply felt need for an account of the Church which would see her not merely as a fact of history (from the apologetic point of view) but also as the object of faith, an account which would go deeply into the mystery of her being, setting out from the sources and from her life in the Holy Spirit, and which would manifest the diversity of her aspects in a just equilibrium. In the search for her own identity and for her own essential characteristics, the Church has been led, in some measure, to cease to center her life upon herself, in order to center it more upon Christ and upon the Holy Spirit.[13]

Of all the themes touched on by *Lumen Gentium* the one which at depth most renews our vision of the Church is that of the Church as the sacrament of salvation and the mystery of communion. The Church is the sacrament and sign of salvation; for she represents and effects the invisible grace of salvation. She is Christ's salvation itself under the form of a social body. One cannot, therefore, separate in her, institution and grace, the Church visible and the Church invisible. And this spiritual reality of which the Church is the sign or sacrament is our communion in the very life of the Trinity. The Church is "a people made one by the unity of the Father and the Son and the Holy Spirit" [14] in whose life she shares. In this mystery of communion the bond

---

13. The bibliography on the subject of the Church is enormous. May we suggest the following: E. Ménard, *L'Ecclésiologie hier et aujourd'hui* (Bruges & Paris, 1966); U. Valeske, *Votum Ecclesiae* (2 vol., München, 1962); J.-L. D'Aragon, *L'Eglise dans la Bible* (Bruges & Paris, 1962), pp. 169-202. On the theology of the Church and the ecclesiology of the second Vatican Council see especially: Msgr. Philips, *L'Église et son mystère au deuxième Concile du Vatican* (Paris, 1967); *La nouvelle Image de L'Église*, a symposium edited by B. Lambert (Paris, 1967); A. Dulles, *The Dimensions of the Church* (Woodstock, 1967); G. Martelet, *Les Idées maîtresses de Vatican II* (Bruges & Paris, 1967); F. Holböck and T. Sartory, *Mysterium Kriche in der Sicht der theologischen Disziplinen* (2 vol., Salzburg, 1962); B. Barauna ed. *L'Église de Vatican II* (2 vol., Paris, 1966).

14. Const. *Lumen Gentium*, n. 4.

which unites Christians with one another and with God is a bond of love; it is the Holy Spirit. It may be said that this theme of the Church as the mystery of communion orientates and inspires the whole of the Constitution on the Church. It may be said too that it throws on every chapter of ecclesiology an entirely new light.

Since the Church is a mystery of communion, ecclesiology today is elaborated in Trinitarian and pneumatological terms. God's design in his Church is that we should share in the sonship of Christ and in the mutual love of the Father and the Son, that is in the Holy Spirit. In giving us his Spirit, God bends over us and extends to us the love which he has for his Son; he infuses within us the love with which the Father loves the Son and the Son the Father; he makes us able to come to the Father in the Spirit of the Son saying with him, "Abba, Father." The Church is the Church of Christ only in being the Church of the Holy Spirit.

In the ecclesiology of the immediate past there was a tendency to identify the Church with the hierarchy, with the seat of power and law. Henceforth it is the whole community, the sacramental community of brothers theologically one in faith and hope and charity, which is seen as the Church. All, pastors and faithful, are part of the Church by the same fundamental right, the right of those redeemed and baptized in the blood of Christ the Priest. The function of the hierarchy is to make the communion begun by faith and baptism grow. The hierarchy is defined in terms of service, taking its place in the prolongation of the redeeming action of the Servant of Yahweh.

The themes of the Church's holiness, of the religious life and of eschatology are also connected with the theme of communion with God; for holiness is nothing else but sharing in the life of God. This communion, here on earth, in the Church and in individual Christians, remains fragile and imperfect, always threatened by sin. Hence there is a tension between what the Church is inchoatively, at the present time, and what she will be in her perfection in the kingdom of heaven, a tension between the fundamental holiness with which she is endowed through the blood of Christ and the gifts he has given to his Bride (the Holy Spirit, faith, the sacraments), and the sin of her members. In this dialectic between the present time and the world which is to come the religious life witnesses to the reality and the substance of the gifts possessed in hope.

The theme of the people of God stresses the terrestrial, historical and social character of the mystery of the Church. But through the theme of the covenant, with which it is connected, it is at the same time the mystery of communion with God who is holy and who prepares for himself a holy people, given life by the Spirit of love, "a chosen race, a royal priesthood, a consecrated nation, a people obtained" through the blood of Christ (1 Pet 2, 9-10). If the expression "people of God" made its fortune at the Council, it is because it gathers together certain aspects of the Church not so well expressed by the images of the Body, the Temple, and the Bride. In particular it stresses the transcendence and the initiative of God with regard to his Church, the continuity of the divine plan and the dynamic character of a Church missionary and pilgrim to the end of time, working unceasingly to reassemble the peoples as one people.

The mission of the Church is seen in its full significance when it is defined in relation to this mystery of communion. For it is men of all times who are called to constitute the holy people of a holy God. The mission of the people of God is the expression of its concern that all the nations of the earth should enter into the communion of love instituted by Christ. It is born in the impulse of the Holy Spirit which "instills into the hearts of the faithful the same sense of mission which impelled Christ himself." [15] This mission is fulfilled by the people of God above all through the clear witness among men of an authentic communion of love.

In the thought of many Catholics local or particular Churches are only branches of the great universal Church which is composed of all the faithful throughout the world united under the authority

---

15. Decree *Ad Gentes* on the missionary activity of the Church, n. 4.

of the pope. Without rejecting the sense in which the Church is universal, *Lumen Gentium* stresses the importance and function of the particular Churches: "it is in them and through them that the one unique Catholic Church exists." [16] The Eucharist, which is the sacrament of communion with God, and the action through which each assembly of the faithful enters into living communion with the universal Church, is accomplished in the local or particular Church, which is therefore, the privileged place of the Church's life.

In the measure in which this vision of the Church as the mystery of communion prevails in the consciousness of her members, obedience will be rooted not in fear, or in anxiety to maintain an external order, as in a well-ordered city, but chiefly in the union of faith and charity. This sort of obedience is in its turn encouraged, if authority is exercised in a spirit of service. From the ecumenical point of view, moreover, this mystery of communion makes of the assembling of all Christians in one single Church, no longer an ideal of juridical reconquest, but an ideal of love. When the Church labors to realize unity among all Christians, it is the desire to accomplish her mission which upholds her; it is the depths of her being which press her on, towards the realization of the perfect unity of all with the Father, the Son and the Holy Spirit.

The Council obviously did not wish to say the last word in ecclesiology. It has left for theologians many unanswered questions or questions without answers that satisfy. For instance, in the theology of the mystical Body, how are we to interpret the bond between Christ and his members? The theme of belonging to the Church needs new investigation at depth. What, in the concrete, is the relationship between the collegiality of bishops and the primacy of the Roman pontiff? No doubt the Church needs a rather long experience to define this relationship better. How are we to resolve the paradox of a Church really holy and really sin-

---

16. Const. *Lumen Gentium*, n. 23.

ful? What is the specific quality of the religious life? What is the nature of the tension between charism and ministry? In the theology of the Church the chapter on Pneumatology is not yet written.

4. *Relations between the Church and the world*

Since the Council and the constitution *Gaudium et Spes,* the problem of the relationship between the Church and the world has assumed such proportions that it now constitutes a special chapter of ecclesiology and a totally new field of research.[17]

As a consequence of the increasing secularization of society, the Church and the world, which in the Middle Ages were a relatively homogeneous unity, were dissociated and became two distinct realities. After being for a long time opposed to each other these two realities are now entering into dialogue. In *Ecclesiam suam,* and then in *Gaudium et Spes,* the Church recognized the secular world as a free partner in an open dialogue.[18] She affirmed the autonomy of the world and of its values.[19] Though conscious of the help she gave to the world through the blessing of the Gospel, she recognized also the help she received from the world.[20] Because it is a new world, the world today poses for the Church a whole gamut of questions which unsecularized periods could scarcely pose. The answers to these questions must be inspired

---

17. See, for example: E. Schillebeeckx, "Ecclesia in mundo hujus temporis," *Angelicum,* 43 (1966), pp. 340-352. Id., "Foi Chrétienne et attente terrestre" in *Gaudium et Spes, L'Église dans le monde de ce temps* (Paris, 1967), pp. 119-158; M. D. Chenu, "Les Signes des temps," *Nouvelle Revue théologique,* 87 (1965), pp. 29-39; Id., "Les Signes des temps" in *Gaudium et Spes, L'Église dans le monde de ce temps* (Paris, 1967), pp. 97-118. At the international theological conference held at Toronto from the 20th to the 25th August, 1967, several papers read bore on the subject of the relations between the Church and the world, in particular that of E. Schillebeeckx, 21 August, 1967, and that of K. Rahner, 24 August, 1967.
18. Const. pastorale *Gaudium et Spes,* n. 40.
19. *Ibid.,* n. 37.
20. *Ibid.,* nn. 4 & 44.

by the Gospel, but they will be new answers because the questions come from a context of life very different from the past.

From the very fact of its existence the world, with its values, is a mass of intelligibility. The events and phenomena which make up the course of human history and scan man's progress constitute an implicit language which the Church can and must decipher. When they are seen in the light of the Gospel, these events become signs: the signs of the present time. A faith which is on the watch can read in them, says Chenu, "the purpose of God, the Creator and Savior who guides the course of sacred history." [21] So the rise of the working class, the emancipation of the colonies, the development of an international conscience and many phenomena of this sort become, when they are seen as signs, so many appeals made to the Gospel, the Church and theology, so many stimulants to action. There is no doubt that the Church's dialogue with the world enriches the Church.

On the other hand the Church can serve and enrich the world, and she can do this first of all as a society. For the Church as a great entity, visible, historical and social, can influence the course which the secular world takes and thus co-operate in the good of humanity. There is here a new field of action for her. For the Church in virtue of her insertion into the world, is in a position where she cannot remain indifferent to the situations and problems which arise there: she cannot for example be indifferent to anything which concerns peace, over-population, or the help needed by any nation or the nations as a whole. She cannot find solutions to these problems directly derived from revelation. The solutions which she offers, though they are inspired by the spirit of the Gospel, are derived rather from an analysis of the Church's present position and of the constantly changing situation in the secular world. In order to study this relationship between the

---

21. M.-D. Chenu, "Les signes des temps" in *Gaudium et Spes, L'Église dans le monde de ce temps* (Paris, 1967), p. 113. *Gaudium et Spes* says, "motivated by faith ... the people of God tries to discern among the events, demands and desires of our time ... which are the authentic signs of the presence or purpose of God," n. 11.

Church and the world, says Karl Rahner, we need a special branch of theological reflection, "a practical ecclesiological cosmology." [22] This discipline, he explains, would take its place within pastoral theology, and its task would be to study the constantly changing relationship between the Church and the world. It would be directed towards discovering what forms the action of the Church should, given this relationship, take in particular circumstances, and to proposing directives and decisions in the practical order, which would help the secular world to advance in a way conducive to man's salvation. This advisory role in relation to the secular world is part says K. Rahner, of the Church's prophetic duty in serving the world.

If the Church takes as seriously as this the structure of future life on earth and collaborates with the world in forming it, it is because she sees a mysterious connection between the progress of the human family as such and the establishing of the kingdom of God. Are not the best fruits of human exertions (equality, freedom and brotherhood) prepared and ripe for purification and transformation into the fruits of justice and peace and love? [23]

Apart from this form of collaboration with the world in the construction of its earthly future, the Church must obviously pursue unremittingly within the world her task of evangelization. But a better understanding of the world, and of the temporal actions required of Christians in the world, has led the Church to a recognition of the decisive role which the laity should play in this task of evangelization.

The laity are asked, in the midst of their family, professional and social occupations, to show the world by the witness of a life fully in accord with the Gospel, that salvation in Jesus Christ has come to men to transform them and give them life. It is a

---

22. K. Rahner, *Réflexions théologiques sur le problème de la sécularisation,* a paper read at the international theological conference at Toronto, August 24, 1967.
23. Const. pastorale *Gaudium et Spes,* nn. 38-39; E. Schillbeeckx, "Foi chrétienne et attente terrestre" in *Gaudium et Spes,* L'Église dans le monde de ce temps (Paris, 1967), pp. 119-158.

question of an apostolate by insertion and permeation after the manner of leaven.[24]

5. *Grace and the sacraments*

Personalism, which has made so deep a mark upon contemporary theology, has exerted a particularly beneficial influence on the theology of grace and the sacraments.[25]

The treatise on grace has become a supernatural anthropology, an anthropology of man redeemed and saved, which stresses the existential and personal character of the union of grace.

Post-Tridentine theology used to explain that man is divinized in that he receives an "accidental quality," conferring upon him a special likeness to God, and making him capable of acting supernaturally. In this way, it said, man participates in the divine nature. Today theology stresses the fundamental act of self-communication by the divine Persons, and the new relations which the just have with them. It is not a question only of an ontological change which takes place in the just, but of their sharing in the personal life of God.[26] On the analogy of the beatific vision, theology talks about an "actuation" of the soul by the Persons of the Trinity (after the manner of a quasi-formal cause). Other theologians explain that it is in our union with Christ that we enter *ipso facto* into the inner life of the Trinity.[27] When a man opens himself to Christ in faith he becomes a member of the mystical Body of which Christ is the Head, and through Christ he reaches the Father. He is divinized: he shares in the filial relationship of the Son to the Father, and in the love of the Son and the Father, that is in the Spirit. Contemporary theology lays equal

---

24. Const. *Lumen Gentium,* n. 31; R. Latourelle, "Les laïcs, ferment de la société," *Relations,* January 1967, pp. 3-5 and February 1967, pp. 34-37.
25. B. Langemeyer, *Der Dialogische Personalismus in der evangelischen und Katholischen Theologie* (Paderborn, 1963).
26. J. Alfaro, "Persona y gracia," *Gregorianum,* 41 (1960), pp. 5-29.
27. See on this subject M. Flick, "Il Cristo nel trattato *De Gratia*," *Gregorianum,* 47 (1966), pp. 114-121.

stress on the individual character and the social character of grace, on its anthropological quality and its cosmic quality. It studies, apropos of the life of grace themes such as its organic structure (the theological virtues, and the gifts of the Holy Spirit), the sovereignty and gratuity of grace, law and grace, freedom and grace, growth in the life of grace and dangers which threaten it, the ecclesial aspect of the life of grace (in terms of charism, vocation, witness) and so on. As can be seen, the treatise on grace tends to annex a number of questions which used to be associated with particular disciplines and with other treatises.

Contemporary theology sees the sacraments, as it sees grace, from a personalist and christological point of view. The dialogic structure of revelation is prolonged throughout the entire sacramental economy. Man meets the invisible God under the species of the primordial Sacrament which is Christ, the saving presence of God among men, and through the mediation of the sacraments which are the earthly prolongations of Christ in glory. Redemption is accomplished once and for all through Christ's passion and death and resurrection, but he remains for ever the Mediator. So grace operates only through contact with him and this contact is made now through the sacraments, which are the place where each one of us can localize and perceive with our senses our encounter with the risen Christ. They constitute a contact which, though veiled beneath signs, is real, and possessed by both body and spirit. The Eucharist is the culmination of this contact with Christ. In its vision of the sacramental economy, theology binds indissolubly together Christ, the sign of God, the Church, the sign of Christ, and the sacraments, the actions of Christ accomplished in and through the Church. In this way it makes it easier to understand the meaning of the *opus operatum* which is inseparable from the sacramental rite.[28]

---

28. E. Schillebeeckx, *Le Christ, Sacrement de la rencontre de Dieu* (Paris, 1962); Id., "Les sacrements organes de la rencontre de Dieu" in *Questions théologique aujourd'hui III* (Bruges & Paris, 1965), pp. 239-267.

6. *Eschatology*

After being long in disrepute, the subject of eschatology has come to take a privileged place in contemporary theological thought. This renewed status has been made possible only by subjecting the eschatological theme as it was enshrined in the traditional *de Novissimis* to profound transformation. First of all it had to be disengaged from all the intrusive questions with which it was encumbered. There has been an effort to discover, beneath the images, and symbols of scripture, in the context of the literary form, the revealed message in its sheer and sublime state, a legitimate demythologizing of a sort which the Church has in any case never ceased to practice. Then above all there has been an enlarging of perspectives. Whereas the classical treatise on the last things used to study death, judgment, heaven, purgatory and hell as it were in isolation, theology today sees these realities as elements in a whole. While the *de Novissimis* was practically speaking interested only in the fate of individuals, present-day theology is interested also in the ultimate destiny of humanity (the social aspect) and the ultimate destiny of the entire universe (the cosmic aspect), in their relation to the drama of redemption and the whole history of salvation. Theology today sees the events of the end of the world in relation to Christ who is their source and principle, the eschatological Event *par excellence* in virtue of his Death and Resurrection. We have in fact come to realize that eschatology is more than the subject of a special treatise: it is rather a dimension which affects the whole of theology. For theology must talk about salvation not only in its phase of restoration and renewal among us now, but also in that of its development and temporal consummation. There is an eschatological value in revelation, in redemption, in the Church, in the sacramental economy, in grace, in the theological virtues, in Christian morals. Eschatology today is constructed by taking into account the entire structure of theology and the incidence of eschatology on the whole of theology. This eschatological dimension seems of capital importance in the eyes of twentieth century theology, since it is part of the very nature of a salvation which is realized in time. It is the consummation of time and the passing of time into eternity which is the criterion by which we can measure everything else.[29]

These new perspectives have already affected many of the problems of the *de Novissimis*. The theology of death,[30] profiting from Heidegger's analyses, sees in death a separation of the soul from the body, but more than that a personal event; not only the end of earthly life, but also a consummation that is the accomplishing in the Christian of the paschal mystery of Christ (the mystery of death and resurrection), the entering into possession of the salvation which was given initially through faith and the sacraments, the passage to the Father and to full communion with God. Purgatory[31] is conceived as in the eastern Fathers, as a condition and process (rather than a place) of painful purification, taking place within a deep experience of union with God and preparing the soul for glory. A requirement of love rather a punishment, purgatory suggests the passive purifications of the great mystics. The theology of hell,[32] after disposing of the erroneous representations of a fierce and avenging God who takes delight in taking poor human beings by surprise and damning them, rightly insists on the mystery of the man who turns towards himself and becomes fixed in his refusal of God. Hell is first and foremost the eternalized contradiction of a freedom which closes itself to what alone can fulfill it, the vision of God who is love. This vision is presented today as a meeting and personal communion

29. On recent points of view in relation to eschatology, see: K. Rahner, "Eschatologie," *Lexikon für Theologie und Kirche*, 3:1094-98; J. Galot, "Eschatologie," *Dictionnaire de Spiritualité*, 4: 1020-59; H. U. von Balthasar, "Eschatologie" in *Questions théologiques aujourd'hui II* (Bruges & Paris, 1965), pp. 271-296.

30. K. Rahner, "Pour une théologie de la mort" in *Écrits théologiques III*, (Bruges & Paris, 1963), pp. 105-167; G. Martelet, *Victoire sur la mort* (Paris, 1962); P. Grelot, "La théologie de la mort dans l'Ecriture sainte," *Vie Spirituelle*, supplément, n. 71 (mai, 1966), pp. 143-194.

31. A. Bourçois-Macé, A. de Bovis etc., *Le Purgatoire profond mystère* (Paris, 1957); Y. Congar, "Le Purgatoire" in *Le mystère de la mort et sa célébration* (Paris, 1951), pp. 279-336.

32. G. Bardy, W. Carrouges, et Al., *L'enfer* (Coll. "Foi Vivante," Paris, 1950).

with Christ in glory, a total meeting in which the whole man body and soul is united to Christ, a perfect meeting for Christ reveals and gives himself wholly, as man and as God, in his created and in his uncreated beauty as the Son united to the Father in the Spirit.[33] Finally, the consummation of the world, with the return of the world, with the return of Christ and the universal judgment is seen from a christological point of view;[34] it is Christ who freely and supernaturally consummates in himself the world and its history, manifests himself to the eyes of all as the Lord and annihilates the opposing powers (sin, death, Satan). The "how" of these events remains wrapped in mystery.

Many points in this theology still call for elucidation and investigation at depth (for instance the relationship between time and eternity, the mystery of the separated souls, and the mystery of the resurrection of the body but it can be said that eschatology has now emerged from the blind alley in which it has for long been immobilized.

Theology today is carrying out a difficult duty of *aggiornamento* and of moving on ahead to confront the world which is just coming to be. For the Gospel must not disappoint the world. The Church must go to meet men with an alert and youthful step. At each instant of time her word must spring into being as new and illuminating as on the morning of Pentecost, forever contemporary. If theology is to fulfill effectively its role as the servant of the Church, it must allow itself to be directed by the wind of the Spirit.

---

33. J. Alfaro, "Die Menschwerdung und die eschatologische Vollendung des Menschen," *Catholica,* 16, (1962), pp. 20-37; Id., "Christo glorioso, Revelador del Padre," *Gregorianum,* 39 (1958), pp. 221-271.
34. R. Schnackenburg, *Le message moral du Nouveau Testament* (Lyon, 1963), pp. 153-168.

GENERAL BIBLIOGRAPHY

ADNÈS, P., *La théologie catholique*, Paris, 1967.
ASVELD, P., « A propos de saint Thomas et de la théologie comme science », *Ephemerides theologicae lovanienses*, 37 (1961) : 450-461.
AUBERT, R., *La théologie catholique au milieu du XXᵉ siècle*, Tournai et Paris, 1954.

BEUMER, J., *Theologie als Glaubensverständnis*, Frankfurt, 1953.
BILZ, J., *Einführung in die Theologie*, Freiburg i. Br., 1935.
BOUILLARD, H., « Croire et comprendre », dans : *Archivio di Filosofia*, diretto da Enrico Castelli, Roma, 1966, pp. 285-314.
BURKE, E. M., « Dogmatic Theology », *New Catholic Encyclopedia*, 4 : 949-956.

CANO, M., *De Locis theologicis*, 1563.
CHENU, M.-D., *La théologie comme science au XIIIᵉ siècle*, Paris, 1945.
CHENU, M.-D., *La théologie au XIIᵉ siècle*, Paris, 1957.
CHENU, M.-D., *La théologie est-elle une science?*, Paris, 1957.
CHENU, M.-D., *La Parole de Dieu*, I, Paris, 1964.
CHENU, M.-D., « Position de la théologie », *Revue des Sciences philosophiques et théologiques*, 24 (1935) : 232-257.
COLOMBO, C., « La metodologia e la sistemazione teologica », in : *Problemi e Orientamenti di Teologia dommatica I*, Milano, 1957, pp. 1-56.
COLOMBO, C., *Scritti teologici*, Venegono, 1966.
CONGAR, Y., « Théologie », *Dictionnaire de théologie catholique*, XV, 1 (1946) : 341-502.
CONGAR, Y., *La foi et la théologie*, Tournai, 1962, pp. 121-272.
CONLEY, K., *A Theology of Wisdom*, Dubuque, 1963.
CORBIN, M., « La fonction et les principes de la théologie selon la

Somme théologique de saint Thomas d'Aquin », *Recherches de Science religieuse*, 55 (1967) : 321-366.

CROWE, F. E., « On the Method of Theology », *Theological Studies*, 23 (1962) : 637-642.

DAVIS, C., *The Study of Theology*, London-New York, 1962.

DEMAN, T., « Composantes de la théologie », *Revue des Sciences philosophiques et théologiques*, 28 (1939) : 386-434.

DUMONT, C., « La réflexion sur la méthode théologique », *Nouvelle Revue théologique*, 83 (1961) : 1034-1050 ; 84 (1962) : 17-35.

EBELING, G. und RATZINGER, J., « Theologie », RGG³, 754-838.

FRANSEN, P., « Three Ways of Dogmatic Thought », *The Heythrop Journal*, 4 (1963) : 3-24.

FRIES, H., « Theologie », *Handbuch theologischer Grundbegriffe*, 2 vol., München, 1963, t. 2 : 641-654.

FRITZCHE, H. G., *Die Strukturtypen der Theologie*, Göttingen, 1961.

GAGNEBET, R., « La nature de la théologie spéculative », *Revue thomiste*, 44 (1938) : 1-39, 213-255, 645-674.

GAGNEBET, R., *De natura theologiae ejusque methodo juxta sanctum Thomam*, 2 vol., Romae, 1958.

GARDEIL, A., *Le donné révélé et la théologie*, Paris, 1910 et 1932.

HAYEN, A., « La théologie aux XIIᵉ, XIIIᵉ et XXᵉ siècles », *Nouvelle Revue théologique*, 80 (1957) : 1009-1028 ; 81 (1958) : 113-132.

HAYEN, A., « Science sacrée et vie théologale », *Sciences Ecclésiastiques*, 15 (1963) : 21-38 ; 17 (1965) : 111-134.

JOURNET, J., *Introduction à la théologie*, Fribourg, 1947.

KOESTER, H., *Vom Wesen und Aufbau katholischer Theologie*, Stetler, 1954.

KOLPING, A., *Einführung in die katholische Theologie*, Münster, 1960.

LABOURDETTE, M., « La théologie, intelligence de la foi », *Revue thomiste*, 46 (1946) : 5-44.

LANG, A., *Die Theologische Prinzipienlehre der Mittelalterlichen Scholastik*, Freiburg-Basel-Wien, 1964.

LECLERCQ, J., *L'amour des lettres et le désir de Dieu*, Paris, 1957.

LE GUILLOU, M.-J., *Le Christ et l'Église. Théologie du Mystère*, Paris, 1963.

LONERGAN, B., *De Deo trino*, 2 vol., Romae, 1964, t. 1 : 6-14 ; t. 2 : 7-61.

LONERGAN, B., « Theology and Understanding », *Gregorianum*, 35 (1954) : 630-648.

MALEVEZ, L., « Théologie contemplative et théologie discursive », *Nouvelle Revue théologique*, 86 (1964) : 225-249.

MARCOTTE, E., *La nature de la théologie d'après Melchior Cano*, Ottawa, 1949.

MARLÉ, R., *Le problème théologique de l'herméneutique*, Paris, 1963.

MEHL, R., *La théologie protestante*, Paris, 1966.

METZ, J. B. und MADRE, A., « Theologie », *Lexikon für Theologie und Kirche*, 10 : 62-76.

MICKS, M. H., *Introduction to Theology*, New York, 1964.

NÉDONCELLE, M., « Théologie et Philosophie ou les métamorphoses d'une servante », *Concilium*, n. 6 (1965) : 93-102.

NEUHÄUSLER und GÖSSMANN, *Was ist Theologie?*, München, 1966.

RAHNER, K., « Zur Frage der Ausbildung der Theologen heute », in : *Sendung und Gnade*, Innsbruck, 1966, pp. 334-358.

RAHNER, K., « Dogmatik », *Lexikon für Theologie und Kirche*, 3 : 446-454.

RÖHRICHT, R., *Theologie als Hinweis und Entwurf*, Gütersloh, 1964.

ROSCHINI, G., *Introductio in sacram theologiam*, Romae, 1947.

SCHILLEBEECKX, E., *Révélation et théologie*, Bruxelles, 1965.

SCHMAUS, M., *Katholische Dogmatik*, München, 1948, t. I.

SOIRON, T., *Heilige Theologie*, Regensburg, 1935 ; *La condition du théologien* (vers. gall.), Paris, 1953.

STOLZ, A., *Introductio in sacram Theologiam*, Freiburg i. Br., 1941.

THILS, G., *Orientations de la théologie*, Louvain, 1958.

THOMAS D'AQUIN, S., *Somme théologique*, 1a, q. 1.

TIHON, P., *Foi et théologie selon Godefroid de Fontaines*, Bruges-Paris, 1966.

TOUILLEUX, P., *Introduction à une théologie critique*, Paris, 1967.

TSHIBANGU, T., *Théologie positive et théologie spéculative*, Paris-Louvain, 1965.

VAN ACKEREN, G., *Sacra Doctrina. The Subject of the first Question of the Summa theologica of St. Thomas Aquinas*, Romae, 1952.
VAN ACKEREN, G., « Reflections on the Relation between Philosophy and Theology », *Theological Studies*, 14 (1953) : 527-550.
VAN ACKEREN, G., « Theology », *New Catholic Encyclopedia*, 14 : 39-49.
VON BALTHASAR, H. U., « Der Ort der Theologie », in *Verbum Caro*, Einsiedeln, 1960, pp. 159-171.

WINGREN, G., *Die Methodenfrage des Theologie*, Göttingen, 1957.
WYSER, P., *Theologie als Wissenschaft*, Salzburg, 1958.

XIBERTA, B., *Introductio in sacram theologiam*, Matriti, 1949.

INDEX